Sierra Liona at abt 2 Leagues distant
from the Shoar

D The Village of Sierra
E Fishing Bay
F
G.

Cape Tagrain at E ¼ NE. about 8 Leagues
A. Here is a pass
B. Cape Tagrain

Negros going aboard Ships with
Provisions in their Canoos

Captain Ino Thomas house

an Idol
or
Grigri

a Negro praying to ye Idol

Negros drink
ing and smoaking

THE CORONA LIBRARY

SIERRA LEONE

THE VILLAGE

SIERRA LEONE

A Modern Portrait

BY

ROY LEWIS

LONDON

HER MAJESTY'S STATIONERY OFFICE

1954

First published 1954
Second impression 1957
Third impression 1958

Crown copyright reserved

Published by
HER MAJESTY'S STATIONERY OFFICE

To be purchased from
York House, Kingsway, London w.c.2
423 Oxford Street, London w.1
13a Castle Street, Edinburgh 2
109 St. Mary Street, Cardiff
39 King Street, Manchester 2
Tower Lane, Bristol 1
2 Edmund Street, Birmingham 3
80 Chichester Street, Belfast
or through any bookseller

Price 25s. 0d. net

PRINTED IN GREAT BRITAIN BY THE CURWEN PRESS LTD., LONDON, E.13

THE CORONA LIBRARY

A series of illustrated volumes under the sponsorship of the Colonial Office dealing with the United Kingdom's dependent territories, the way their peoples live, and how they are governed. The series has been designed to fill the place between official Blue Books on the one hand and the writings of occasional visitors on the other, to be authoritative and readable, and to give a vivid yet accurate picture. The books are being written by established authors whose qualifications include, where possible, experience of colonial administration and first-hand knowledge of the territory concerned. Neither Her Majesty's Government in the United Kingdom nor the Governments of the territories necessarily associate themselves with the personal views expressed by the authors. Each volume will contain maps and be fully illustrated.

FOREWORD

By the Rt. Hon. Sir Winston S. Churchill
K.G., O.M., C.H., M.P.

NOT since the days of the Roman Empire has a single nation carried so great a responsibility for the lives of men and women born outside her shores as Great Britain does today. Within her forty or so dependent territories dwell eighty million people for whose welfare and enlightenment Britain is, to a greater or lesser degree, answerable.

There has been no lack of critics, at home and abroad, to belittle Britain's colonial achievement and to impugn her motives. But the record confounds them. Look where you will, you will find that the British have ended wars, put a stop to savage customs, opened churches, schools and hospitals, built railways, roads and harbours, and developed the natural resources of the countries so as to mitigate the almost universal, desperate poverty. They have given freely in money and materials and in the services of a devoted band of Civil Servants; yet no tax is imposed upon any of the colonial peoples that is not spent by their own governments on projects for their own good.

I write 'their own governments' advisedly, for however much diverse conditions may necessitate different approaches, the British have for long had one goal in view for their overseas territories: their ultimate development into nations freely associated within the Commonwealth framework. The present state of the Commonwealth is the proof of the sincerity of this policy.

It is because I believe that Britain's colonial record is too little known and her policies too little understood that I welcome the books of the Corona Library. The aim of these books is to present a contemporary portrait, at once reliable and attractive, of each territory. I warmly commend the series to the attention of the public at home and abroad, for if these publications do even a little to clear away the clouds of misunderstanding and prejudice that have gathered round the very idea of colonial government, they will have been well worth while.

ACKNOWLEDGEMENTS

I owe a quite unrepayable debt to Mr. Gordon Ash, the Public Relations Officer of Sierra Leone, who not only arranged my tour, gave me hospitality and introductions, allowed me to make free with his office and proved an endless source of information and suggestions, but also aided and abetted me in breaking entirely loose from official connections, and encouraged me to meet whomsoever I liked and do whatever took my fancy. It is only proper to acknowledge the courtesy and patience of scores of officials to whom I went for information, and who proved amazingly ready to turn their files upside down for me. It would be invidious to mention names among so many—and especially so many District Commissioners who accorded me so much time and hospitality—but I must express my thanks to His Excellency Sir George Beresford-Stooke, then the Governor, who took a personal interest in the evolution of my doubtless often heterodox views, to Mr. Norman MacRobert, the acting Chief Commissioner, to Mr. F. A. Montague, the Administrative Secretary, and to Mr. G. W. Lines, the Director of Agriculture, who put the facilities of his department at my disposal in the Protectorate.

I received a great deal of help from the staff of Fourah Bay College; especially from an old friend, Mr. Robert Peel, the Bursar, and from Mr. Frederick Dain, the Principal. Mr. Thomas Decker and Mr. Ekun Davis gave me invaluable instruction in Krio; Dr. M. C. F. Easmon and the Hon. A. Casely-Hayford, Minister of Agriculture in the Gold Coast, gave me much useful information and permission to reproduce a few of Gladys Casely-Hayford's creole poems (which I hope will soon find publication in their entirety). Mr. Ralph Wright has given his permission for the reproduction of the music and words of the 'Lyttelton Calypso'. It is, however, impossible for me to thank individually the many ladies and gentlemen who have told me so much about Freetown and creole life—so much more than I can put into this book.

Nor can I individually thank the many Paramount Chiefs who gave me help and *laisser-passer*, though I must mention Paramount Chiefs Jaia Kai Kai, Kai Samba, Bai Kobolo, and Alimami Lahai. To the Rev. T. Harris of the Methodist Mission in Daru, and to Father Joseph Jackson of the Mission of the Holy Cross in Serabu, I owe a special debt of gratitude. And while I was in Freetown, I repeatedly took problems and queries to Mr. E. F. Sayers, whose kindness, like his knowledge of the country, seems to be illimitable. To 'Pa Sayers' I owe permission to reproduce his translations of two poems which appear in the text, and which were first published in *Sierra Leone Studies*.

R.L.

January 1953.

CONTENTS

CHAPTER   PAGE

1. Landfall 1
2. The Stones of Freetown 11
3. Colony 19
4. Creoledom 31
5. Palaver Sauce 41
6. To the Protectorate 52
7. The Wisdom of Bo 62
8. The Wisdom of Njala 74
9. Georgic 85
10. South West 95
11. South East 105
12. The North 114
13. Borboh 123
14. Borboh Grown Up 133
15. Mariama 143
16. Modern Times and Missionary Influences . 151
17. Art—and Arts and Crafts 160
18. The White Man's Grave 165
19. Children and Teachers 176
20. Mount Aureol 186
21. The Mines 194
22. The Childs Plan 204
23. Africanization 217
24. Self Government 226
25. The Wherewithal 236
26. Stirrup Cup 243
BOOKS CONSULTED 249

ILLUSTRATIONS

PLATES

I	The village (*coloured*)	*facing title-page*
II	Farmer and palm fruit	*between pages* 56 *and* 57
III	(a) Suppressing the traffic in slaves (b) Releasing slaves	
IV	Creole street traders in Freetown	
V	Freetown prospect	
VI	The slums of Freetown	
VII	(a) The cotton tree (b) St. Patrick's Church, Kissi	
VIII	The railway leading to the interior	
IX	(a) A district council (b) An up-country market	*between pages* 120 *and* 121
X	(a) Soil erosion (b) Hillside burnt for cultivation	
XI	Njala agricultural college	
XII	Village in the interior	
XIII	'The white man's grave'	
XIV	Doctor, nurse and patient	
XV	(a) Iron ore mine (b) Modern saw-mill	
XVI	(a) and (b) 'Bullom boats'	*between pages* 168 *and* 169
XVII	The deserted village	
XVIII	(a) and (b) Two views from Kent	
XIX	Two views of Shenge	
XX	Bonthe	
XXI	Winnowing newly gathered rice	
XXII	(a) Boiling oil palm fruit (b) Blacksmith	
XXIII	Cutting down the mangroves	
XXIV	'Country cloth'	*between pages* 216 *and* 217
XXV	Infants' school	
XXVI	(a) and (b) New schools	
XXVII	(a) Fourah Bay college at Mount Aureol (b) The building in which the college was originally housed	
XXVIII	A would-be Chief states his claim	
XXIX	Cocoa farmers	

ILLUSTRATIONS

Plates *continued*

xxx   (a) Pioneer oil mills
        (b) The primitive 'method of cracking nuts'
xxxi   Freetown Junior Dinner Club

Acknowledgement is made to the following for the use of photographs: Dr. Spitz, Plate IX (a) and (b); Sierra Leone Development Corporation, Plate XV (a). The photographs in Plates VI, X (a) and (b), XVII, XVIII (a) and (b), XIX (a) and (b), XX, XXII, XXVII (b), XXX (a) were taken by the author.

DRAWINGS

Divination figures	*page* 10
Drums and 'bush piano'	*page* 18
Game of warri	*page* 61
Warri board	*page* 73
Nomoli figure	*page* 84
Poro crocodile mask	*page* 132
Bundu mask (i)	*page* 142
Bundu girls	*page* 159
Bundu masks (ii)	*page* 203
Scarf dance	*page* 242

Drawn for this volume by Levett-Prinsep

MAPS

The Colony	*page* 22
Tribal areas	*page* 58
Mineral resources and vegetation	*page* 77
Lakka village	*page* 90
Main crop areas	*page* 207
Sierra Leone	*at back*

Black-and-white maps drawn by Reitz

1. LANDFALL

Il kabo na kabo
All welcomes are welcomes
CREOLE PROVERB

AT three thousand feet the forest is a vegetable empire reaching to the horizon. A vast, lumpy, tufted mattress of greenery, its leaf-woven surface absorbs the hot sunlight. Here and there a winding ravine, whose brown floor is languidly-moving water, reveals the depth of the pile under that surface: seventy or eighty feet, contested every inch by a host of tropical plants—trees, creepers, parasites, undergrowth—wrestling in a massed embrace upwards for life. For three hours the infinite forest slides slowly eastwards under the wheels of the aircraft—Gold Coast, Côte d'Ivoire, Liberia, Sierra Leone; a broad swath of the West African rain belt.

The plane is squarish, with large oblong windows and unadjustable upright seats like a bus; a slip of paper is handed backwards from passenger to passenger. It gives the course and expected time of arrival, and tells us that we are about to cross the Mano River into British territory. Everybody stares out, to locate another brown lane cutting through the green plateau. Soon after, the appearance of the ground begins to change. It is as though a mowing machine had been roughly thrust through the forest, which looks less dense and matted. Hitherto, little brown clearings in the forest, with the oblong or rounded excrescences which were African huts, had been infrequent; now the intervals between them lessen. They appear in clumps like so many haystacks. Large cleared brown or black patches grow in number and size, like a leaf-blotch on the surface of the green vegetation; at this height the white boles of cut trees look like spilled matchsticks. A spreading vein-structure of red roads or paths asserts itself, and red-brown rivers succeed one another, all flowing slowly southwards and seawards, with an occasional glitter of rapids or shallows.

As we lose height, the land becomes a mottle of lighter and darker greens and browns; the rivers and roads are furred with dark trees along their edges. Among the trees the feathery tufted head-dresses of the palms are more conspicuous. The rivers widen and brighten and merge into broad estuaries fringed with unmistakable mangrove; the water holds a mirror to the flocculent scenery of the clouds as we glide over it, and the engines change their note.

Southwards a line of green hills wears a kerchief of pale vapour; northwards the green mosaic stretches to the horizon; within the cabin the 'Fasten Seat Belts' sign flickers up. Palms —palms—palms flash under and up to the wheels, then tarmac as the plane touches down and bumps to a stop. When the doors open, the warm mugginess of West Africa envelops one's limbs relaxingly.

This first view of Sierra Leone as an aerial map is today the usual one for the busy traveller; and provided he can interpret the meaning of the mottle of greens it is not an unilluminating one (though airplane officers are prone to advise him that 'There's nothing to see'). It is certainly more revealing than the first glimpse of West Africa given to the traveller by sea. For him, skirting the shores in a liner, as the Carthaginian explorer Hanno did in a galley 2,500 years earlier, West Africa presents itself as a low, flat, uninviting coast, for much of its length defended by mangrove swamps, and furnishing no clue to the nature of the interior.

On the Guinea coast, the Sierra Leone range of mountains is, indeed, the one salient feature, which, when approached from the sea, appears, in the words of an eighteenth-century visitor, 'to rise gradually from the sea to a stupendous height richly wooded and beautifully ornamented by the hand of nature with a variety of delightful prospects'. Freetown is clustered round its base. The air traveller, like the sea traveller, now approaches it in a boat, for the Lungi airport is on the northern side of the Sierra Leone or Rokel river, and he must be taken across in a launch. His first view of the mountains of the Colony penin-sula was from above, now he sees them from sea level. As he enters the huge harbour from the Bullom shore, the line of white foam on the harbour bar appears from the landward side. Skirting the long waterfront of the town he lands at Govern-ment Wharf as thousands of Europeans have disembarked before him from steamers, from sailing ships, from steamships that carried sails: a long line of officials and Governors, business men and missionaries, doctors, explorers, prospectors, scientists and simple sailors; and, like them, he lands near the steps where thousands of liberated slaves came ashore as free men and women.

For anyone with a sense of the past it is logical to start a visit to Sierra Leone with its historic little capital city, where the first shadow which falls upon the visitor will be cast by the bulk of the Lower Commissariat, a long, low, red early Victorian building, in which pale-faced red-coats were once housed. But to gain the best perspective of the whole territory today, I think it might be better to arrive in Sierra Leone from somewhere in Liberia, and reach Freetown last. The past is potent in Freetown, and in the Colony peninsula; but in terms of the forest it is a recent past, going back no further than a little before the French Revolution. The processes of the forests develop more slowly than that; and their longer memories, perhaps, are the stronger and wiser for being mainly unconscious. The missionary, the anthropologist, the naturalist, the enthusiastic administrator have good reasons for spending as little time as possible in the Freetown atmosphere before they go up-country. But Freetown is the gateway to the country, indeed almost the only one, besides being a traditional port of call on The Coast. It belongs, I came to feel, more to Europe and America than to Africa; its immense harbour, exceeded in capacity only by Rio and Sydney, has sheltered their argosies in the world expansion of the West, while in two world wars it has witnessed the fateful events of Western, especially of British, sea-born hegemony. It is the site of the first effort by the West to redeem three hundred years or more of piracy and plunder in Africa—to work out a new policy towards its peoples based on the Christian component of our Western civilization: a policy in harmony with the emergent ideals of a new British Empire, a gunboat-guarded evangel of Reform, Humanitarianism and Progress. The stones of Freetown heard the British ideal formulated before Lugard or Curtis were born; and many of the bold things said today in a dozen cities in Africa were said here when those cities were mud-and-wattle villages. It is not easy in Freetown to say anything new about the opportunities which the Commonwealth offers Africans.

The Union flag, as flown at Trafalgar, without St. Patrick's cross, was hoisted here in May 1787. This was five years after

3

Britain had renounced the American colonies for ever, a year before the flag ran up the flagstaff at Botany Bay. The British Empire was a small affair of islands, strong-points and settlements on the edge of unexplored continents, an Empire of the sea and vague if profitable Indian hegemonies operated by well-armed joint-stock companies. To this somewhat unpromising sketch of the second British Empire was added twenty square miles acquired from King Tombo, the Temne chief of the Sierra Leonian mountain peninsula, in exchange for rum, muskets and an embroidered waistcoat. This area is now the centre of Freetown, Britain's oldest African possession (Gambia excepted). Britain has been here for 170 years. In Freetown the traveller sees one of Britain's oldest overseas cities which, outside the West Indies, is probably the oldest founded by Britons which is still flying the Union flag.

It is a small place, though in 170 years it has spread from King Tom's first concession up the hills and round the bays where the pirates used to land for water. But it has the serene unhurried pace of a small English port, further slowed by tropical languor. Grass grows still in wide main streets which are shaded with cassias and another yellow-flowering tree, *Peltoferium*, while bright orange lizards run under the sightseer's feet. The streets were originally laid out on a grid plan, yet there is nothing planned about Freetown, which has grown gently round its first beginnings as an English town grows round its Roman layout. There are no central squares or Government cantonments. No attempt has ever been made to impose any architectural unity; fine buildings have been put up here and there as a site offered, and they must be sought out for their historical or other interest. For the rest, convenience, fashion, commerce and the law of freehold possession have dictated its growth. At first one gains the impression that there is nothing much to see, yet it is impossible to grow tired of the scene. Freetown charms by its oddments and out-of-the-way corners; many surprising details, as they are discovered, make up the individuality of the whole—for example, the significant number of slate roofs in a town 3,000 miles from Welsh slate workings, which mellows and lessens the effect of endless tin shanties produced on the eye by the usual African city.

Slate roofs are a reminder that Freetown possessed dignity

and comfort—except for servants sweltering under the slates in the attics—before corrugated iron spread through the world, playing its great though unsung role in subduing the wilderness. British cars in the streets, green double-decker buses which might belong to Bournemouth Corporation, street names and notices in English, somehow do not add up to the impression of British influence in this tropical place; it lies in something infinitely subtle—in the way the place has grown, the square castellated church towers, the church bells, the punctual arrival of civil servants at the Secretariat, a Victorian flavour in everything, and, above all, something in the bearing of many—not all—Africans in the streets. It is hard to find words for it. I can only say that I felt that many of them, slightly overdressed for the climate, would have welcomed the return of the top-hat. I learned later that many creole families possess ancestral toppers, though it is now rare to be buried in one. There is, in fact, a genuine vein of uncomfortable antimacassar respectability in Freetown—worn thin, no doubt, but perceptible, and the more redolent of England in its contrast to the prevailing air of laxity and indolence.

But Freetown is essentially a creole metropolis. Its most typical, most revealing aspect is its domestic architecture: the thousands upon thousands of little homes of every sort and size. Big houses, like that built by Sir Samuel Lewis, are witness to creole success in the past; the rest vary all the way from stone or concrete down to wood and flattened kerosene tins, down, on the outskirts, to the indigenous African house of wattle and mud-daub with palm-thatch roof. But the average is between the two: the little gabled house, with a laterite or brick first floor, and a wooden second storey, its wall space so filled with lattices that it resembles in size and shape an English signal-box. Lit up at night by municipal electricity, these upper floors provide enchanting peepshows into creole *décor* and life; furniture of the Decorated 'Eighties period mixed with modern Tottenham Court Road style imported by the United Africa Co., or even made by the P.W.D.; square, oval and circular picture frames—whole walls of family portraiture; scenic wallpaper; coloured china ornaments and curios either imported in bulk or landed in odd lots by every incoming vessel from every port in the world; tiny magpie-nests of rooms, crowded with possessions and people. These houses line the roads to the suburbs, Fourah Bay, Kissy, Congo-Cross, Pademba. Some are in the last stages of dilapidation. Others are in various stages of construction—it is not lucky to build a house all at once. Many now have concrete walls; but everywhere are to be seen the most ingenious little houses made of the sides of packing cases, old iron, flattened drums and hessian sacking, often neatly painted.

In the main thoroughfares are the shops, built on the eastern or mediaeval plan: a large or small chamber at street-level with a counter bisecting it and merchandise on shelves behind; or even with a glass counter and elegant furnishings—but closed by stout wooden shutters. Freetown has only a few plate-glass windows; window shopping is as yet undeveloped, as are the wiles of advertising. The smallest English village seems to carry more signs and hoardings than this capital. Even the proprietor's name is small, and his business baldly stated or compressed into an epigram: 'general dealer' or 'sympathetic bootmaker'. From the moment of landing the Syrian grip upon retail trade is impressed on the mind by the succession of Levantine and Muslim names over shops. Most of them sell almost anything that will sell; there is little specialization. To the newcomer it seems bafflingly difficult to buy anything; like the shop in *Alice in Wonderland* the place is chock full, but you can never pin down just what you want. But that is because shopping attitudes are different in West Africa. People know what they want; the range of their wants is narrow. Shops that seem vivid with colour and variety are found, on closer examination, to hold a limited stock-in-trade.

In the streets the people weave an unending fabric of colour and variety; though Freetown is neither Delhi nor Port Said as a meeting-place of races, there are classes, occupations, and twenty or more tribes to be distinguished—and above all, faces. Who's creole and who's not? There are African girls slim and assured in print frocks that might have been bought in London's Oxford Street; African girls in native dress of every hue that Manchester can print, as well as some that are obviously locally dyed—a skirt and a blouse, but worn in half a dozen styles in accordance with the custom of half a dozen tribes; older women in long dresses resembling Regency smocks; schoolgirls walking in

6

twos, and even crocodiles, wearing adaptations of English school uniforms of mauve or puce, with straw hats or berets; and then the eye is caught by a girl wearing only a cunningly-wrapped skirt, some necklaces and a coif of braids done up with cowrie-shells, who presents with serene confidence a perfectly sculptured ebony torso to the world.

Men's dress is no less varied in the streets, though the flowered cotton toga, the *Kente* of the Gold Coast, is regrettably absent. Shirt and shorts predominate, but may be vividly patterned, and the shirt may be worn outside or tucked in. Clothing may be reduced to a loin cloth or consist of volumin-ous and dignified robes sweeping the dust; these may be plain white or embroidered richly. There is every variety of Euro-pean attire, but tending to colour, patterning and lightness; trousers as well as ties are often vivid; fedoras may be turquoise blue or even scarlet. It is as though a choreographer had dressed his *corps de ballet* in burlesque variations upon a theme of double-breasted lounge suits. But up towards the Law Courts move dignified gentlemen carrying papers, in Geneva bands, pin stripe, and jackets blacker than their faces.

They move slow-footed through the humid air, with eddies of lounging idlers at every corner where large women sit with small wares spread before them on a mat laid on the pavement or on boxes or trestles. At twilight the streets are thick with a dark citizenry thus informally garbed. They can be followed to the little box-like houses or, more of them, to the tin shanties which lie behind the railway and East Street, or the slums of Kroo Town. They are the people for whom the place was founded; the inheritors of the Abolitionists' dreams and the Reformers' plans; voters, ratepayers, townsfolk, the dwellers between the ships in the harbour and the inland of Africa stretching mottled green and brown endlessly eastwards.

Freetown climbs the hills which look down on its harbour and estuary. The civil service lives at Hill Station, breathing a cooler and more rarefied air, and the Public Works Department runs up more bungalows around it; a signpost warns lorry-drivers that they cannot enter the precincts without a signed authorization from the Director of the Public Works Depart-ment. The Army has barracks on Tower Hill, somewhat lower. On Mount Aureol the academic forces of Fourah Bay College can

7

look down analytically on the whole sweep of the town from Frenchman's Bay to Kissy; the thousands of tin and hundreds of tiled or slated roofs, the occasional office block, the churches, the crumbling slums: the world's third largest harbour, with anchoring for 200 ships, which possesses one small wharf and a new deep-water quay under construction to take the place of the boats and lighters which for 170 years have been adequate to load and offload the few ships that are in normal times enough to carry away all that Sierra Leone can produce.

For all its harbour, for all its long start on Accra, or Lagos, or Dar es Salaam, it is a small place; its charm is the charm of a small place; its pace and pulse is that of a small place that has grown slowly. Once it had two hotels; but today the traveller has the choice of staying with hospitable friends, or in the Transit Camp, or in the City Hotel. Hospitality is rarely lacking, but generally takes one up the hills above the town. The Transit Camp is said to be comfortable; but I find something nasty and post-war and Orwellish in the idea of being in transit. The City Hotel, on the other hand, is a remarkable hostelry where much that is true, and much that is entirely false, can be learned about Sierra Leone in quite a short time. At its bar can be heard the authentic voice of The Coast. The Coast knows why Freetown has remained small while Accra and Lagos have developed so fast; The Coast knows what goes on up-country and in the Legislative Council and in the Governor's head; The Coast knows why the Government Fishery trawler was sabotaged and how, and just what is going wrong or right with half a dozen other pretty projects for raising Sierra Leone by its bootstraps. The Coast can tell the newly-arrived traveller why there is no water in the town pipes just before the rains come, and who made a mess of the water scheme. The Coast can tell him also the meaning of the throbbing of drums and the cries and shouts which he heard in the region of Pademba Road on his first night—the sounds of the secret rites in the Bundu Bush where girls are initiated into womanhood in the traditional African way. For there is a Bundu Bush in Freetown, and the newspapers, while deprecating the noise and inconvenience to the neighbourhood, do not denounce it; for after all quite a number of the mauve- and puce- and green-uniformed but nubile-looking schoolgirls who walk in crocodiles through the streets will be rushed through Sande in the holidays.

And while The Coast has been explaining these things, and hinting the unchangeableness of Africa and the African, clouds have gathered and suddenly lightning cleaves the sky; thunder detonates in the mountains and over the city like the firing of 8-inch guns from the vacant emplacements of the ruined forts on Aureol. The rain smacks down hard, vicious, torrential, hammering on the iron roofs with millions of tiny fists, peppering the roadways and making the dust jump in the gardens. It roars down, a forest of driven liquid rods, bombarding the earth and loading it with water. Now the deep gutters, two or more feet deep and as wide, which run down either side of the Freetown streets, show their purpose; they become swirling rivers. In heavy enough rain, it is said, children have been swept away and drowned in them. But the so-called 'tornadoes', which are common at the beginning and the end of the rains in Freetown and the Colony peninsula, are not regarded as serious rain by the inhabitants of an area which receives 150 inches ($12\frac{1}{2}$ feet) a year—mostly in July and August. There will be no sign of the downpour tomorrow morning, and it will be perfectly safe to go to bathe at Lumley beach without taking an umbrella.

But the newcomer has been presented with another important element in the life of the place to which he has come. Let him watch the jump of the bare earth in the garden of the City Hotel, as the sprays of bougainvilia and hibiscus bow in supplication; let him meditate what becomes of it as it floods off the road and soaks into the soil. For the rain and the forest govern much in West Africa. The rain has much to do with the size of Freetown, with the lighters unloading the ships, with the idlers on the street corners, with the throb of the Bundu drums, with the weary wisdom of The Coast, with the remoteness of Hill Station, with the Syrian names over the shops, with the lush greenery of the mountains, with the failure of well-planned schemes, with what goes on in the Legislative Council and in the Governor's head.

It has everything to do with what Sierra Leone is now, and can become as part of the British Commonwealth in the years ahead. Most people would consider that November, after the rains have fallen, the skies have cleared, and the harvests have been gathered, is the best time to visit Sierra Leone. But rain is one of the principal characters in the great drama being enacted here, and the first tornado of the year is a suitable overture.

Divination figures of the 'Yassi' secret society used to determine guilt in chiefs' courts. The taller one was brought back by Alldridge at the beginning of the century.

2. THE STONES OF FREETOWN

> *Yu dro rop, rop dro bus, leppet kam na tong*
> Pull on a rope, the rope pulls in the
> forest, and with the forest the leopards
> come to town   CREOLE PROVERB

NEAR the Law Courts, at the junction of Westmorland Street and Pademba Road, there stands a colossal cotton tree, nearly a hundred feet high, which has seen the city grow from rows of wattle houses plastered with clay. The great buttresses which support the huge silvery-green trunk take on the quality of a drape, and the branches overspread the road-crossing, where a policeman in a flat peaked cap directs the traffic and a neat telephone box stands. In the branches, if you look up, and if you have the Four Eyes, you will see witches' capes hanging by the hundred; possession of one confers magical powers, but they are trying things to own as once you have one you cannot get rid of it, and if you show it to anyone else (invisible as it is) it will kill you. The telephone box is also very magical; whatever number you dial you get a different one, and while you are waiting for your wrong number you can hear calypsos or the news on the rediffusion programme.

Across the way, the steelwork of the new Government House is being fleshed in concrete on the foundations of old Fort Thornton which was first built to repel attacks by 'Timmanee' war-boys—in 1801 they nearly captured it and wounded Governor Dawes as, sword in hand, he led the defence. Its architecture is beginning to suggest a pavilion at an international exhibition, but at least it will enable the Governor to descend again from the clouds of Hill Station and live once more among his people—and not only his people, his ministers. For though no Houses of Parliament are yet being built by the P.W.D. to the designs of the Government Architect, the Legislative Council is now controlled by an African majority, while in the Executive Council six African 'Ministers-in-training' are learning how to run their departments and the country.[1]

[1] This probationary period ended as I passed the proofs (May 1953) of this book. See postscript on p. 235.

As concrete-and-steel construction comes in, as aerial surveys are set in motion, as science is applied to fisheries, to agriculture, to everything, European power is beginning to pass away. It is passing, however, not to the descendants of the ex-slaves who built Freetown—but to the people of the interior who are, in the fullness of time, reclaiming what was once sold for an embroidered waistcoat. Even in the capital, the creoles are in a minority. Self-government on any representative basis means government by the peoples of the tribes—by the Temnes, who owned the soil on which Fort Thornton was built; by the Mendes, the largest tribe in the country; by the Bulloms, who were thrust into the coastal swamps at the hands of the Mendes and Temnes, by the Korankos and Limbas and Susus and many others who make up the tribal blend of the country.

Freetown seems dominated by Anglican churches. The foundation stone of St. George's (so named in recognition of George IV) was laid, together with that of St. Patrick's in Kissy, by Sir Charles MacCarthy, in 1817. It was Sir Charles who, as Governor of the West African settlements controlled from Freetown, was defeated by an Ashanti army, and his embalmed head became a potent medicine of theirs. Thereafter, seven governors laboured on St. George's, and spent £5,000 on it, and meantime permitted the persecution of the Muslims who had the effrontery to set up mosques in a Christian city-to-be. But today the strength of Islam in the city shows itself in Eid-ul-Fitri, when the drums beat and vast crowds take possession of the streets carrying paper lanterns and dragging enormous illuminated set pieces—battleships 30 feet long made of laths and coloured tissue paper—on carts and barrows. It takes a State occasion, or the recent visit of the Archbishop of Canterbury, to fill St. George's now: at one time the Governor led the Colony into church twice every Sunday like a Victorian paterfamilias. But if the churches become emptier, the new Welfare Department is extremely busy, running approved schools, youth movements and community centres, dealing with marriage problems and child guidance; struggling to bring service and discipline into modern African life.

In 1938 a medical expert urged, during the annual Health and Baby Week, the construction of a cinema to improve Freetown's morals by providing a healthy outlet. Freetown now has its cinema, but the rates of insurance rise as crime takes increasing toll. The disintegration of the war years, so lovingly delineated by Graham Greene in *The Heart of the Matter*, sets a task for cinema, Churches, Welfare Department and police. Goods are stolen from the wharves; the clothes of bathers are stolen from Lumley beach; indeed the clothes of sleeping people are snitched from their very bedsides by rod and line; I was frisked of my pocket-book as sweetly as a sleeping babe. But then, diamonds are smuggled out of the country with impunity by a ring of dealers, while even respectable British traders thought it commonsense to smuggle coffee in view of the unwillingness of the British Ministry of Food to pay a fraction of the French price. 'Tief tief, God laf,' say the creoles: When thief robs thief, who cares?

This is no more than a sign that Freetown mirrors conditions everywhere today. It may be a small place, and the pace leisurely. None the less it is cosmopolitan, and the pace quickens. It has a historic past; but that does not mean that history has finished with it. The restless winds that disturb every part of Africa blow here.

There are many social Freetowns. The Freetown of the official world spends the day in the secretariat (or in spill-over offices in the Nissen huts left over from the war), and the evenings and nights in its bungalows in Hill Station. A mountain railway carried it to and from its work between 1904 and 1925, traversing Water Street, Westmorland Street and Brookfields; and seats were taken in the train with strict regard for seniority in the service. Today everyone has cars with which to cover the distance between the world of official files and committees and the world of official cocktail parties and bridge. Hill Station is often accused of being remote and standoffish, and the Governor is returning to Freetown. But in fact African officials who can do so are only too happy to live in Hill Station. There is no social barrier in Hill Station, though until recently few even among the educated creoles dined there frequently. But The Hill Station Club is open to Africans now, and Government House parties, which set the tone, are uncompromisingly multi-racial. European and African judges, scientists, journalists, doctors, business tycoons and visitors of all nationalities meet there in lively if select discussion.

Cline Town Club, however, insists for its own reasons that it is the meeting place of friendly folk as against the exclusiveness of Hill Station. Here you meet the railway people, the executives of banks and shipping firms, technical men down from 'the mines' to do some shopping, business people of all kinds. Here the visitor meets The Coast, if he has not already met it leaning against the City or Normandy bars. He will also meet here the representatives of 'The Firms', whose exalted position in the trade and development of this territory compels one to capitalize respectfully throughout. The Firms are the four or five powerful trading companies who buy the produce in all West African territories, and sell everything from jeeps to toilet goods. They stand quite apart, both in history and scale, from the multitude of Syrian traders and the innumerable African small shopkeepers. Though there is competition, of a sort, between them, they hold the door in West Africa—and, hitherto, without much regard for newfangled ideas of public relations, though the advance towards African self-government has made them more sensitive.

The leader among them, of course, is the United Africa Company, whose hand is everywhere, hidden or open, and which maintains most of the plate-glass frontages in Freetown, since it controls G. B. Ollivant and Pickering and Berthoud; followed by Paterson Zochonis. But the famous 'French Company'—Compagnie Française de l'Afrique Occidentale, or 'C.F.A.O.', and the other French firm Société Commerçiale de l'Ouest Afrique, or 'S.C.O.A.', also operate in Freetown and up-country.

The Firms and the Syrians dominate the trading section. Many of the older brick houses in Freetown were built by creoles. Although from the first creoles found themselves in keen competition with the Fulas, within living memory all East Street and Kissy Road was a creole trading area. Now the Syrians' shops stand shoulder to shoulder, and the Fulas operate from shanties in odd corners. Creole trading is reduced to marketing along the roads and railway line, and in the market facing Kroo Bay, whither the country boats under their lateen sails bring rice and fish and fruit and a hundred minor necessities from the Bullom shore. These boats, capable of carrying 70 people at 10 knots before the wind, themselves enshrine history, for their design has not changed since the Portuguese taught the Bulloms to build them. In the market the full variety of African produce is spread out and tells the story of life in the African home. Here you will see, besides the cheap imported utensils and textiles, palm oil soap at 1d. the small tablet; cassava balls, or foo-foo, for starch; cassava leaf for spinach; alligator peppers; red camwood for rubbing on babies' skins or use as a dye; charcoal made from mangrove wood, preferred for baking bread; cowries to be crushed to make medicine; ginger, also medicinal, recommended for the coughs which are increasingly afflicting the poor of Freetown; cinchona bark, to be boiled to make a medicinal tea and to be taken as a purge; *brokobak* nuts; dried snails, a delicacy to take home for your husband's tea; *gbongo*, an unpleasant stuff used to grease children's sores; goats' horns, which have peculiar uses that embarrass the market mammy to explain; crude African wooden spoons and combs; spices with a score of names; raffia; cloves; roots to be boiled for children with malaria; *malombo*, a red bark, sovereign against the piles; *finga*, to be boiled as a morning pick-me-up; garlic; porcupine quills, still preferred for writing Arabic script; beads innumerable and fascinating, and liable to sprout, if planted, into every variety of tropical plant; iron rings of Loko manufacture, to keep witches off babies; peanuts; clay pots, crude but serviceable; calabashes and sea salt; and a hundred other things which, if their origin and uses were fully traced, would throw a searchlight upon the medicinal herbs and plants of West Africa, and the lives and beliefs of the people. Above all you will see tins of the rich red palm oil that is Sierra Leone's blood and sap, her true wealth; and heaps of kola nuts which are West Africa's stimulant and sedative in one—aspirin, nicotine and caffein together.

All around there is chaffering in a language that the visitor will mostly not understand, though he may catch the drift occasionally:

'Omos fo dis fisse?'

'Four coppa' [2d.].

'Yu nor go lo me?'

'Nar so dem all day sellum!'

'Ar don se betta pris!'

'Orit: takum fo tree coppa!'

In this market building was held, in 1865, the Great Industrial Exhibition, which looked forward to the colonial advances and triumphs to come. The crafts of British and French West Africa were on display—cloth of intricate design, mats, carpets, baskets, leather bags and cases, war pouches and saddlery; lovely work by the Joloffs who had their shops in East Street. The Fulas at that time could make the locks of rifles, however intricate; steel spectacles; rings that a white bride did not disdain to wear. Craftsmanship was on show such as could not be collected now. Freetown has lost its craftsmen and hardly gained a factory.

Yet it seems by nature designed for greatness, with hills that soar into the cooler air, and 4,000 acres of eight to 14 fathoms of sheltered water and a bottom of good holding ground. Barbot in the seventeenth century described 'the fine bright colour of sandy bar, looking at a distance like a large spread of a sail of a ship. The strand there is clear from the rocks, which renders easy the access of boats and sloops to take in fresh water. A few paces from the sea is that curious fountain where a ship may fill 100 casks a day.' By the first traders this harbour was selected as the gateway to West Africa. From 1672 to 1762 the Royal Africa Company had at Bunce Island a fort whose walls and cannon remain. Along the shores of what is now Cline Bay was a town containing the fine houses of thirty European traders, who with rum and dancing girls entertained pirate captains and Royal Africa Company captains with a fine indiscrimination. Master Crackers, for example, saluted all craft entering the river with his three guns.

As early as 1799 Freetown had a mayor and aldermen. It had a long start in civic development on any other West African settlement. By 1811 it had a population of 2,000; by 1851 of 18,000; by 1891 of 30,000. Its streets echo its history. Pademba Road, along part of whose length is cast the dark shadows of the prison, commemorates a headman, Pa Demba, to whose village the terrified ex-slaves fled when a French ship, flying the tricolour, sacked the settlement against the orders of the National Convention which had promised to respect it in the name of the Goddess of Reason, Liberty, Fraternity and the Rights of Man. George Street is called after George III, Wilberforce Street, and, of course, the Wilberforce Hall, from the man who led the anti-slave trade forces; Bathurst Street from a colonial secretary whose name is perpetuated in towns in Canada, Australia, South Africa and Gambia also. Walpole Street recalls General Walpole, who defeated the uprising of the Negroes in Jamaica, and brought many of the rebels to be resettled in Sierra Leone. Freetown's streets are redolent of the Regency and early Victorian England. It had the first railway terminal in West Africa, and the first railway—leading to a country the size of Ireland.

Is Freetown a city which has somehow missed its rendezvous with destiny? Is the charm of its historic associations, its Sunday quiet, the symptom of some fatal malnutrition at the growing-point? What is there about its hinterland that keeps trade around the figure of £6 per head, compared with Gold Coast's £30?

'All the same, there's been progress', said an elderly resident to me. 'I can remember when starving natives from up-country begged in the streets of Freetown during the hungry season.' He added: 'And before the war, the Secretariat officials used to drop in here for a drink about twelve. You couldn't get near the bar. Now they're too damn busy with all these economic plans and making a good impression on their African ministers. . . .' Now, indeed, men from up-country come to wield political power, to think of Freetown as their capital, not as the amazing creation of 'White man's Juju'. As a Mende expressed it to Dr. Little, the anthropologist: 'I became a sort of idiot as we moved along . . . I took a very keen interest in gazing at two-storey buildings, I admired people moving in them, and often asked my brother if they would not fall from there.' Freetown found it hard to influence the interior in the years of Victorian supremacy; now that it has succeeded, the people from the interior begin to crowd the streets ever more thickly and to claim it as their own.

African cities like Accra, Lagos, and Dar es Salaam are straightforward enough—booming, shantified, suburban, boring, extroverted. Freetown is not. It has a complex, with-drawn, faintly melancholy character, scarred with failure and disappointment. It has suffered. It tried, perhaps, to do too much too soon. It sees through modern clichés, while submitting to modern pressures. Welfare—certainly: though it can recall that the high ideal of African liberation in fact made Freetown itself for years the finest slave-market on The Coast. Deep-water quays—certainly: though Freetown recalls that it took 40 years to build Government Wharf, and it fell down several times, even then. Freetown is subtle, as people who know failure and disappointment are subtle. For all its colour and bustle, it wears an expression of whimsical disbelief; in its soft and humid air one seems to catch sometimes a long-drawn sigh.

Two drums and xylophone or 'bush piano' (see p. 163).

3. COLONY

Da say we kan tie cow na dey go et grass
A cow must graze where she's tied

CREOLE PROVERB

THE 20-mile chunky range of green mountains which harbours the thunder and dominates the flat coastline has been called Sierra Leone since the early Portuguese explorers likened the mutterings along its summit to the roaring of lions. Only within the last 60 years has the name, incongruously but for want of better, been extended to the whole hinterland put under British rule. (Only one lion has ever been seen in the whole country, and none in the Colony: nor have any 'tygers', anticipated by early navigators.) The Colony is spoken of as a peninsula, an accurate description for the children's geography books, and preferable at a time when all men of good will are trying to give the territory a new unity. But to me it appeared an island—an island racially, culturally, politically: a British-made island anchored off the West African coast. When the settlers first landed, it was part of the Temne country which stretches northwards up the river for 100 miles; but communication was always by water rather than by land. Bounded on the west by the sea and on the east by the river, on the landward side the mountains were cut off from the mainland, rather than connected to it, by a neck of peculiarly difficult country—mangrove swamps and a network of ravines. Not until 1940 was this neck of land crossed by a motor road, and when in 1906 it was for the first time crossed by the railway, officials were lavish in their praise of the achievements of engineering genius at such places as Orugu gorge:

'Only those who have travelled on foot over a deep tropical gorge know what it can mean,' wrote Travelling Commissioner Alldridge in 1909, 'and it is only they who can be at all adequately thankful for these railway viaducts. The gorge used to be one of the most formidable obstacles of the traveller, especially when he came upon one unawares. Perhaps after he had managed to struggle through a long stretch of bush or heavily timbered forest, he suddenly saw an enormous chasm yawning before him. How deep it might be he could not tell; it appeared a bottomless abyss. Or he might be in a hammock going along the edge of a gorge, as I have frequently been, when his men would cry, "Massa, suppose we go fall down dem place they no go find we again!" . . . This broad, rocky wilderness spanned only by a delicate iron bridge little more than the width of the train is a terrible place to gaze down into even from the security of the railway carriage.'

Between the settling of the Colony and the laying of the railway Sierra Leone was to all intents an island, comparable with Zanzibar or Trinidad: a tidy geographical entity for the Colonial Office to contemplate with satisfaction—a national home for Liberated Africans, with limited liability. A happy ending for a rather reckless adventure in philanthropy. Britain seems always to have liked islands, perhaps because she is an island herself. Her collection of islands is a representative one, with specimens from every ocean and climate; and she wears it as a necklace that goes well with the trident. It is continents, not islands, which, in Disraeli's phrase, become millstones about her neck; and these have mostly been given independence, or have taken it, as he foretold. For a hundred years the Colony was consciously or unconsciously thought of as separate from the hinterland.

This, perhaps, was the easier inasmuch as it gives the impression of an island. Though it has a coastline for only three-quarters of its boundaries, the mountains give it cohesion and individuality. And what a coastline! A series of curved beaches like burnished scimitars honed and ground by the surge; tropic greenery pressing down to high-tide mark; promontories crested with palms thrust out into turquoise waters; islands like emeralds set in platinum lying offshore; every association with *Robinson Crusoe*, *The Tempest* and Technicolor travelogues continuously titivated. And behind lies the Sierra, foothills and mountains rising to 2,500 feet, densely clad in forest—indeed, in some of the indigenous forest. Above the 600-foot level you find, besides the buttressed cotton trees, towering African mahogany, ironwood trees, golden walnut and pearwood. In the past, especially on the steeper slopes, they were protected by the difficulties of access, and now they are protected by law.

A rush of bizarre impressions make up the total impact of this tropic luxuriance. Dark, densely-leafed mango trees overhang the roads, their fallen fruit impregnating the air with an aroma of sickly ripeness. The ungainly breadfruit seems artificially decorated with the green globes that depend from its upcurving branches. The monkey-apple displays an unhealthy-looking fruit of yellow streaked with crimson. In the valleys the pulpy flesh and bedraggled fronds of the bananas, and the fibrous, ringed stems of the paw-paws, loaded with golden lusciousness, suggest the hydroponics of vegetative growth in the porous, water-leached soils. Here and there may be seen the light bark and the dark, secretive leaves of the kola tree, bearing in clusters the coveted nuts which have social significance throughout West Africa: kola that is the symbol of friendship, proper offerings at meetings and departings and religious occasions—kola whose quinine-bitter taste accompanies a power to keep hungry porters on the march beneath their 80-pound head loads, to nourish sick men unable to take or keep down food, to underpin the jaded bridegroom's prowess, to prolong the Bundu dancer's strength from midnight till dawn and on into high noon again.

Flowers gleam like jewels in the disordered network of coiled creepers, 'country ropes' and convolvulus: the yellow, sweet-scented blossom of the acacias, the white tassels of the rose apple, the pale stars of the amaryllis, the delicate rubescence of the damask roses, the garnet flowers of ginger, the deep purple of the straggling guava, the brassy vulgarity of the African marigolds, the crimson balls that swing from the locust tree, the diverse blooms of cactus and anemone, of tree and creeper, ground orchid and flowering grasses. Brighter than flowers, and beyond description in shape and insignia, flit butterflies whose wings seem cut from flowered taffetas, shot silks, brocades, sequin-studded voiles, intimate lace-edged satins; snips of iridescent fabrics beyond the synthesis of the textile chemist, the versatility of looms, or the palette of printer or dyer. Perfumes of orange, frangipani, lilac and pineapple suffuse the air palpable with heat, humidity and languor, musical with the mechanical hum of insects, the intermittent song of birds, and the frou-frou of tumbled foliage in an occasional breeze.

In this green island are set a score of Colony villages. They possess in miniature the same indefinable charm as Freetown, but nostalgia impregnates their picturesque quiet like the frangipani; it is almost too much. They nestle in valleys or

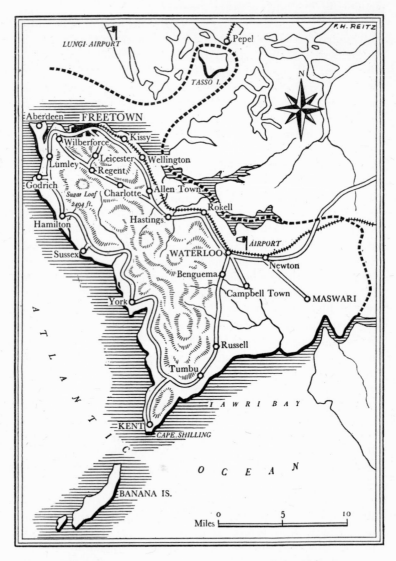

The Colony area, showing Freetown and the Colony villages. Other small coastal areas included in the Colony include Bonthe, Sherbro Island, and Turner's Peninsula (see end map). The rest of Sierra Leone is a Protectorate.

find a hollow behind the sounding shore. They shelter against mountainsides, or stand back in the shade of mangoes and monkey-apples from the main roads from Freetown to the Protectorate, clusters of little box-like houses, with gables and fretted half-screens, overgrown with bougainvilia and set in gardens vivid with yellow allemanda, the delicate red pagoda flower brought from Ceylon, and the brilliant purple blossom of the pineapples which wear their spiky crests like gatherings of warriors. Each village has one or more little rose-red churches, built in Regency Gothic style; the windows are set with panes of plain blue or red coloured glass, and the square towers hold no bells. These are usually mounted in a small stone or wooden structure at one side. The walls are often thickly embossed on the outside with the simplest of memorial plaques—a 9-inch square of concrete or plaster incised with a name and dates. In some cases these commemorate the families who subscribed to build the church.

The larger villages have a *barri* in the native style—an open-sided building whose roof is supported on pillars, like a small English market; it is designed for the hearing of court cases, and for other gatherings, in reasonable coolness. Among the wooden or stone houses will be dotted some native houses with palm-thatched roofs and mud walls; mostly square in the approved style, with verandahs, but some circular with conical roofs. There will be a school. With Mr. Maurice Jones, the Commissioner for the Rural Areas, I walked through the village of Kent, a group of houses, some inhabited, some deserted, scattered along a branch road. We passed the shell of a large mission house, the walls gaping, the roof sagging, and went towards the shore through a gap in walls built as though they had been intended to enclose a gentleman's park. From a long, low brick building came the sound of children's voices singing:

> All things bright and beautiful,
> All creatures great and small . . .

They had no idea of the tune; their voices were a series of little cracked bells as the teacher marked time; in the dimness behind them, another class was engaged on some other task. The school had been there for over 100 years, and was designed in accordance with Victorian ideas of a single classroom under high master, ushers and monitors. The song itself had probably been sung for nearly 100 years, apt to the hauntingly beautiful vista of the Banana Islands, shrouded in a rainstorm, which could be seen almost from the school door across a foreshore under whose tangle of bush and creeper lay old seaward defences against pirate raids. A single cannon was visible.

The charm of the Colony villages is the charm of decay. Their populations are declining. Waterloo, the largest Colony town outside Freetown, with a population of less than 5,000, has seven churches, one of which is abandoned. In every road a third of the houses seem to be boarded up, or split and collapsing like rotten teeth. But vegetation quickly covers them; the villages sink imperceptibly under the green tide. The houses go; the little congregations dwindle, and the churches themselves will disappear in time. York, with its superb rest-house perched on a spur of the hills which divide two bays, is hardly more than a single street. Regent, now a tiny place in the hills, had in 1850 a congregation of 1,000, as compared with an average Sunday attendance at St. George's in Freetown of 500. Only those that have become suburbs of Freetown grow and prosper and contribute to the import of corrugated iron, such as Lumley, where the Europeans play golf and bathe, and Kissy, which was originally founded to settle a consignment of Kissis, then considered a peculiarly savage, slave-dealing tribe.

Enough is left of the Colony villages to see what they once were: pioneering settlements intended to give Freetown a hinterland of trade, agriculture and market gardening. To the colonizers' minds, the green hilly island ought to be dotted with little towns and villages resembling the greater island whose power and conscience in alliance had freed the slaves and now was to elevate them to the full enjoyment of civilization. Like their benefactors, they had freedom, they had the English Common Law, they had the Anglican—and the Wesleyan—Church, they had an island home; there was no limit to what they might become if they lived, as their benefactors did, in villages industriously cultivating the land and developing crafts and manufactures and trade.

The first village to be founded was in the mountains above Freetown. It was built in 1809 and called Leicester. Regent and Wilberforce were settled in 1812. As the slave ships were brought into Freetown harbour in the years that followed, and more land and housing had to be found for the Africans, new villages were started and roads or tracks made to them: Gloucester, Leopold, Charlotte, Bathurst, York—names that recall the England of Prinny and Mrs. Fitzherbert. In 1819 Wellington and Waterloo were founded for discharged soldiers of the garrison, the West India Regiment. Hastings and Kent were set up soon after. Managers ran the villages and started education. Church-building went ahead actively. Many existing villages, occupied by Temnes, mostly fisherfolk, were left undisturbed.

When plans were being made to develop Sierra Leone as a colony for the Black Poor, it was believed that the hilly country was fertile and suitable for agricultural settlement—and yet thinly populated. Dr. Smeathman in 1783 published a plan of settlement, in the course of which he reported that 'the woods and plains produce spontaneously great quantities of the most pleasant fruits and spices' and that 'it is not necessary to turn up the earth more than from the depth of 2 or 3 inches with a slight hoe in order to cultivate any kind of grain'. People then supposed that tropical luxuriance of vegetation was synonymous with the fertility of tropical soils—as many people do today. The villages were expected to become so many Eveshams and Ketterings, centres of rich farming districts.

They prospered at first, but never at farming. The only farming the settlers knew was what they had learned on West Indian plantations or had practised in West Africa before they were enslaved; the latter experience proving a great deal more useful than the former. The Government was supposed to provide them with implements and instructions—but the latter were never given for the simple reason that the officials did not know. The villagers set about cutting down the greater part of the huge stand of indigenous timber which clothed the land from water's edge to the hill summits, and indeed this is the usual way to keep going while a farm on virgin soil is being broken. The first crops may have been good—but thereafter the infertility of the soil was revealed to the colonists, though not to the officials. They turned to manufacture—such as the making of roof shingles at Hastings, or fishing, or trade. They grew for themselves cassava and a few vegetables and exchanged their fish or wood for the rice which they could not grow. 'There is', complained the 1887 Blue Book, 'abundance of land in the Colony favourable for agricultural purposes, etc., but trade and barter has a greater attraction for the country. A state of affairs in which everybody sells to everybody else cannot be regarded as satisfactory; so long, however, as huckstering pays, there is little likelihood of manual labour finding favour with the masses.'

The failure of the rich green valleys and hill-slopes to produce either food or an export crop baffled a succession of officials, when they gave the matter thought. They put it down to laziness, 'to the unconquerable repugnance . . . to engage in any employment apparently menial, or that requires the slightest exertion'; and I myself heard officials put down to laziness the absence of great herds of dairy cattle waxing fat on the herbage of the Colony hills (in spite of an obvious lack of dry season feed). But the settlers quickly discovered the truth: that to produce quite a small crop you need in the Sierra Leone hills a great deal of land. The land that will support dense forests will barely permit the lifting of successive crops of cassava root from the same plot; after that it requires to be fallow for seven years and more. It must go back to bush, preferably back to forest. It is infertile. Dr. Smeathman could not have been more unfortunately in error.

Lazy or not, the villagers did what they could: they cropped the land as intensely as it would allow them, cutting the timber and burning off the bush. They returned to the land as often as possible; and presently whole areas produced little more than grass. It was, from their limited knowledge, completely exhausted, however green it seemed. They waited for the Europeans to demonstrate how to make it do better. But they waited in vain. Model farms were talked of, and one or two were even started—but came to nothing. A few small plantations of sugar, ginger, cotton, tobacco, cinnamon, cocoa and coffee, and even rubber, were run by enthusiasts, but they never precipitated the growth of whole export industries. Some of the first settlers made a fair start, but the incoming hordes of liberated savages stole their crops, cut down their plantations and gradually reduced them to beggars by the 1840's. The mountains remained green, and the villages looked charming but stayed poor.

Freetown grew, but the villages remained the same, and then began to shrink. They had sent young people to Freetown who became leaders in the community; who became rich and respected, and who in some cases returned to the villages to retire and die; but who in any case sent money back to their old homes. About the turn of the century this process was interrupted; and in the 'twenties and 'thirties the difference between the life to be enjoyed in the decaying villages and Freetown was much accentuated. Freetown had piped water, electric light, motor cars, the cinema, and, above all, jobs. Freetown was no longer the capital of an island 20 miles by 14 as it had been in the 'eighties; it had grown into the capital of a country the size of Ireland. There was no longer anything the villages could sell Freetown, and a life of fishing and of farming the grudging laterite soil was something for the ambitious young man to escape from—and forget. The world was moving on; and the nearest a creole boy or girl could get to the moving world was Freetown.

In the village of Benguema, whose houses seem to retire from the broad road into groves of mango and kola and orange trees, I talked of the decline of the Colony villages to Bishop Johnson, who was young when they were in their prime, and who deplores their decay. In a house whose dark, polished beams show the marks of the settler's axe and adze, he spoke of the packed churches and of a clergy respected and influential, paid a living wage; of the young men going out to found businesses and preach the gospel, not only in Freetown, but in the untamed Protectorate and down the Coast, and returning later in life; of the cultivation of virtue in a purposeful setting—and of the sad decline since those days. Could anything be done, he asked with gentle wistfulness. England had been urbanized, yet had returned in some measure to her villages: a bus service between the Colony villages might work wonders. Would not public servants be glad to live cheaply and cultivate their gardens if they could get to and from their work easily? Such spare-time agriculture had always produced the best results in the Colony, for educated men knew the importance of fertilizers and the value of vegetables in the diet. The villages were so eroded now that they lacked leadership of any kind; sunk in ignorance, some of the inhabitants inevitably drifted back to fetish . . .

Community centres were needed, welfare, uplift, vigorous administration, women's institutes, mobile cinemas, or at least
film-strips, extra-mural university work, all sorts of things . . .
The Bishop is nearly eighty, but as he outlined his plans his
voice took on an energy and power which belied his years and
recalled his leadership in the Church.

Much, indeed, is planned for the Colony villages. At one time
the Colony was treated as a district with a European D.C. in
charge. He dealt with the villagers through their headmen. Now
they are to be taught local government; the Colony is to become something like an English county. Democracy is to be the
active principle. There are to be village committees, elected by
the ratepayers of the area (either a village or a group of small
hamlets); the village area committees of a district elect six of
their number to become the district council and each of the
six district councils elects one member to go to the Rural Area
Council. The President of the Rural Area Council is at present
the D.C., who is a creole, Mr. Jones; in 1953 this office, too, will
be an elective one. The pyramid of local government will then
be complete. Each authority will have its own treasury and
finance, and the improvement of the Colony will be in the hands
of the rural dwellers themselves. If they can find dynamic
leaders, and if the finance will run to it, they will be able to
better their position.

But money is hard to find, since the Colony has run down.
Even in the past, the villages received considerable sums from
the central government to undertake all important works, pay
for education and social services. They received large sums of
missionary money subscribed in Britain. A rate of tenpence in
the pound today will bring them little more education, roads or
bus services; it will pay for only a little more than the administration itself.

The Colony is no longer predominantly creole. People from
the Protectorate have been migrating to the villages for many
years. They are of all tribes, and have brought many tribal
customs with them to mingle with the creole customs and rein-
terpret the Christian religion. The creoles have withdrawn more
and more to Freetown; but considerable intermarriage has
taken place, and the Colony is not tribal. The 'secret' societies and
other social organizations have established themselves, but not

chiefdoms. Paganism has sprouted between the laterite paving stones, as the mud-and-wattle house has filled the gap when a wood-and-tinpan house has crumbled. But nearly all the villagers have taken English names, while at the same time the old Temne names of some of the villages have been resuscitated for unofficial use. Those who study life in the Colony villages find nearly everybody and every place has two names—which is a convenience as the feeling returns that for strangers to know your real names gives them an undesirable measure of power over you.

In the end, the land dictates the kind of culture that grows from it. Colony agriculture will only support settlements of the simplest kind. Cassava is the main crop, with yams, sweet potatoes, okra and the products of the oil palm. This leaves the cultivator with little to sell in Freetown, except starch made from cassava, and foo-foo, or ground cassava, made into balls for cooking and sold for a ha'penny each. The most lucrative crop comes from the sea. Along the Colony coasts, as well as north and south of it, live a hardy if illiterate race of fishermen whose skill with line and net is unequalled, but whose principal equipment is a one-man dugout canoe costing £3 to build. The size of the catch and the cash income of the coastal villages therefore leaves no surplus for development. The stable pattern of the fisherman's life is such that education confers no advantage on those living it; those who raise themselves seek to leave it. After a hundred years, in many of the villages, so far from the agriculture of England or some tropical adaptation of it having taken root, as Governor Denham and others hoped, the native system of agriculture which they considered so backward has proved the only one of which the land and the people are capable; and the people ready to endure the consequences have quietly moved in and possessed themselves of the land of those who were not.

The island has proved a piece of the mainland after all; as a self-sufficient hinterland for the capital it has always been inadequate. The house of the District Commissioner for the Rural Areas stands on a hillside above Waterloo at the eastward end of the Colony, and looks toward the mainland. From that eminence a land of greens and browns stretches to the horizon. An African D.C. lives there now, and with him I

discussed the plans for the renaissance of the Colony, local government, better roads, social services, development. One of his
English predecessors acquired a lamp-post from old Waterloo
Bridge when this was being dismantled in 1937, and set it up
on the lawn near the inevitable cannon and flagstaff. It was
cast, I suppose, about the year that Waterloo village was
founded, and in which the confines of the Colony, except for
acquisitions on the south coast, was finally drawn. But leaning
against that lamp-post and watching the rain rolling over the
land, I reflected that the creoles had never acquiesced in that
tidy delimitation of their island home. It could not, they quickly
found, provide for them; it could not support the expansion of
their city of hope and personal advancement, Freetown. It had
to be the trading centre of a far larger area if it was ever to
fulfil its destiny or theirs.

The creoles knew this instinctively before the Colonial Office
did, for they left the villages, almost as soon as they were
founded, to build up trade in Manchesters and palm oil with
'the interior': with the country of the unsubdued indigenous
tribes and chiefdoms, the Mendes, Temnes, Sherbros, Lokos, and
those that were still wilder and further into the forest. For then
the forest rolled up to the foothills at Waterloo, and the view
from the hills was of trees to the horizon, not, as it appeared to
me, a brushwood country interspersed with palms. The creoles
knew that Freetown had to by-pass the poor mountains and
their struggling villages and become the entrepôt of a far larger
hinterland, as well as the capital of a maritime empire along the
Guinea coast. To grow, to become rich and progressive, to make
citizens of them, it had to drain West Africa, as the fabulous
London of their dreams drained not just a small island in the
German Ocean, but the trade of the globe. Colonial officials
might condemn the creole propensity of everyone trading with
everyone else; but it was a sound English mercantile instinct,
however inherited. From Waterloo, as from Freetown, they
went eastwards with the missionaries and the European traders;
and the Government found it expedient to send expeditions
after them. The Colony was Freetown's backyard; but from the
first Freetown sought to make herself the capital of a far bigger
Sierra Leone.

4. CREOLEDOM

*If yu nor no ussi yu dey go, yu fo no usai yu
komot*
If you don't know where you're going,
you do know whence you came
CREOLE PROVERB

IT is difficult to imagine, from their history, any more
interesting community than that of the creoles of Sierra Leone.
Like the Anglo-Indians, they are the creation of the British,
though the British are not always as proud of their creations
as they might be. For many creoles still speak of Britain as
'home'. In Freetown, as in scores of towns in Australia, New
Zealand and Canada, children have for a hundred years been
tantalized by stories of that greater fairyland, Britain. Cultural
experts are, of course, against such myth-mongering; the cinema
has done a good deal to dispel it. Liverpool Docks in a drizzle
have often proved a sore disappointment after half a lifetime of
anticipation; and it may be that creole fantasy and yearning
builds up a vision of a green and pleasant land that not even a
Blakean crusade could materialize. Reading through some school
essays on the subject of the Industrial Revolution, I was
interested to be instructed that such glories as the Homeland
may possess are founded on the sufferings of enslaved factory
children in the past: every essay, however it varied in detail,
agreed on the shocking essentials—the children had no education and no shoes.

Over half the Colony children get some education; the proportion who wear shoes must be smaller, though use and possession are different things. Education, and a higher standard of
living—particularly as expressed by European attire and by
the independence and respect accorded to women—are the
formative influences of 170 years of creole development. From
the first, a decisive break was made with the past—with a
hundred thousand years or more of tribal tradition. The first
settlers came from all over West Africa. The pioneers consisted
of many Negroes who had served in British regiments or war-
ships against their colonial American masters, and after the
war were discharged in Nova Scotia, Canada or in London,

where they suffered from the climate and lack of employment. Their immediate history was that of the American plantations; many were educated and had experience of growing cotton and tobacco. They were soon joined by the Maroons descended from the tribes of the Gold Coast, and by discharged soldiers of the West India regiments; they were steadily reinforced thereafter by Africans liberated from captured slave ships; the last slaver was captured in 1862. The Liberated Africans came from all parts of the West Coast; most had fresh memories of the countries of their birth and upbringing, the very young had none; they were all mixed and mingled in Freetown and the Colony villages in the mountains and foothills. Widely different customs, traditions, ideas, racial stocks were fused and melted together; Victorian missionaries laboured among them to make Christianity the main cement.

To the Victorian mind it was an almost ideal experiment in civilizing unfortunate savages. There was the vital break with the unregenerate past, caused by an evil trade, but marvellously transmuted by Providence into an abiding good. There was a clean sheet to begin; and to the early Victorian mind it was a *clean* sheet—there was no limit to what might be fairly writ upon it. To the early Victorian, the Negroes were black, but that was the only inherited difference between them and other men—after all, Negro and white alike had only been created about 6,000 years previously. Darwin was still in velvet knickers, *The Golden Bough* was unwritten, and though there was some trouble over fossils, which had forced a few Churchmen to speculate reluctantly upon the possibility of pre-Adamic man, the general view was that shoes and education would bring Africans ultimately to the general level of Victorian England. The comparative lack of temptations suggested to some that in spiritual achievement they might quickly make pupils of their pastors and masters. 'Nor do I think,' wrote Mrs. Fauconbridge, contemplating the Colony in 1793, 'nor do I think nature has been so unkind as to endow those people with capacities less susceptible of improvement and cultivation than any other part of the human race.'

In any event, the new Colony was to be a beacon on the coast of savage Africa: a light to lighten the Gentiles still sunk in superstition. The Freetownese, it was thought, by their mere example would make the hinterland tribes envious and receptive of the new teaching. They would show what an African could become: fully the equal of the white in all essential matters. From fairly early days, the course was set. In Trevelyan's *Life and Letters of Lord Macaulay* it is reported: 'The town was built; the fields were planted and the schools filled; the Governor made a point of allotting the lightest work to the Negroes who could read and write'. Not long after that (in 1827) Fourah Bay College was founded to train Africans for the priesthood. The Church Missionary Society had been teaching Hebrew for nearly 20 years at Fourah Bay before a short-lived School of Agriculture was established at Kissy. Creoles quoted Theocritus as the crops failed to come up.

These facts have been used for the past 50 years to explain creole traits and shortcomings, and creole misfortunes. Victorian policy, designed to produce a superior Negro race, freed from the past and free to shape its own future, merely succeeded, it was said, in producing a relatively small cadre of semi-educated clerks and a general distaste for manual labour and farm work. The creoles, therefore, never struck root, never developed. Indoctrinated with the notion that they were somehow better than the rest of Africans, and that they would without effort endlessly enjoy rising standards, they renounced all real effort and certainly all self-criticism. If the Colony failed to prosper, the reason was this fatal early impression given to creoles that learning was more honourable than toil; that the professions (especially Government service) were above trade; and trade above farming. The soaring Victorian faith, which pumped money into the little settlement, sent missionaries out to die of dysentery or malaria in a few years in the sure knowledge of a martyr's crown and of a brother by the next boat to step into his shoes and keep trim his grave, dwindled to an official whine that the thing had not come off; that the material was disappointing and unsatisfactory; that creoles were inherently lazy, boastful, improvident and fatally enamoured of clerkships in the secretariat. 'Education has been supplied on a generous scale,' observed F. W. H. Migeod severely in 1926, 'and the present-day creole, the descendant of three generations of literate people, has in all probability reached the highest point to which the African black man can attain.'

But the strongest critics of the creoles are the creoles themselves. More than once I have heard creoles reproach their own folk for a 'slave mentality'. 'In the early days of the Colony', a member of the Executive Council said to me, 'we were given everything by the English: land, implements, administration, schooling, language and culture, endless help. When money ran short, appeals went out and the African Institution or some other body found it. It seems to me that we have never recovered from that dependence. We still expect everything to be done for us. We have only ourselves to blame if the Syrians take the trade and the Protectorate people assume the leadership in Leg. Co. If we creoles had the energy we should be running this country now, and not kicking up a fuss about the new Constitution because you British won't hand it to us on a platter.'

Stern words said with a thrill of anger and authority by an elderly man who had laboured for his people in the last sixty years—laboured in trade, in education, in politics, in social welfare, in self-realization. I shall not quickly forget the impression that he gave as he spoke: his white hair, his kindly face set in judgement, his precise sentences—and behind him the vista of the harbour at Bonthe, a sheet of blue water to the further mangrove-fringed shores, the fleet of white Government launches at their buoys, the flagstaff and the men on the waterfront working in the boats. A vista incongruously suggesting Pangbourne and Venice and Hickling Broad, sun and ease and boats and nothing mattering. An hour or two later the sun and the blue vanished and it thundered and rained as it cannot do in England, save when England turns Africa: inches in an hour.

Perhaps the impression produced by Victorian policy upon the creole character is deep. Certainly the origin of the Colony as a slave settlement has a profound effect on the creole mind. A few elderly folk still alive remember grandparents who spoke to them of the slavery from which they had been liberated. But many of the Liberated Africans were slaves only for a short time in any case; the history of freedom is far longer than that of captivity. The Victorians thought more of the glory of being free than the antecedent degradation. They thought of opportunity offered, of expansion, of self-help. In Bonthe there was a creole merchant called MacFoy in the last years of the Victorian era, when Bonthe did half the trade of all Sierra Leone;

to carry his palm oil and piassava to England and America,
MacFoy chartered ships. They stood at anchor nearly opposite
Bonthe itself, and their captains came and waited on him. He
was the greatest merchant of the south. His name is now a
memory; his children were trained to be lawyers and professional people, his house and fortune faded away, and no creole
came to take his place.

The creoles followed the English tradition with fatal fidelity.
When they made money, they sought to raise their children
above shopkeeping that they might advance that superior Negro
culture which was the great hope of the original founders of
the settlement. They still seek to redeem that promise; they
believe now, as they did then, in education. They believe,
with the Victorians, that education makes all things possible
to Africans, as to Europeans. They are not disillusioned with
it upon results; what they want is more of it. If the experiment
started by the British failed in Sierra Leone, in their view it was
because it did not go far enough, or have enough spent on it;
it was the British, not the creoles, who lost heart. But creoles
do not think the experiment has failed. In essentials, they feel
it has succeeded. Within a hundred years of Freetown's founding, creoles had shown what they could do as missionaries,
catechists, lawyers, architects and teachers in Sierra Leone and
along the coast. Their wealth showed that many were good
merchants and carried on much of the trade with the interior.
Fergusson, a mulatto, had been Governor; Sir Samuel Lewis
had been knighted; MacFoy's name was good on any bill;
senior administrative posts were held by creoles; the African
had proved himself, and the tribal natives in the Rising of 1898
murdered them in scores just because they were Englishmen
and Englishwomen.

Those who achieved distinction were few; but education was
limited and everything was on a small scale. And after the turn
of the century, creole prospects began not to improve but to
worsen; opportunities were reduced, not increased. The Syrians
began to arrive and take the trade from the local traders;
beginning as 'corals' with their wares—coral necklaces—
hanging round their necks, they grew in riches by sheer under-
living and undercutting the creoles. The British did not exclude
them (as the Australians would have done), but allowed them

to ruin their protégés simply by hard work. The British officials themselves moved up into Hill Station, where they began to see everything differently (so creoles told me) from that superior elevation and with the regular arrival of the latest books of Mr. Kipling. With the Protectorate to rule, they felt truly imperial. They also felt a good deal better, as the result of Dr. Ross's work on malaria, and were less ready to tolerate the happy-go-lucky conditions of the past. They lived longer—which meant that Africans had fewer chances of promotion via dead men's shoes. They were greedier of the jobs available now that it was possible to live in the White Man's Grave with the chance of retiring on a pension. Creoles whose years enable them to recall the past have told me that the old comradeship of the Liberated African and the Briton suddenly died.

The creole community virtually ceased to grow—their numbers have increased very little since about 1890, even if the census is somewhat inaccurate. The reduction in opportunities increased the demand for clerical jobs; jobs became the problem and the obsession of creole life. Men tended to marry late, as in the tribal areas. Education became so important, in getting the jobs available, that its cost became one of the first burdens on the family budget of the ambitious. Education led to the law, teaching, and Government service only; there were few other careers open to talents, except for the handful of families who could send children home to take medical degrees—some 67 Sierra Leonians became doctors up to 1950.

So far from the creoles becoming the envied and imitated among Africans, the tribal natives began to lose their respect for the black English people. The natives steadily immigrated into the Colony and Freetown, and there was much inter-marriage. In some ways, the tribal influence in creole life became more pronounced; the creoles became more African. In origin they are almost purely African: the word 'creole', which denotes a person of mixed racial origin in the West Indies and South America, was applied to the Liberated Africans for want of a better. The admixture of European blood is certainly slight, though it exists as the result of intermarriage and less formal unions as well as the close relations between Sierra Leone and the West Indies; to be a 'West Indian' has a certain cachet in Freetown to this day. In the first days of the settlement, there being a shortage of African women among the first shiploads of Black Poor, settlers were supplemented with about 60 Englishwomen, mainly 'of the lowest character', shanghaied from the streets of London, to serve them as wives. Evangelical opinion was profoundly shocked at an occurrence which probably seemed a practical arrangement to most eighteenth-century minds.

From these various materials, and upon the loom of this environment, the creoles have woven their own life and culture. It is a blend of African and European: perhaps the closest blend that is to be found in Africa outside the Cape. In the villages, the little box-like houses suggest the privacy and keeping-oneself-to-oneself of English family life—yet these villages tend to degenerate into groups of mud huts where life is lived communally. Creoles are mostly Christians, but many, even among the educated, pour a libation to their ancestors. Among the poor, witchcraft receives the same credence as the Bible, and many Mende or Temne festivals are solemnized as well as Christian ones. Christian and Muslim festivals are attended by the same people. Eid-ul-Fitri brings out paper lanterns in the hands of the same people who pour into church at Christmas and Good Friday. In the Colony villages, the influence of tribal customs is stronger; dancing societies exist to put displays on both Muslim and Christian festivals, and medicine is a potent influence in deciding the course of events. Where the life is as hard, and the methods and rhythm of agriculture the same as in the Protectorate, it is natural that customs should approximate to the native; in the villages are to be found the same living on credit between crops or catches, the same communal organization of life, the same simple training of children in herds, as may be seen in villages in the interior.

Thus, when a child is born, it is, at the fixed and proper fee, christened; and a magnificent ceremony this may be. Christening outfits can be hired—a frock and other accoutrements for the child and possibly (I never could find out for certain) for the proud parents also. But when the christening is over, a string is tied round the baby's middle and charms are hung upon it: verses of the Koran, for instance, wrapped up in leaves to ward off the kaw-kaw bird (a large bat), which, as everybody knows, is a witch that sucks the blood of small children and is

D

responsible for the many deaths among them. A child loaded with charms has a good mother, for good charms cost money.

Then, when a girl is engaged to be married she begins to get her white bridal gown and trousseau ready and the banns are called in the little church with the cheap coloured-glass windows. Her fiancé has a ring made or sends for one from a London mail-order house; she goes about with a dignified air. And three days before the wedding her parents-in-law-to-be bring her a calabash containing a needle, beans (or some copper coins) and kola nuts, to remind her that their son will expect her to be a good housewife, to look after his money and bring him luck in his work, and to bear his children. The wealthy put every denomination of coin into the calabash to signify that there should always be money in the house of which she is to be mistress.

Nor does the burial service end with the final words 'dust unto dust' . . . for creoles know that the spirit remains in a vulture's body and cannot 'cross over' without the additional ceremonies 'Tri-day', 'Seven-day' and 'Forti-day'; hymns and wailings must be heard at sunrise, cold pure water and crushed *agiri* will be left by the grave. Only then is it possible to say 'Lord, let thy servant depart in peace' with any comfortable certainty that this will in fact occur; and it may even be advisable to chant hymns by the grave at the New Year. In villages where the Mende influence is strong, a widow, while attending to all the Christian rites for her dead husband, may think it well to make a mud pack with the water used to wash her husband's corpse and smear herself with it; then, when it is washed off, all his proprietary rights over her are washed off with it and she can marry again.

In the villages there is relatively little home life. Houses are sleeping rooms and refuges from the rain. Life is conducted in view of your neighbours and thoroughly and continuously discussed with them. Conversation in Sierra Leone is conducted even more than in Stepney on the lines: 'And then she said . . . and I said to her . . . but he said that she told him . . .'; endless repetition of conversations. But what else gives impulse to the Drama? In the poorer parts of Freetown, too, much creole life is conducted outside the house, and of home life there is little; family affection is vague and diffused, rather than concentrated. Children are early set to work. The girl who comes home in a neat school uniform with an embroidered badge and an armful of books quickly changes into a booba and lappa and goes out to market with a basket on her head, or takes charge of the younger children. Life is in the streets; news is one's neighbours' doings. Mother is out in one part of the town; father in another. Meals are casual affairs, cooked as required; not fixed rituals which divide up the days. A more carefully cultivated family life begins higher in the social scale, but the emphasis is generally on the clan rather than on man, wife and children. Creoles are perhaps less conscious of blood-ties than natives, but the claims of relationship are strong and are enforced socially. What belongs to one, belongs to all; a man has no right to refuse to take in a relative, or share his meal or his money with a relative. This is the African social tradition. It is reinforced in Sierra Leone by Muslim views on fellowship and alms-giving. I have heard it said that Africans are not particularly hospitable; that they do not, for example, return European hospitality. My impression is that European hospitality—especially in Africa— is the product of a high standard of life; most Africans cannot afford it. They are too busy, and too straitened, in affording it to relatives. Perhaps, too, they are sometimes a little ashamed of their homes, of which it is useless to be house-proud; another sign of their allegiance to European standards. But those who show understanding can go anywhere. 'At no to bon' runs the proverb—the heart isn't made of bone.

A Freetown household will often include children from poorer branches of the family. The breadwinner's salary will be helping to educate as well as to support nephews and nieces or cousins once removed. The little houses are crowded; there are continual goings and comings; a settled routine is something for the rich to enjoy. Education plays a big and characteristic part in it. It is inevitably looked on as largely vocational, as training for the job and the salary. The more you pay, the better the training, and therefore the bigger the job and the salary. This attitude echoes the tribal attitude to the Poro and Sande societies. For education is vested by creoles almost entirely in the teacher; it has little or nothing to do with the parents. The teacher is paid to do the whole job. In poorer homes, where children are being educated, the parents are too illiterate to discuss the child's school life; in richer homes they are usually too busy—some of them never think of it. The child therefore lives in two worlds: the formal, academic ritual of schooling, and the warm, irregular complex of family relationships. These worlds rarely touch; and in after-life the processes by which the salary is earned, and the processes by which it is spent, also bear little or no relationship one to another.

This is hardly what the founders of the settlement intended, or what the more hopeful of the creoles imagined would be the destiny of their people in Africa—to produce a culture and a life that would neither be wholly African nor wholly European. Today many creoles voice their frustration at this outcome. Some look nostalgically backward to a more hopeful past, and blame the British—occasionally themselves—for missing the road somewhere: but just where? Others are more concerned to see how creole culture can be used in the development of African nationalism. Some spoke movingly to me of a sense of oppression at the mental effort required to master the intricacies of Western civilization, advancing with giant strides along the road to somewhere, pouring out inventions and discoveries with a breathtaking fertility. Once it was sufficient to be a good Christian; that would unlock all the doors and make a man equal in stature to any other man. Now the West appears a great deal less earnest about Christianity, and ready with a dozen new and conflicting explanations of the whole duty of man, black or white. The importance of the great experiment in African development in Sierra Leone, the act of restitution for the wrongs done by the Slave Trade, seem to have been shouldered aside. All's to learn again.

Something of this frustration welled up in the creole protest against the new constitution for Sierra Leone which gave control of the country to the representatives of the Protectorate. 'Do you want to be ruled by Mende men?' shouted a political orator at an election meeting in 1949. 'No!' shouted the crowd. They had been faithful, in their fashion, to the white man and the white religion; and now they were being thrust on one side. The British were full of the rights of pagans and Muslims. The Protectorate was everything; but who showed the British the importance of the Protectorate—who but the creoles of Freetown? Yet the British did not think the creoles good enough to inherit the land and the power. It was hard to bear.

5. PALAVER SAUCE

Monkey tok, monkey yeri
Only monkey understands monkey
<small>CREOLE PROVERB</small>

THE soul of a people is expressed in its language; mother-tongue is the first and most sustaining possession. When the Liberated Africans were given a home in Sierra Leone the British philanthropists assumed that their language would be English. They had no common language, for they came from a variety of West African tribes speaking a dozen languages or more; and the ex-soldiers from the American plantations had, in most cases, no knowledge of any language but the English of the Negroes. The West Indians, too, were mostly Caribbean born and bred, and they spoke the basic English of the sugar plantations. It was pidgin-English; but the Victorians took the rational view that education would enable the settlers, and certainly their children, to speak the tongue that Shakespeare spoke—the most flexible instrument ever devised to express human thought, etc. The Irish had given up Erse; the Hindus were to give up Hindustani; English was to replace the miserable 'Taal' of the Cape. Of course the Liberated Africans would start their clean sheet speaking English, thus receiving, as a capital bonus, the treasures of English literature and the commercial lingua franca that would enable them to trade with the world. They would be the first Africans to have a European language absolutely at their command; it would be the decisive step in their advancement.

To this day many English observers regret the existence of the language of the creoles, created in the 170 years of creole adjustment to their environment. It is held up as the concrete example of the failure of African mentality to cope with European thought. I was assured that it was a corrupt pidgin, an impoverished dialect, which is insusceptible of precision of meaning and quite incompetent to handle abstract concepts. A friend instanced as typical an occasion when a creole had warmly thanked her for speaking grammatical English to him, instead of 'talking down' to him in pidgin.

Whatever truth there may be in these allegations, a strong section of educated creole opinion rebuts them with indignation. 'Krio', they declare, is no patois; it is a language in its own right. It is a language to be understood and even revered: for it is the creative achievement of the Liberated Africans. It is no more pidgin-English than English is pidgin-Anglo-Saxon. It is an honest, thorough, and comprehensive reconstruction of English from its roots to suit African requirements—a language that is still living and growing. It contains within itself the elements of an African accommodation to Western civilization.

From that point of view Krio is certainly worth more study than philosophical philologists seem to have bestowed upon it. The visitor, unless he has much time at his disposal, is not likely to reach any worthwhile conclusions. It is, however, fair to say that true Krio is not pidgin. Pidgin is spoken in Freetown alongside Krio, and indeed can be heard being translated into Krio. It is spoken by Europeans to their servants and other Africans in the fond delusion that they are speaking the local language. They are not. The tribal native may well speak pidgin but be unable to understand Krio. Indeed, some creoles get angry if tribal natives try to speak Krio. A simple example may show the difference. In English we say, 'This is the man' (Ecce homo). Pidgin puts it in form, 'Dat be de man'. But the Krio is, 'Nar de man dat'. Again, the English sentence, 'I am going to my house', becomes in pidgin, 'Ah de go for me house'. The Krio is, 'Ar de go nar me ose'.

Krio is, of course, 'corrupted' English; but it has suffered a sea-change into something rich and African. It now requires long practice to become proficient and, just as important, creative in it. There are no grammar books; moreover, grammar alone would not suffice, for the language is creole lore and life, and creole lore and life are the language. At first hearing, it seems to have less grammar and inflexion even than English. The whole English passive tense, for example, has been dropped —perhaps naturally, since it does not exist in other West African languages, except Hausa. The sentence, 'It has been said by them of old', is incomprehensible to an African child who yet knows the meaning of each individual word and would understand the thought in the form, 'This is what old people used to say', which in Krio is, 'Nar dis den de ole people den kin say'. But in the active voice Krio possesses a full complement of tenses, past and future. 'Ar see' (I see) has its past 'ar bin see'; its past perfect 'ar done see'; its pluperfect 'ar bin don see'. The future 'ar go see' makes its conditional 'I shall have seen' in the form 'ar go don see'.

It has a full set of words or expressions for casual or conditional events: thus 'so tay' develops the meaning 'until' from the English verb 'stay'. 'Ar go wait for am so tay e cam' means 'I will wait for him until he comes'. But 'ar wait for am so tay e nor cam', which apparently means 'I waited for him until he didn't come', is not an Irishism, but the Krio idiom for expressing the idea, 'I waited for him *a long time* but he didn't come'. Again, 'nar way e libwell' means 'because things are easy with him'.

The vocabulary of Krio is derived from many sources. Much of it consists of English words shorn of any difficult syllables or altered to suit African pronunciation. 'Th' becomes 'd'; long vowels are shortened. Brother becomes Bra. But many words have been inherited from Spanish and Portuguese, via the slave plantations. 'Sabby', the verb to know, is from the Portuguese *Sabeir*; 'pikin', an infant, is a further simplification of the Anglicized 'picaninny' from the Spanish *pequeno nino*; 'borku', meaning 'much', is the French *beaucoup*, and from the French *palabre* comes that essential West African word *plabba* or *palaver*, meaning both trouble and discussion of the trouble. English will perhaps annex it, it is so useful, like the invaluable Hindi 'bandobast' meaning 'comprehensive and inclusive arrangements'. But a considerable proportion of its vocabulary as well as its grammatical forms come from the native languages of West Africa. The word for rogue is 'akata', from the Yoruba, which means a hawk, or stealer of chickens. The words for bride and bridegroom, 'yawoe' and 'okoyawoe', are also from the Yoruba.

Krio is indeed a fascinating language, as any visitor to Freetown discovers who discusses it with one of its best-informed defenders, Mr. Thomas Decker, of the Public Relations Department. To Thomas Decker I am indebted for what little I learnt of it. In a monograph, Decker writes: 'When the mind of the West African aborigine appears to lack the faculties of reasoning and inventing, it is not because there is a real lack of these

43

faculties, but because the West African aborigine is at present besieged and beset by European reasoning and invention, which he has found so satisfactory for the time being that it is somewhat unnecessary to use his own. . . . Whenever the time comes in which the West African aborigine will be able to shake off European mental tyranny in the same way as the British shook off Roman tyranny, the necessity and scope for using his faculties of reasoning and inventing will arise, and he will surely use them to go on living.'

No one can doubt the possibilities of Krio who has seen Decker's translations of Shakespearian lyrics. Krio suffers, in English eyes, from English spelling and the ghosts of the English words which the spelling evokes. It should, strictly, be read in a phonetic script or heard by ear. It then emerges as a melodious, liquid tongue, almost devoid of the gutturals and the lip-hiss of the English s, sh, and th. I have listened with care to a story in Krio, which was told me with every concession to my ignorance, and with that superb miming which makes any African tale in the mouth of a professional story-teller a regular Ruth Draper performance, but I barely caught the plot and dramatis personae. Written in English, it is easier to follow, but loses most of its quality. This Krio lullaby may convey something of its homely power:

Slip gud-o, bebi gial: *Ar wan fo si da ting*
Opin yai lilibit   *We kin de shain insai*
En luk me wan minit   *Insain yu fain fain yai*
Bifo yu slip.   *En kot mi at.*

So! Set yu yai nau no
Ar tink se a don si
Wetin ar wan fo si
Gud nait, slip gud . . .

It is in songs and tales and proverbs (called 'paraibuls') that the Krio language is preserved. It has no written tradition, alas; for it is the language of a numerically small group which was always educated—so far as it was educated at all—in English. The fully educated creole, when he wrote, wrote for the market and for his intellectual peers—in English. But the oral tradition is still strong and living: the language of childhood, of the fields, of love and courtship, of the wisdom of the wise, of market-place and family reunion. It is the language of gossip, of 'congosa'—that malicious 'den say' which provides spurious authority for the discussion of other people's business.

It certainly possesses enough currency and development to challenge the Afrikaaner claim that Afrikaans is the world's most modern language. It is a pity that so little of it is written, but orthography is a problem. Nonetheless Krio finds its place in modern creole entertainment. Nothing is so typical of creole delight in gossip as the calypso—the unpremeditated verses made to celebrate some local occasion or person's achievement, and sung to a thudding rhythm of drums, saxophones and castanets. The creoles declare that the calypso did not originate in the West Indies, but in West Africa, where it was developed from the impromptu songs sung to chiefs on state occasions. In support of this theory I can urge that I myself heard such a calypso sung to drum and balangi when a dance was put on in my honour at Kabala. Nobody cared to translate exactly, so I presume it made one or two references to me, no doubt of a satisfyingly topical kind.

Most of the calypsos which gain popularity in Freetown now start with the 'Variety Time' radio rediffusion programme, and most deal with such stirring events as the introduction of double-decker buses or the tour of Mr. Oliver Lyttelton, Secretary of State for the Colonies. This latter is reproduced here (p. 50) with the permission of the composer and lyric-writer, Mr. Ralph Wright; it was regarded in conservative creole quarters as positively Aristophanesian in its political innuendo. It vindicates the freedom of political comment allowed on Freetown Radio. It is, like most Freetown calypsos, in plain English. But many are composed in Krio, and these are among the most popular, and are sung and hummed everywhere. 'Lef me bo, ar nor de pan dat' (Leave me alone, I don't want you) has a haunting lilt:

Wen we two bin lili
Ar bin call yu Rosi—
Wen we two de grow
Yu de tri for tak me low—
Lef me, bo; ar nor de pan dat.

Wen ar ask for marrad yu
Yu nor wan for tell me tru—
Dat nar wen we jes lef school
Yu bin tink se me nar foul—
Lef me, bo; ar nor de pan dat.

45

Wen we go dans nar Lumley   Crismes tem nar Wilberforce
Yu bin ask for money   Wen yu bin mak yu fuss
Wen ar se leh we dans   Nar me buy da suss—
Yu de tri for marrah me—   Way yu run go harbuss
    Lef me, bo; ar nor de pan dat.   Lef me, bo; ar nor de pan dat.

It is in these sad or lively passages of everyday life in creole villages and towns that native songs in the native tongue best capture the sweet and sour taste of existence in the hot and humid air, the smell of poverty in the aromatic tropical breeze, the drawl of time through sun-sodden afternoons, the quick drop of darkness and the changed heartbeat of soft nights under diamanté ceilings of stars. The ballad, song, fairy-story are appropriate vehicles for the traditions of such a people as the creoles, and are more impressive than the polemics in mixed metaphor which form a not unentertaining feature of their newspapers. A few creole intellectuals have written in Krio as well as in English. The late Gladys Casely-Hayford, sister of the present Minister of Agriculture in the Gold Coast, was outstanding among creole literati. She was a vivid and active spirit, artist, traveller, African patriot, who died in Accra recently while still young—eagerly observing and criticizing the work of the first responsible African Government. A manuscript book of her poems was lent to me by Dr. M. F. C. Easmon, and proved a profoundly interesting study of an African girl's response to creole life and to the creole predicament. The verses in the vernacular came nearest to the heart of the matter, and two of them may best bring out the flavour of creole love and creole domesticity.

E tin ap; meself tin ap; tay ar put e'en cal'bash don.
Ar say 'which si yu komot, bo?' 'Ar komot Fullah Ton.'

E shet en mot; me shet me mot; e tan lek spirit pass
So tay ar draw am clos me, for cam sidon na de grass.

Den not to common yarn, we yarn. Ef yu ear way I dey shoot
Whilst me one yai jes dey spy am, from en hed tay reach en foot.

E luk me; meself luk am. Ar say 'Ar lek yu, bo';
E drap en sweet yai onetime; e say 'meself lek yu, Jo.'

E kiss me; meself kiss am. Na so me at de beat
Den we tell gudbye. I watch am—tay e los go don de treet.

The second poem supplies not only a coloured miniature of dinner time in one of the little matchwood interiors of Freetown, it also provides examples of some Krio idioms which Gladys Casely-Hayford explained in footnotes which I reproduce with the lines in her own Krio spelling (which is, as yet, far from being standardized):

> *Jane go pull[1] de fufu.[2] Ayo, tun[3] de pot;*
> *Bobo, you go wash dem plate, make de soup go hot;[4]*
> *Maria no come back yet? Lor de pikin slow—*
> *I jes sen am for buy rice from longtime[5] way e go.*
> *Sonny dey play ball na treet. E tink say en dey wait*
> *For make I call am. I no fool. I bissen[6] ef e late.*
> *Tunu, tell you sisi, say ef e no go stop*
> *For knack da piana bom, bom, bom, en try come don an chop?*
> *Who humbug me,[7] no go get wan grain dry fis self*
> *Jane, you pass day cober[8] dish whey da pantap[9] dah shelf*
> *All man for go was den pan! All man take den spoon*
> *E luk lek wouna[10] all no want go school dis afternoon?*
> *Jane, Bobo, Tunu, Ayo, Maria, Sisi, Sonny, Sweet—*
> *Say you grace en take you plate, tell tankee en go et.*

[1] pull=dish up; [2] fufu=cassava starchy food; [3] tun=stir up; [4] make de soup go hot—i.e. so there will be no delay in dishing up; [5] from longtime, i.e. she's been absent too long; [6] bissen=not my business if she's too late; [7] who humbug me=those who are caught; [8] cober=cover; [9] whey da pantap=that is on top of; [10] wouna all=seems as if none of you want to.

Peoples express themselves in their national dishes as well as in language and proverbial lore. The creoles have a cuisine at least as individual as, for example, the Afrikaaners. It owes something to the West Indies, and a good deal to the French influence which is noticeable in creole life and comes largely to Freetown from the Gambia. I have enjoyed creole cooking both in Sierra Leone and Gold Coast, though it finds no mention in Mrs. Beeton's international section. I know of no better dishes than groundnut soup and stew, palava sauce, or foo-foo rice. Rich, spiced and oily to the English taste, but correspondingly satisfying, they take advantage of the profusion of local vegetables and fruits. No excuse will be needed to include a few creole recipes among poems, examples of proverbs and music, language and literature: they are intimately connected with all these things. Anyway, plenty of people read a recipe as others do a musical score, and catch internal gustatory harmonies as musicians catch internal rhythms and assonances. Sierra Leone has its own quality on the tongue and palate: its own remembrances from the stomach upwards after the meal. . . .

To make palaver sauce: Take one pint of water, add pinch of salt, put in about 1 lb. brisket of beef; take ¼ lb. tripe cut into slices and add. Bring to boil for about ½ hour, and add 1 pint palm oil, allow to boil for 10 minutes and add to taste a penny-worth of powdered *locos* or *ogiri*. Keep boiling while *bologie* leaves are boiled in separate casserole: strain off water, allow leaves to cool, squeeze leaves dry and add to main dish with about a shillingsworth of powdered *egusi*; add two shillings-worth of dried *bonga* or snapper (fish) after boning; beat up onions and four red peppers and put them on top of the mixture which must simmer for one hour thereafter. Keep boiling until the water is all steamed off leaving only the oil and the ingredients of the dish. Serve.

To make foo-foo chop: Peel and wash raw cassava and soak the tubers in water for two days till they become soft, and then pound into flour, make into balls. Beat again to a fine pulp, strain through a sieve into water and allow to stand for one hour. Squeeze in half a lime, strain off water and cook the starchy porridge which remains until thick, and eat as a dumpling—with palaver sauce or other dishes.

Joloff rice is really a Gambian dish, but everyone eats it in Sierra Leone: Boil rice with tomato purée, pork, chicken or other meat fried in advance, simmer over a slow fire and serve with cooked cabbage, pumpkins and egg-plants.

To make groundnut stew: Take a chicken, cut up; one onion; peppers; garden eggs; pumpkin; groundnut oil, one cupful. Fry chicken in hot oil with onion and when brown strain off the oil; grind the groundnuts to a paste, dilute with hot water and salt, and strain through a fine sieve, pour on to chicken and allow to simmer for one or two hours until tender, when water should have thickened; add ground rice flour. (For this a hand-ful of husked rice is ground to a flour and thickened with groundnut gravy.) Add vegetables and serve.

As an antipasto, Sierra Leone provides paw-paw, grapefruit and melon, besides all the ingredients for hors d'œuvre if

butterfish are substituted for sardines; but avocado pear (introduced from the West Indies) is considered the best palate pre-
parer. It is usually eaten like paw-paw with a spoon, but with
vinegar, not sugar. Connoisseurs take only a pinch of salt or
pepper to develop its flavour. There are many creole sweets,
mostly composed of coconut and brown sugar. Rice bread is
made by soaking rice into a flour, drying it in the sun and
mixing sugar, nutmeg and a little bicarbonate of soda; it is
then mixed with a paste of bananas and baked as a heavy cake
with raisins and currants. Made with plantain paste it has a
different flavour, pleasant but sourish.

Creole culture has an unquestionable charm—it is fatally
easy to say old-world charm. Whether it can survive in present
conditions is another matter. The pressure from both overseas
and the Protectorate is growing. A technical civilization is
demanding proficiencies which do not fit well into the creole
rhythm—and the young among the creoles are attracted by
it. America, rather than Britain, is their Mecca. They turn
from Krio to pidgin interlarded with Americanisms, from proverbs to wisecracks. They require a language that will enable
them to master machinery, and in that respect, at least, what
the Victorians intended is nearer to coming to pass. On the
other hand, purely tribal customs and attitudes dilute the
creole community more and more. Creole culture was, perhaps,
the product of rather special conditions, of a slow-moving
parochialism, for one thing, that is fast vanishing; of a creole-
run, old-fashioned education which is now thought inadequate
and denounced on all sides. If it disappears it will be a great
pity. Something gentle and unexpected, unplanned by any-
body, yet spontaneously and essentially African will have been
lost. As an educated creole lady said to me: 'Of course we must
know English and French, it is necessary if one is to get anywhere or understand the world; but somehow when we are by
ourselves it is *nicer* to speak Krio, cosier and friendlier and more
homely, and it says what you mean better. But then, you don't
have to be on your guard and impress people when you're at
home, do you?'

THE LYTTELTON CALYPSO

(by Ralph Wright)

INTRO.

CHORUS

Wel - come to the Sec-re - ta - ry of State Here's what we'd like to

men-tion For his most immediate at - ten-tion If we'd be gi - ven a date With the

INTERLUDE

ve - ry great Mis-ter Lyt-tel - ton.

VERSE

It would be good to have ....

to CHORUS

50

It would be good to have a Gu-ma Va-lley Dam,

And then, for a change, we'd have wa-ter ga- lore;

Be- cause it's bad to have ra - tion - ing for years & years more

Chorus: Welcome to the Secretary of State, &c.

Solo: It would be good to have a Deep Water Quay,
For when it comes to taking the logical point of view,
Because it has been bad to wait till 1952!

Chorus: Welcome to the Secretary of State, &c.

Solo: It would be good to have more schools like the F.S.S.G.[1]
For that certainly would help to ease the situation;
Because it's bad to struggle for our children's education!

Chorus: Welcome to the Secretary of State, &c.

Solo: It would be good to have a lower price of rice
And some help in these hard times of stress;
Because it's bad to see our copper buying less and less!

Chorus: Welcome to the Secretary of State, &c.

Solo: It would be good to have more and more tarmac roads
And bridges instead of those many ferries,
Because it's bad to struggle with our loaded lorries!

Chorus: Welcome to the Secretary of State, &c.

Solo: It would be good to have a 'straighter' railway
With faster and wider-gauged and heavier-loaded trains;
Because it's bad to have losses instead of some glorious gains!

Chorus: So welcome to the Secretary of State,
We'd hoped he'd have stayed for a longer duration,[2]
And learned to love our great little nation,
Which may one day stand alone—Sierra Leone!

---

[1] Freetown Secondary School for Girls.

[2] It is said in Freetown that it is usual for celebrities touring the British West African Colonies to have a month in Nigeria, ten days in Gold Coast, an overnight stop at Government House, Freetown, and lunch in the Gambia. But Mr. Lyttelton stayed longer.

6. TO THE PROTECTORATE

Long rod no kil nobodi
A long road kills no one
CREOLE PROVERB

RAILWAYS, in some obscure manner, are a symbol of civilization and confidence. Unlike aircraft, they have demonstrably and permanently conquered all natural obstacles in their way. Their punctuality imposes system and order upon the wilderness; the railway map turns a geographical area into a vertebrate country. The parallelism of the track suggests the formidable body of theoretical learning behind it. Unlike roads, they incarnate the industrial revolution, the whole technological grand transformation scene of the past 170 years. The sidings, yards, columns of trucks, and the snorting of shunting locos at the terminus and docks, suggest the wealth of the hinterland tapped by the railway and sucked seawards, while the loaded trains making for the interior bespeak the input of capital development, of manufactures and consumption goods, ranging from steel sections to corrugated iron sheets, from textiles to bicycles, which are converting jungle and wilderness into farm and garden. To change the anatomical metaphor, a big railway terminal is a mighty heart; from the puffing and to-ing and fro-ing of locomotives can be inferred the systole diastole of its pump action which is felt in the remotest wayside station up-country.

The impression given by the Sierra Leone Railway is therefore a condensed picture of the development and potentialities of the territory: a sort of recapitulation of the history of the opening-up of this red patch on the map of Africa. In scale it is of a piece with the little wooden houses, the grass-grown streets, the succession of all-sorts shops of the capital. One wonders immediately whether the railway is small because Freetown is small, or whether matters are the other way about. Mr. Venner, the able and dynamic General Manager, assured me that a narrow gauge demanded as much, if not more, engineering skill in day-to-day operation as a metre or standard gauge railway. Tolerances are just as fine; in short, Sierra Leone's railway may look as though Mr. Emett designed it, but it is as solid and serviceable as any line in Britain. One must bow to superior wisdom; but the fact remains that the lines of the 2 ft. 6 in. gauge track, which runs through the streets of Freetown towards Cline Town, do not look as parallel as Euclid requires; the driving wheels of the engines look like furiously revolving half-crowns; the coaches overhang the track; and the average speed of expresses—this is incontrovertible—is 18 miles per hour. Uninformed opinion in Sierra Leone on the subject of the railway, moreover, is divided between those who desire it to be torn up and replaced by a tarmac road suitable for use by 10-ton lorries, and those who feel that the loss of such a charming survival would spoil the amenities of the country, one of which is that the pace should not be too hot.

The railway and its history sheds a good deal of light on the country, the Colony and the creoles. A journey from Freetown to Bo, the capital of the Protectorate, a distance of 136 miles, gave ample time to reflect on the subject, as it took ten hours though we were dead on time. It gave leisure, too, to observe one of the richest parts of the country in company with a senior official, a Catholic Father, and the manager of one of the trading firms, so that my thoughts were in a sense assisted by Church, State and Commerce; by God, Caesar and Mammon. We sat in wicker chairs in what the first travellers on the railway regarded as the height of modern luxury, though not in the original rolling-stock; the bogie coaches were dated 1913. And though, on the occasions when the railway ran alongside a road in the Colony, we were easily outdistanced by the most decrepit of mammy-lorries, 18 miles an hour did annihilate distance in 1899, for until then you either chugged up the few navigable rivers in steam launches at $2\frac{1}{2}$ knots, or were carried up and down bush paths in hammocks by relays of porters at between 8 and 12 miles per day. The railway, the first built in British West Africa, transformed trade and government. Spanning gorges, bridging rivers, skirting hillsides in marvellous loops and detours, but always reaching its objective, it was itself an object-lesson in British colonial administration, calculated to impress the chiefs and their war-boys that the future lay with peace, mission schools and Manchester cottons; that the old order—or disorder as the white men perversely persisted in thinking it—had passed away for good.

E

Water Street station is a single-platform terminus, but possesses something of the cathedral gloom of the genuine Victorian terminal train-shed. The train lumbers out, through streets busy with trade, at a speed which enables one to buy bananas in passing, to Cline Town, which is Freetown's Clapham Junction, and will one day be the new terminus, close to the new deep-water quay, to the railway administration offices in Fourah Bay College, and to what is expected to become the industrial area of the town. From Cline Town the train leaves the city, skirting Kissy, where a fine church stands half-way up the hill and a score of Admiralty Nissens dot the riverside. From then on, the mangrove swamps stretch down to the Sierra Leone river in acres of dark green flats on one side, while the Colony hills grumble with thunder on the other. Waterloo is almost the old creole frontier and now the furthest suburban station, lively with passengers and trade. Girls walk up and down with baskets of mangoes, avocado, peanuts and tangerines. Small boys, naked but for a ragged pair of shorts and a bright English school cap, sell pineapples and Vimto. 'Fain pineyapple dey go! Fain pineyapple dey go!' and they are—at two for threepence. Youths saunter up and down, hand in hand, in grave converse, or shadow-box with open hands, laughing.

Market mammies waddle past with unmanageable burdens —too miscellaneous to catalogue—or a single small umbrella on their heads; a young lady smartly attired in a green silk skirt and tartan brassiere gives me a witching smile. Syrian gentlemen rush up and shake Father Jackson by the hand and present him with a refreshing bottle of Vimto. Railway officials wear large dome-like topees as dated as the coaches; a light panama and perhaps sunglasses are considered adequate protection against the tropic sun in this informal and scientific age. Every kind of headgear may be seen, however, on Waterloo and other S.L.R. stations, from purple trilbies to embroidered deerstalkers. . . . The shirt, in every style and colour, may be seen worn negligently outside, or dressily inside the trousers or shorts.

Between Waterloo and Songo Town the railway crosses the frontier between the reign of the Common Law of England, as modified by Colonial Ordinances, and the rule of native law and custom, as modified by Colonial Ordinances. In 1898, when the

Protectorate was in revolt, the railway rushed troops to Songo, then the railhead, to defend that frontier and to prepare a base for rescue operations. We rumble over a succession of bridges, glimpse brown and turbulent streams torn to white lace over worn boulders, the slender-set bodies of men bathing or bright patterns of kirtled women knee-deep washing clothes, like a mass of water flowers. In these next few hours the traveller to Sierra Leone gets an impression of the scenery and vegetation of the interior which may stay with him during all his subsequent journeys and cause him to impose on it a monotony of undifferentiated greenery which in fact it does not possess.

It consists in rolling vistas of brushwood and thicket, woven into a dense mat by creepers, the trees or saplings rising to 20 or 25 feet, but rarely more. The only trees of any size which seem to raise their crests above the bush are the oil palms, rising to 40 feet and surmounted by their bunches of feathery fronds, and occasionally even taller coconut palms, the green nuts among their untidy foliage a promise of cool, sweet refreshment. In the distance the oil palms dominate the green bush rather like dandelions in a very weedy lawn. The oil palms, as the traveller soon learns if he has omitted to prime himself with a glance at the statistics before he started, are the main wealth of the country—yet they grow like weeds; in many parts of the land they are treated as casually, milked of their riches as haphazardly as if they were weeds. Here and there may be seen a glass bottle or calabash protruding just below the heart, or cabbage, where the head or fruit of the tree grows a mass of wine-dark nuts; this bottle is inserted into the tree's sap-stream so that the sap runs into it. This is 'palm wine', whether drunk fresh or fermented. The tree can stand this drainage if the tapping is carefully done, but along the railway, especially on the Colony's boundaries, trunks without foliage, or with yellowed and drooping fronds, show that the tree has been killed. Many of the trees, too, show blackened trunks where fire has licked them, and the lower leaves are shrivelled and dead. To the casual glance there seems a high mortality among them.

Four hours out from Freetown, at Masanke, the train runs past a plantation of oil palms, some 100,000 of them in regular lines, their leaves intersecting in a green fan-vaulting which covers long shaded aisles. It is a common enough sight in other parts of West Africa—but the only example of such a plantation in Sierra Leone. It was established by the Forestry Department but was managed for many years by the United Africa Company. I was told it had never flourished as had been hoped; and that this, rather than tribal dislike of capitalistic exploitation of tribal land, was the reason why there were no others. Always in Sierra Leone one hears that sad *envoi* to a story of ventures started in high hopes of creating a new industry or boosting the output of an old one—'somehow it didn't pay; it came to nothing'. I heard it when the history of coffee-growing in the Colony was discussed; I heard it again as we left Masanke behind. 'It doesn't pay—it doesn't pay—it doesn't pay' the wheels of the train echoed; but it was perhaps speaking of itself.

The green bush grew to various heights, and every now and then we ran through tracts of elephant grasses. At intervals there were large burned patches where every bush and tree was reduced to a charred stump, and occasionally great masses of charred debris were raked to one side to become bonfires. The half-consumed supine carcasses of oil palms lay in these blackened patches like Hindu corpses in the Benares burning ghats. And here and there amid the charred stumps nature was putting forth a thin covering of bright green, grassy shoots— the young rice. Elsewhere, the cleared land had been raked into lines of low earth mounds—where the coco-yams or cassava cuttings had been set. Gradually it came to me that in this succession I was seeing at ground level what had struck me from the air, and when gazing over the plains from the District Commissioner's house at Waterloo: the mosaic of light and dark greens and browns which composes the Sierra Leonian landscape. *This* was the pattern of shifting cultivation: the brown areas were the land cleared for cropping, the green were the graduations of fallow—land that had gone back to bush, one, two, three or more years of ever denser and greener growth.

Even then I did not understand the full significance of what I was seeing. It still seemed to me—though I should have known better—that most of the land was unoccupied, unfarmed, un-owned even; that primitive tools and agricultural ignorance were responsible for these pathetic little cassava patches in the

The land's wealth: farmer and palm fruit

Auspice Britannia liber—'The centre of operations for suppressing the traffic in slaves on the African coast, and asylum and foster mother of the captives when emancipated from the chains and confinement of their prison ships.' (Rankin, *The White Man's Grave*)

'Man liv bai man': creole street traders in Freetown

'I lek os tait sotay, fol go lay' (However full the house, the hen finds a corner to lay in): the slums of Freetown

The heart of Freetown: the cotton tree under which the first freed slaves gathered still casts its shade over a free people; the Churches, such as St. Patrick's, Kissy, still witness the devotion of the first missionaries who built up the Colony

'Only those who have travelled on foot over a deep tropical gorge . . . can be at all adequately thankful for these railway viaducts . . .' After fifty years, the narrow gauge railway is still Freetown's trade artery with the interior. Modernization will cost £6 million

tangled, fast-growing undergrowth. I still wondered that no beasts were to be seen munching the stretches of tufted sward through which the line sometimes ran. The land seemed lightly populated. Here and there narrow paths were beaten through the undergrowth, and the train sometimes surprised a naked girl with a naked baby on her hip, or a group of women in faded wraps, some with babies bound to their backs by a cloth tied round their middles; but the significance of carrying one's baby like that escaped me—it didn't occur to me that it might have something to do with the burnt patches of land in the bush, or with towering rain-clouds that were piling up for an evening downpour as the afternoon wore on. Nor did it occur to me that it might have a good deal to do with the size and speed of the train itself. My companions knew, but I was asking them the wrong questions, or at least questions in the wrong order, as we ground to a halt at station after station.

I was too taken up by the people and the towns, by the things that were being bought and sold or loaded on the train, by the strange trees which clustered round the houses and railway buildings. The Colony was far behind. Creoles were still in evidence: but most of the women were in tribal attire or the long Regency dress with puffed sleeves called the 'Cabbaslot'—so called, I understand, because generations ago the ladies' outfitter in Freetown who made them ready to wear was called Cabba, and his place of business was on the lot granted him as an immigrant Liberated African; but I do not vouch for such pleasant etymology. As you travel through Sierra Leone you gradually begin to distinguish the tribal styles of dress by variations in the way in which the women wear their two-piece costume, the skirt, or lappa, and the blouse, or booba. The Temne women are more careless than Mende women in tying their lappas, which are bunched up; Mende women tuck the booba into the lappa. Mandingo women affect a double ruffle on the booba with a much lower neckline and sometimes an off-the-shoulder effect. In Kabala, in the north, I met two ladies who were wearing both booba and lappa in a manner I had never seen before—it was the same, yet it had an indefinable something . . . The lappa seemed to fit more tightly, the booba to be subtly wound with a vague impression of interesting stresses; the hair was done up with ivory combs, the ensemble produced an unmistakable suggestion of—what was it? I enquired. 'Oh, they are French', was the reply. 'They come from French Guinea, over the border.' All was explained. An unmistakable suggestion of the Boulevard St. Germain.

The villages consisted of mainly square huts made of wattle and daub with palm-thatch roofs; some were under construction, which revealed how they were put together. An average house requires between 100 and 150 poles of 3 to 4 inch diameter driven into the soil and bound by lateral poles fixed with

Map to show approximate tribal areas. Where the dotted boundary-line extends across the Sierra Leone frontier, the same tribe and language extends into French Guinea or Liberia. Names are pronounced as spelt, except that Mende is pronounced Mendi, and Temne is pronounced Tim'ni (and was first spelt 'Timmanee').

palm fibre rope. The rafters are similarly bound to the eaves and to the roof tree. There is space for two or three partitions, and usually a verandah, in which in occupied houses commonly hung a hammock, in which the occupier generally lay. But as we ran on, circular houses, with lower walls and conical roofs, became common. In larger towns the wood and tin-pan construction, ugly but serviceable, was in evidence. Wherever road and railways intersected, lorries crowded into the yards, with shouting, bustle and trade. Conspicuous were the olive complexions of Syrians in shirt and trousers, the cotton frock and headscarf of Syrian wives and daughters; always several Syrian groups with velveteen-clad plump children, getting off or on trains or into large new American cars, looking out from unshuttered shop doorways or latticed windows in wood and concrete houses.

'They make a lot of money', said the Church, with a sigh, as yet another bottle of Vimto was handed into the carriage; the State and Big Business nodded agreement, and were heard to murmur something about a necessary evil. Sixty years from corals to Cadillacs—and the railway had a good deal to do with it. But it was a creole who first urged a railway—Dr. Edward Blyden, who led a good-will expedition to the King of Falaba in 1872, wrote a report suggesting a line from Freetown to Falaba to open the country up to commerce. In fact long before that time creole traders were deep in the country and with the missionaries opening it up. Their labours did much to force a reluctant Government to extend its influence ever deeper into the interior. Trade dribbled out in head-loads; but it held the promise of more. Definite proposals were put before the traders of Freetown at a meeting in the Wilberforce Memorial Hall in 1888 by Philip Lemburg, a European merchant. This was for a railway across the hinterland to Timbuktoo in French territory, but it was before the British protectorate had been declared or even contemplated with distaste by the Colonial Office. Even more ambitious schemes were suggested in subsequent years, but in the end a line was decided upon to open up the Mende country towards the south-eastern confines of the area which was approximately in the British sphere of influence. The density of the bush and the need for cheapness decided the Government upon a line of tramway proportions.

59

The surveyors, toiling in difficult and unmapped country, took the line round every conceivable obstacle and saddled it with expensive gradients.

The revolt of 1898 strengthened the Government's view that the railway was an administrative necessity even if a commercial speculation. The permanent way reached Rotifunk in 1900, the scene of the worst massacres by the tribesmen; though the official opening of this section had to be postponed when the tribes rose again. By 1902 the line reached Bo. In 1906 it reached Pendembu, 'the town under the Counter tree', but never was taken over the border to link with the French. In 1916 the branch line from Moyamba to Kamabai was completed, but the railway never went as far as Kabala, as Blyden had wished; indeed the work done in the First World War was partly undone in the second, for the rails between Makeni and Kamabai were torn up in 1942.

The railway certainly enabled the Government to run the Protectorate. It also opened up the country commercially. It has provided jobs for creoles. But it never paid. It met working expenses, and works financed out of revenue; but after 50 years of running the total deficit on operations reached £2,600,000. Partly this was the consequence of periodic bouts of ramshackle inefficiency, such as that disclosed by the Hamilton report of 1923. Partly it was caused, in two world wars, by inability to maintain the railway, which by 1943, indeed, was reduced practically to scrap-iron. But mainly it followed from the failure of trade to materialize on a scale which would enable it to pay, narrow gauge, gradients, hairpin bends and all. Technically, the railway still has a capacity of twice the present requirements, given certain improvements. It was completed before there were roads or motor vehicles in the country, and, at least until recently, road-building has fed traffic to the railway rather than away from it.

Railway history is a study of the dashing of high hopes. A better-designed railway might possibly have paid better through lower operating costs; but it would not have handled much more traffic. Why? The appearance of the country supplies one answer. The great riches promised by Dr. Smeathman for the Colony in 1792 were rather freely predicted for the railway in the 1890's. After an initial response, the 'twenties and the depressed 'thirties recorded stagnation. And the railway stopped short; if it had tapped the country as far as the Niger basin and French Sudan it might have induced a heavier flow of traffic, canalized trade to Freetown which went to Conakry and Dakar. But the railway, which the creole traders called for, was in the end fatal to them; for it rendered the country penetrable by the Syrians, who entered the territory in growing numbers and were able to trade on the larger scale now made possible. The Protectorate secured Freetown a more adequate hinterland for the capital than the Colony offered, but it brought in two elements which ultimately involved the eclipse of the creoles—the Syrian trader and the awakening of the tribal natives to their own potentialities and importance.

Game of 'warri' in progress

7. THE WISDOM OF BO

He that refuses a gift
will not fill his barns
TEMNE PROVERB

WHEN the mammy-lorries strike the tarmac roads of Bo, and the frantic protests of the machinery and chassis die to a mere chattering fit, the drivers sometimes call out: 'Ha! Bo! Coal Tar! Black Man's London!' Bo has electric light as well as metalled roads; it has Bo School, the black man's Eton; the Bunumbu Press which prints books in the tribal languages; the office of the *Sierra Leone Observer*, voice of the tribal natives; and the residences of the Chief Commissioner and of Dr. Margai, leader of the Sierra Leone People's Party and Prime Minister-in-Training. Bo is the administrative centre of the Protectorate, though Freetown is Dr. Margai's capital. At Bo a determined effort is made to efface from the mind of the enquiring traveller any false impressions that he may have received in Freetown about the country. In the genial company of Mr. Norman MacRobert, who was acting Chief Commissioner while I was on my travels, and other officials, this process may easily go on to three o'clock in the morning.

Bo and Njala (which is about 40 miles away) are key centres. Which should be visited first depends on whether you think agriculture comes before government, or politics before economics. At Njala, headquarters of the Agricultural Department, they can answer the questions that grow insistently as you wander through the decaying Colony villages or watch the primitive cultivation of rice on the blackened patches of cleared land along the railway. At Bo, they can tell you how the Protectorate is run, how it was run before it was declared a Protectorate, how it will be run as the British withdraw, and its relationship to the Colony. At Bo they know the native mind; at Njala they know the native soil.

Bo (which means the potter's clay) was created by the railway, its importance deriving from its location half-way between Freetown and Pendembu, making it the convenient overnight stop, where the 'land canoe' could 'tie up'. It began with the erection of a rest-house; it was selected as the site of a school to train the sons of chiefs in the art of rulership under the system of indirect rule. It became associated with rule through the chiefs, by the appointment of a Provincial Commissioner to watch over the southern province, followed by the appointment of a Chief Commissioner to watch the whole development of the Protectorate for the Governor. Finally the Protectorate Assembly was set up, and met in Bo, as a body representing the chiefs and their tribal authorities. Bo is growing fast as the Protectorate grows in self-consciousness and takes the lead in the political control of the whole country. Yet it is a curiously characterless town—suggesting, to me, the curiously character-less approach of the British officials in the past to the political future of Freetown's hinterland.

That approach was reluctant, and was always made to the chiefs as the real authority in African states or societies. From the first, the establishment of the colony of ex-slaves implied that the tribes of the interior should change their ways. The British Government was pledged to the suppression of the slave trade, and it quickly became apparent that the suppression of the European slavers and their factories, the capture and des-truction of their ships, was the easier part of the job. The real difficulty was to discourage the slave trade in the interior. If the African societies had opposed the slave trade, it would have quickly died once the preventive service was instituted. It kept going for so long because the African communities were partly organized on a slave-raiding, slave-dealing basis. Their resent-ment against those who spoilt the market was keen. By treaty, and to some extent by minor purchases or cessions of colonial territory such as Turner's peninsula, the British Government secured the coast and the frontiers of the Colony. The treaties with the chiefs in the coastal areas were designed to further good government, the suppression of slavery and the encourage-ment of trade, but left it to the chiefs to run their tribes and carry out treaty obligations in their own way.

Matters could not stop there. Chiefs further into the interior raided those that were in treaty relationships with Her Majesty's Government. Disputed titles to chieftainships caused the rupture of treaty relations. Traders and officials from the Colony were mur-dered from time to time, which called for punitive expeditions.

Slowly the area of treaty relations deepened. To maintain it, exploratory missions had to be sent. The 'little wars' that were fought by naval amphibious expeditions up the rivers, or by detachments of Frontier Police or the Army, led to further treaties. Inevitably the British, armed with Congreve rockets and breech-loaders, upheld the law-abiding, spared the conquered and warred down the proud. Chiefs who were threatened by invaders and needed allies asked for protection. More and more treaties stipulated that traders should be allowed to trade, that missionaries should be allowed to teach and preach, that 'abominations'—or at least those that appeared most outrageous to the Victorian mind—should be suppressed.

If responsibility and paramountcy had been actively sought, the area of British influence would have grown rapidly. It would in the early 'sixties have been possible to have asserted British jurisdiction or made treaties which would have so far extended the British spheres of influence that the hinterlands of Sierra Leone and the Gold Coast would have met, leaving Liberia and the French Ivory Coast as small enclaves in British West Africa. But any such process would have been abhorrent to Gladstone and Bright. A Select Committee of the House of Commons on the subject of relations with African chiefs declared in 1865 that: 'All further extensions of territory or assumption of Government, or new treaties offering any protection to native tribes would be inexpedient'. Repeatedly chiefs from the interior approached Governors offering suzerainty as a means of stopping tribal wars, and had to be refused. The chance to include in the British area an enormous territory controlled by the Alimami Samodu, for example, was lost to the French. The long start obtained by British and creole efforts on the Coast was overtaken by the French, who extended their influence to the basin of the Niger and made contact with the undefined territories claimed by Liberia on the east, thus hemming in Sierra Leone as they had hemmed in the Gambia. When the home Government had decided to join in the scramble for Africa, little remained to do but send men like Alldridge to make hurried treaties with the remaining chiefs of the interior to secure at least the basins of the rivers running to the Atlantic. The size of the country was settled more by the French and Liberians than by the British—or by any logical attempt to consider the natural area for which Freetown was adapted to be the capital, linked by waterways, roads and railway systems. It ended about the size of Ireland; it *might* have been the size of Nigeria.

In 1898, the Protectorate was declared over all the area with which treaties pre-empted British influence. Relations with nearly all the chiefs were then as between equals—'Good Friends' in forms of address. Some of the chiefs, it is true, had been approved or deposed by British Governors. But a Protectorate implied administration. Five District Commissioners were appointed, the railway was put under construction, and the question arose: who was to find the money? A hut tax was imposed to the astonishment of the chiefs, who had no thought of raising the rate of British income tax. Bai Bureh, a Temne chief, refused to pay and troops had to be sent to deal with him. The Frontier Police began collecting tax forcibly with supplementary vails intended for their own pockets. The Mende chiefs, organized by the Poro society, gave the signal to their war-boys at a concerted time, rose, and tried to sweep the white men into the sea. It was—perhaps—the last big protest by African society[1] against Western civilization; against the suppression of slave-dealing, tribal wars, many sanctioned customs; against railways, District Commissioners, economic development and taxation. Creole traders and missionaries were murdered in hundreds, and but for the railway Waterloo itself would have fallen to the war-boys. The Government reacted vigorously and soon put down the rebellion, hanging 33 chiefs.

The reign of D.C.s, working through paramount chiefs, was thus firmly established upon a demonstration of power. It was suggested, when the rebellion was suppressed, that the moment was favourable for the incorporation of the whole territory into the Colony. A new legal code (as in India) would be introduced, English legal customs would prevail and be developed by creole lawyers, it would be possible to buy land from chiefs (by plantation companies, for example). The conquered natives would become British subjects. The Government was not prepared for any such radical measures, or the cost of administering them. The chiefs were reinstated, though not always from the legitimate ruling families. The District Commissioners were

[1] Omdurman was fought in the same year.

instructed to interfere with native customs as little as possible
—beyond upholding law and order, suppressing slave-dealing,
cannibalism and human leopards, collecting tax, encouraging
agriculture and holding the ring for the civilizing efforts of
missions and traders. Chiefs were forbidden to put the Poro
taboo on kola and other trees in restraint of trade in produce.[1]

The District Commissioners got to know their people and to
respect the values and apparent self-sufficiency of African tribal
life. They became the fathers of their people, uniting in themselves executive and judicial power. The British-trained lawyers
of Freetown and the Colony police force were kept out. Instead,
the D.C.s relied, and still rely, for police work, detective work
and general executive duties, upon a remarkable semi-military
body, the Court Messengers. This force developed out of the
Government-paid messengers who maintained contact between the Governor in Freetown and his Good Friends, the
Chiefs in treaty relationship to Her Majesty. After the Protectorate was declared, they were put into uniform and given
proper training; men who have served in the West African
regiments often become Court Messengers, and ex-C.M.s usually
obtain high positions in the chiefdoms from which they come,
even to being elected paramount chief. They carry out their
duties generally quite unarmed; and no witchcraft or ordinary
threat of resistance prevents them from going to remote areas
to make an arrest. They serve as interpreters, as foremen of
public works, as general go-betweens; and the traveller in tribal
country finds them a mine of information, folk-lore and anthro-
pological detail. They are thus more than policemen; and their
morale, it is hard to deny, is far higher than that of the ordinary
African constabulary.

The maintenance of tribal law also kept out the plantation
companies. Under a different dispensation, these might possibly
have obtained land in Sierra Leone, planted and cultivated the
oil palm and perhaps coffee tree scientifically, and thus developed the export trade and the resources of the country more
rapidly. Bo set its face steadily against any such introduction
of modern methods, deferring to native tenacity of land-rights
and choosing to rely on the slower growth of agricultural and

---

[1] In fact, the origin of this custom was largely to ensure that people should do
farm work in the right order.

commercial skills among peasant cultivators. These were indeed of slow growth, and mineral rights could not be treated in the same way; diamonds and iron in the 'thirties at last brought the big City interests into the tribal areas, and with them just the sort of impact that the older generation of D.C.s had feared and distrusted.

So well did the Protectorate administration shield the tribes from hasty interference with their settled customs that it was not until 1927 that the newspaper-reading public discovered that Britain, while taking a high moral tone in the League of Nations, was firmly upholding a relic of domestic slavery in the hinterland of Sierra Leone itself—the Colony created as a home for liberated slaves, the living monument to Britain's noblest piece of humanitarian evangelism. So firmly upholding it indeed that a *British* court had reversed a D.C.'s decision that a slave who had run away to Freetown from his tribal owner was thereafter free and could not be claimed as a slave on his return. Nobody cited Mr. Justice Mansfield's decision of 1772! It wasn't relevant! Wasn't it, though—with all Europe laughing at British hypocrisy? The Governor received a curt telegram from the Colonial Secretary to put matters on an eighteenth-century basis instantly. Considerable numbers of dejected 'slaves' were turned by their indignant owners and providers into the less fertile farm-bush to fend for themselves. Others refused to go—Ordinance No. 24 of 1927 or no Ordinance No. 24 of 1927. (Even recently, a Vai chief was heard to remark: 'No, we don't have slaves now—we have *cousins*'.)

But the principle that the protected natives must be free to live their own lives in their own way without undue pressure from Europeans prejudiced in favour of Western ideas was never tenable for very long. The chief and his authority is the taproot of African social organization, but it was cut through when chiefs became, in greater or less measure, the agents of British administration, their authority subservient to the convenience of the Government. Chieftaincy had been a hereditary office, derived from right of conquest and limited only by the possibility of reconquest. In 1898, expediency suggested that chiefs should be weakened. Some large chiefdoms were promptly broken down into smaller units and the staff of paramount chieftaincy given to men who were section chiefs or headmen

67

in a confederacy. Thus the relative importance of the chief's 'Good Friend', the District Commissioner, was enhanced. Today, this multiplicity of small chiefdoms has become no less inconvenient. As administrative areas they are proving too small and their revenues too straitened. So now the brass-knobbed staffs are being surrendered again (with compensation). I came upon half a dozen stacked unceremoniously in D.C.'s office lavatory. But the enlargement of chiefdoms is not intended to restore power to the chiefs. On the contrary, it is part of the conversion of chiefdom rule into local government, which will ultimately dispense with chief and District Commissioner alike. 'Our chiefdoms will be parishes, or perhaps I should say Rural Districts,' observed Paramount Chief Kai Samba to me, with a ghost of a twinkle in his eye. 'And the Districts will correspond to your counties and county councils. We chiefs? Well, we shall become figureheads, Lord Lieutenants I suppose, with ceremonial duties only. Many chiefs are paid less than schoolteachers as it is.'

Does African tribal society evolve naturally into English local government? It was hardly supposed so by the first generation of District Commissioners. Nevertheless, even from the first, circumstances drove administration, perhaps unconsciously, into some such assumption. The chief's power was progressively curtailed. His court had powers of life and death; but the District Commissioner took over criminal and capital cases, and became the Court of Appeal, even from the chief's decisions on woman-palaver or inheritance of bush-farms. The D.C. exercised wide powers of settlement in chiefdom disputes. But British protection increased the chief's privileges in ways which presently called for further interference. It became harder to oppose or depose the chief, especially when he stood well with the Government, because he had nothing to fear from his rival chiefs. He could therefore settle down to make his chiefdom a source of personal wealth; and many did. The chief and his officers (the speaker, the principal adviser and regent, the sub-chiefs and headmen) were able to live on tributes in cash and kind, on chiefdom forced labour, on benevolences, on the fines exacted by the native courts, and on other payments. They took their pick of the young women. Missionaries believe that chiefs greatly increased the numbers of their wives as their personal riches grew under the peaceful shade of District

Commissioner rule. Some have had upwards of 300 wives, and it has been known for a chief to express a desire for a woman he encountered in the bush, only to be told that he had been married to her for some time. One methodical chief made his wives embroider serial numbers on their lappas; another put his into a regular uniform. The District Commissioners paid no attention to polygamy and its attendant country customs, but found it impossible to leave the swollen privy purses of the chiefs unregulated. Chiefdom treasuries and estimates— proper accounting—have been progressively introduced over 20 years. The chiefdom clerk, literate and able to keep books, was the first local government officer. In some chiefdoms he has become more powerful than the chief.

The conversion of chiefdoms in this way into 'native administrations' has been done against the inclination of chiefs and their people. The first British idea for the improvement of the Protectorate along purely 'African' lines of development was to breed, at Bo school, a generation of enlightened chiefs who would themselves know how to combine Western knowledge with native customs. Bo school, organized as a British public school, has produced some enlightened chiefs. But merely literate and educated chiefs have not always been a success— and are today still often failures. Buedu, near the borders of French Guinea, in the remotest part of Mendeland, is strikingly unlike any town in that area. It is laid out on sound principles of town planning, each house in its own compound with a separate latrine, the roads broad and awaiting only the growth of young trees to become shady boulevards. And it is lit by electric light from Buedu's own power station. Schools, cemented wells and dispensaries meet every requirement of welfare and health planning. But I did not meet the progressive ruler responsible for these innovations, for his people had risen against him, and, after enquiry, the administration deposed him. He had gone too far, too fast, and . . . 'Tck! tck!' they murmured in Bo, 'such a pity. But please don't ask for details'. At Bandajuma near Pujehun the town centre is a charred wreck; at Blama the chief was hurled from power and the Colony police riot squad had to be called in to restore order. 'A . . . particularly regrettable feature of these events', notes the Report on the Protectorate for 1949, 'is that the paramount chiefs who figured in them were in almost every case the product of secondary school education.' Many model rulers are, of course, fully literate; but many perfectly illiterate chiefs are model rulers. In the north and in Kono country, where the chiefs are mainly Muslim and the people relatively more backward, peace has prevailed.

The enlightened chief may go ahead of his people, or use his education to exploit them. In any case he will have spent at school years which, under the older dispensation, were spent intimately in contact with tribal custom and history. 'The fact is,' remarked an official to me, 'by and large, too many of the chiefs are just not up to the job'—of running a modern administration, he meant. It was therefore natural that the Government should turn still more from the chiefs to a form of administration designed to bring the best brains of the community closer into the councils of government. Four years after the abolition of domestic slavery buried the remains of the 'no interference' policy, the creation of experimental native administrations and district councils began. Chiefdoms were converted more and more into administrations run by the elders and with the aid of literate clerks; the money gathered in court fees were turned into the treasury. Tributes in kind were converted into taxes. Today, even the obligation to provide the chief with unpaid labour for his farm and for communal development, such as road construction, has been stopped. Men employed on development must be paid out of the local treasury. (However, they are not always paid at the Trade Union rate—nor do their wages always reach them without sundry deductions.)

At the same time, the chiefdoms have been gradually made into electoral bodies for a representative district council. Just as the villages are represented by their headmen or section chiefs, in the paramount chief's barri, so the chiefdoms are represented in the district council. The district council in turn elects members to the Protectorate Assembly and to the Legislative Council in Freetown. Except to elect the member to Leg. Co. the ballot box is not commonly used; but it is strongly affirmed that African democracy enters and controls the selection process at every point. Ruling families have hereditary rights in the chieftaincy; but the whole method of becoming headman, section chief, and a member of the tribal authority is in fact achieved by the custom of 'hanging heads'. Hanging heads consists in a protracted discussion and bartering of minor and major *quid pro quo*'s, until the most advantageous and acceptable man gets the post. Policies are decided and important pronouncements are made in tribal life by the same consistory method. Those in power in the chiefdoms and district councils assure one that it is an excellent democratic method and the very negation of arbitrary rule; those who are out of power and chafing at restraint do not conceal their view that it is the method by which a favoured and corrupt oligarchy share the lucrative posts provided by the Government.

The chief's position, between the District Commissioner on the one hand ceaselessly pressing his 'Good Friend' to undertake desirable reforms and expensive public works, and the elders (tribal authorities) generally objecting to any change and contemptuous of 'white man's humbug' on the other, has been difficult, and is perhaps becoming more difficult. Among the Temnes the chief at least is crowned and has religious attributes, but the Mende chief has no such sanction or immunity. Yet chiefdom elections have continued to be keenly contested by every member of the ruling families who can advance a claim. For there is still money in the job. The chief is still the centre of native life—the patron of Poro and Sande, the head of a court of notables, servants, singers, drummers and hangers-on; the most uxorious man in the chiefdom—if also its first cuckold; the owner of the largest tin-roofed compound, the man who, if he is politically ambitious, can most easily secure from his position on the district council a seat on the Protectorate Assembly and even in Leg. Co. in Freetown. Though he may be worse paid than a Government clerk, means exist of supplementing his emoluments. Deposed chiefs feel the descent into inconsequence and squalor very keenly.

The chiefdom can be studied in every stage of transformation. In Kono country, as yet unpenetrated by roads, some of the remoter chiefs are despots, obeyed without question, disposing of their treasuries much as privy purses, cool towards new-fangled white man's talk of education and development. But along the railway and in the mining towns the chiefs have little power. They cannot exercise much control over the 'strangers' who come and go. They certainly could not afford to entertain them, normally the chief's first responsibility towards any visitor in his realm. Their administration is truly committee-run, and even so their literate 'young men' are dissatisfied with their share in it.

From these elements of the old society, it is the task of Bo to develop somehow a new self-governing community. The officials are hopeful that it can be done; that the clay of tribal organization can be moulded to a new but serviceable shape. But it is not easy; for where the chief's authority is already partly embodied in new forms, the very circumstances which made this possible has created faction, intrigue and opposition, so that the hand of the District Commissioner must remain on the controls. Where the old ways persist, a disciplined people cling to their chiefs and a long task of 'community development' lies ahead. Though the object of the whole operation is ultimately to withdraw the District Commissioner as ruler, the plain fact is that at present he is as necessary as ever; for he alone can keep political evolution on the prescribed lines. The task of the D.C., if anything, becomes more difficult and exacting.

Moreover, delicate as is this operation, it is urgent. The poverty and lack of resources of the hinterland left the chiefs and tribal customs of Sierra Leone with more authority than was often possessed by the chiefs and emirs of richer West African territories. Their supremacy was unchallenged by a rich trading or professional class. But now, if the circle of poverty and ignorance is to be broken, it is necessary to re-group the territory into administrative units which are at once large enough, rich enough and well enough governed to put large-scale schemes of agricultural and social development into operation. The chiefs, indeed, must become such leaders as they never were; leading their people into completely unfamiliar forms of co-operative association, teaching them new kinds of farming and cropping, new habits of living, working, feeding and even thinking.

For there is no way back. The British officials are as much under pressure from the processes which they set on foot when they gingerly took charge of law and order as are the chiefs and their people. A small, circumscribed country, a backwater off the main stream of economic currents, Sierra Leone did not mark time while chiefs held court in the old way between the visits of 'Pa D.C.', borne in his hammock or striding along the bush paths swinging his stick, behind his singing train of porters. For, free or enslaved, the people farmed and multiplied, multiplied and farmed, and in so doing changed the land and the whole basis of their existence. Long before what was called slavery[1] was swept away because Lady Simon focused the awful power of England's conscience on Sierra Leone, long before the first experimental district councils were set up, the Agricultural Department was warning the District Commissioners about the state of the land, and the District Commissioners were trying to warn the chiefs and elders of impending disaster. The problems of Bo are also the problems of Njala.

---

[1] The Mende word for a slave is Ndole, but in fact means a domestic servant in a feudal relation to the 'owner'. Slaves or serfs were not sold or ill-treated, and often reached high positions in the chiefdom, becoming quite well off. Some became chiefs.

'Warri' board, a game played throughout West Africa, usually for high stakes.

8. THE WISDOM OF NJALA

He who upsets something should
know how to rearrange it
TEMNE PROVERB

ONE of the great arguments used by the railway promoters
in the 'nineties was that the railway would stimulate agriculture. Already the Colony villages were decaying, Freetown was
importing rice, and the city's prosperity, such as it was, mani-
festly depended on middleman profits from the sale of palm
oil, palm kernels, kola, ivory, gold and camwood from up-
country. The Agricultural Department was started in 1895,
with a botanical station in Freetown which was closed after
a few years. The Department continued—a two-man department. As the railhead probed deeper into the interior, agricultural hopes rose. The five new D.C.s were invited to run
experimental and demonstration farms as part of their civilizing
mission, a delightful combination of the technical and administrative which was discreetly abandoned. In 1911 the Agricultural Department was established at Njala, in recognition of
the fact that the wealth of the territory lay in the land. For
over 40 years the Department has wrestled with the climate and
the soil: to begin to understand agriculture in the tropical rain
forest belt it is essential for the visitor to take peripatetic instruction among the green lawns, the screened bungalows and
hygienic pigsties, the experimental plots and nurseries, the
laboratories and botanical collections of the station, which is
set in the rolling hills and a bend of the river Taia. It is the
more instructive if, as was my luck, explanations are given
between showers of rain.

At Bo, you talk before the political map of Sierra Leone;
at Njala before the physical map. To the agriculturist the
eastern frontier, running along the watershed between the
Niger basin and that of the Sierra Leone rivers, is rational,
though the boundaries between the territory and the neighbouring French and Liberian territories are artificial. From the
eastern frontier the land slopes to the Atlantic, a great, uneven
draining-board for the colossal rainfall which varies between

74

100 inches a year in the north to 150 in Freetown. From the eastern hill districts a pattern of rivers and streams carries off the water, brings it down through the rolling country of the central areas on the way, turning many natural depressions into swamps or lakes, and finally loses it through the lowlands and marshes which border the western and southern coasts. The figuration of the land and the fall of water decide the strange fate of Sierra Leone and its peoples. No one could tell me, in terms a layman could understand, why the winds, the climates of the sea, the earth's seasons and currents hurl against this small section of the Guinea coast such terrific tonnages of vapour which are condensed so rapidly that already in the north, when the Harmattan or dry winds blow, one gets a reminder that the Sahara lies not many hundred miles beyond. But it does; and the rain has been falling, falling, falling, year in, year out, for hundreds of thousands of years.

On this earth our lives depend on slender margins: a little too little spells poverty—yet a fraction too much likewise spells destitution. The first lesson in geography in Sierra Leone is the way the rain has fallen. Attached to Mr. Utting's history of Sierra Leone for the schools of the Protectorate is a time scale which purports to show how little we know of the territory's history; nothing before Hanno glimpsed the Colony hills in 500 B.C.; nothing again until in 1462 Pedro da Cintra named them. But we know the important facts, which African children must now learn consciously, and which their parents knew unconsciously: that the rains have fallen and in their falling have decided the limits of living and farming. In the rains the rivers rise to great heights—sometimes 29 feet above dry-season levels—and rush to the sea carrying with them huge tonnages of soil. Over the centuries this soil has been built into the low lands which border the coast, the swampy fens and deltas covered with grass and mangrove. In so doing, the rains have determined the quality of the soil and its capacity to support plant life, animals and men.

The red soils of West Africa are the results of the rains. Laterite, an inexact but sufficient term, is the final state of rocks which have been washed by high rains for eons—it is the insoluble part of the basic igneous rock. Rocks consist of minerals, and the rain washes out the soluble salts. The alkali (sodium and potassium salts) goes first; then the lime, followed by silica. In the end a red-coloured concentration of iron, aluminium, manganese and other insolubles is left. The soluble salts, which are in fact the nutrients which plants draw from the soil through their roots, are almost wholly washed out—into the rivers, into any soil that will hold them, but mainly leached down through the crevices and porosities in the rocks to the water table. The result is an acid soil poor in nitrates and phosphates. Covered with the lush vegetation of the tropics, it looks rich and fertile; it supports the dense forest which the traveller sees from the air, the carpet of green on the Colony hills which the sailor sees from the sea. There seems not an inch of soil but must grow something: yet it is all a strange, cruel illusion. Clear the phalanx of rooted trees, hack away or burn the intricate snare of creepers and undergrowth, bare the red earth and put in the plough, and the soil promptly turns sour and unthrifty. By a quaint device the banquet vanishes. After one crop, the next is starved and poor. The earth powders and blows away; finally it sometimes forms a stiff clayey pan which thereafter grows nothing but poor grass. From the first year that the Colony was founded, the torrents of rain were draining away food from the roots of the crops so hopefully sown. Swift run-off water from the hillsides often made matters worse, carrying away the soil as soon as it was bared to the hoe.

The process can be seen at work. The traveller on the roads waits for a tremendous downpour to pass, and then fears his car will be bogged in mud. It may be. But it is astonishing how rapidly the laterite road surfaces dry again after such a sousing. The reason is that the soil is porous; the water goes through with unexampled rapidity. What the great weight of water does to the soil I saw at a mechanized farm at Demongo in the Gold Coast. After a tropical downpour of some hours I went out to see the skilfully contoured fields, which had just been ploughed. For all the skill of the contouring, the edges were filled with long pools of brown, froth-covered water which had accumulated as the result of the breaking of the ridges. That froth was the salts in the soil, washed out, washed away, lost.

To the geologists of the Geological Department in Freetown, to the scientists of Njala, this is simple causality, plain double-entry chemical accountancy. It supports the paradox of tropic

FRENCH GUINEA

LIBERIA

Predominantly Swamp
Farm Bush (secondary forest growth)
Savannah
Forest Reserves
Iron   Chrome   Diamonds

Map to show mineral resources being worked and
approximate areas of types of vegetation.

lushness on infertile soil. It does more, I think: it helps to explain
what I can only describe as the haunting sense of human
failure, man's impotence to work his will, in a gree-gree
haunted land. This sense that nothing thrives pervades Sierra
Leone; merely to live, in the native mind, requires a constant
propitiation of the angered spirits of the place. For all the care
taken to propitiate the dark forces which hold the land in
thrall, human endeavour continually comes to nothing; and
quick success brings envy and retribution. This sense, I fancy,

spreads even to the European who works here; nothing seems to come right—nothing quite pays—the money and care put into projects seem to seep away, like water, through the soil . . . But at least we begin to realize the reasons for past failures: forty years of work at Njala have not been in vain.

There is perhaps no complete balance in nature: the seas are salt with the land's mineral content, and the sea-bed is covered with the erosion of geological ages. But in the gradual dissipation of the earth's capital, temporary balances between soil, climate and plant-life are struck. In this tropical land, the process is arrested by the tenacity of plant life. The heavy rainfall means that plants can grow dense and grow tall. Forest trees take possession of the soil, bind it, and hold it. Some are shallow-rooted, supported on great buttresses, their roots absorbing the water greedily before it sinks through the soil and carries away the nutriment; others are deep-rooted, and these pump up from the depths, from the water-table, the salts that have been carried down by the leaching process. The great trees soar upwards and spread their interwoven canopy of sugar-synthesizing leaves high above the earth's surface; the rain that smashes so viciously into the bare earth is broken in its fall by millions of tough, half-yielding leaves, and descends to the ground with its force spent and its volume somewhat reduced. The trees, moreover, continuously provide a natural mulch to protect and to manure the soil in their annual fall of leaves. In the tropics their branches are never bare; flush follows flush, and shedding follows shedding, so that a tree usually wears simultaneously a new growth of foliage and a year-old growth, while losing a third. Moreover, the canopy of leaves breaks not only the force of the rain, but also the power of the sun, which directed on bare soil, for example, disintegrates and dissipates a dressing of manure in a few weeks. In the hottest weather you walk through the rain forest in comparative coolness; the earth is not baked hard, it yields springily underfoot.

In that vast, greenhouse shade, an unending proliferation of life has room to work the ceaseless process of death and renewal between the soil, or the soil below the soil, and the great, permeable but protective umbrella above. A fantastic variety of creepers festoons the forest trees, the red flowers of

THE WISDOM OF NJALA

the climber *Musserida elegans* or the *johnsolinus*—like Ashanti Blood—marking their pathway to sunlight; in the wetter parts of the forest the climbing palms grip the leaves and branches of the forest trees by hooks, and when they fall, slip and hang in great loops and coils—slip only to climb and slip again. Tree trunks are wound round like Laocoön with the snakes, or sheathed in a tight corset of spade-shaped leaves. Hundreds of species of orchids lodge themselves high up under the canopy, mostly small growths with sprays of tiny green or white flowers. What light gets down through this green upper level, what food is left in the soil after the root systems of the trees and their dependants have taken all they can, is consumed by plants of the undergrowth—sometimes dense but often sparse. Upon all, trunk and stem and leaf, grow every variety of fungus and lichen.

This is the indigenous forest that grows unbroken (save by swamps and rivers) wherever the rain falls more or less continuously all the year round, with a peak in the three summer months. Then, northwards, as the rainfall is concentrated in the summer and the land is parched from December to April, the forest cover progressively thins, for in the dry seasons the root systems must search more widely for water and food, and the number per acre goes down, the great canopy breaks, and savannah grass establishes itself, and, in seven- or eight-foot heights, by its own means defends and renovates the soil with its matted and creeping roots. Mile by mile, the Lophira trees become sparser, except along the rivers and round the swamps, and great sheets of varied grasses cover the land, lush in the rains, tinder-dry to flashpoint when the Harmattan blows. Upon the hillsides on the road to Kabala, and round Yengema, one of the wonderful processes by which life asserts itself over the lifeless earth can be seen: a rock-sedge (Catagyna) which grows on the apparently smooth, rain-planed rock face by developing a mat of roots and humus which grips the smooth stone, absorbs the rain and fragments of dead matter. The tough grass grows from this pad of soil, strengthened by mosses and lichens, and supports a special orchid of its own. Gradually it covers the rock, the interstices are filled up with rubbish, and a layer of living soil is created even on slopes of over 45 degrees in despite of the ceaseless waves of water pouring down the rock face.

79

The dominion of the trees ceases, also, in the alluvial swamps of the south. Where the marsh gives no foothold for the trees, sudd grasses grow; and near the salt water the mangroves drive their stubborn roots into the ooze and hold back for the land a proportion of the soil carried away to the sea by the rivers. To the very shores of Sierra Leone you can see the battle of the plants with the water for the soil.

But to grow crops man must cut down the forest and bare the soil. After he has taken a crop, or several crops, he must let the forest reclaim the land, protect it from the sun, restore to it a top dressing of humus and, by the deep root systems of trees, pump back into it some of the mineral richness that crops and rain have taken away. This was the primitive system, to move from one small clearing in the forest to another, and return perhaps once in 25 years. Where men are few and farms are small, the forest remains unbroken and the land remains in good heart; the cycle of tropical fertility is unbroken. In the Liberian hinterland the forest rules the land, and men snatch their crops here and there. But to enter Sierra Leone from Liberia is—I imagine, since I have flown over Liberia and stood on her dark and forbidding frontier—to move slowly from forest to thinner and thinner woodland and scrub. The Gola forest in Sierra Leone is contiguous with the Liberian forest and I have walked there; I have come from under that green cover to the broken, patchy 'bush' which is now the vegetation of much of Sierra Leone.

At Njala they interpreted for me the picture I had had from the air: the mosaic of light and dark greens which asserts itself as one crosses Sierra Leone. The land is not wilderness interspersed with small patches of primitive cultivation: the whole area, except for some mountains, some fragments of forest and infertile stretches, is under cultivation. The farm bush is simply the land under fallow, recovering from cropping; the cultivated patches are destined to go under bush again. The forests have almost all disappeared: barely 5 per cent of Sierra Leone is under forest. What is more, the bush is nearly all young growth; for the land is not rested 20 years or even 15; but after four to seven years it is put under crops again. And four years is not long enough. The land does not recover its fertility. In spite, therefore, of the apparent sparseness of population the land is closely cropped and indeed overcropped by existing methods. A soil erosion survey has recently been made and maps prepared which show the extent to which the bush is being degenerated; the maps reveal that whole tracts in the central areas of Sierra Leone have now reached a stage in which the bush can barely re-establish itself in the fallow periods. It is being replaced by grass; and this grass, in tropical conditions, does not restore the fertility of the soil. If it is ploughed, the land produces almost no crop. A process of denuding the soil of vegetation has proceeded to a point at which it is irreversible—except, perhaps, in terms of centuries of slow, natural restoration.

It is not easy at first to grasp the grim meaning of the maps. The contrast between the Liberian high forest and the Sierra Leone degraded farm bush seems to stick in the mind. For when the Colony was founded, the southern half of Sierra Leone was what Liberia is today. Indeed, high forest abounded until very recently. Paramount Chief Caulker of Shenge told me that when he went to Moyamba from Shenge as a young man—just before the great rebellion—he travelled through narrow winding paths under forest much of the way; I travelled the same way, and on either side of the road stretched nothing but low scrub, with occasional large trees. It is well known that the older generation can remember the forests. Alldridge, in his description of the railway journey in 1908 from Freetown to Pendembu, speaks of the hilly country round Moyamba 'covered with great forest trees'; what I saw were mountain-sides brown and raw where the trees and bush had been cut down right to the summits; fast-growing scrub made the land appear green and fertile—but of the great deep-rooted trees there were few. Mr. Harris, of the Methodist Mission in Daru, further east, told me that when he first arrived in Sierra Leone seventeen years ago, 5- and 6-inch diameter poles were used for houses, and small poles rejected; today poles of 2-inch diameter must be used, and even so are not always easy to find. Tree-trunks large enough for shaping into big dugout canoes are so rare anywhere within transportable distance of the coast that they cost up to £8 apiece.

The land has been ruthlessly cleared and thinned; but not by modern sawmills or axe-teams. It has been largely done in

G

50 or 60 years by the native axe, the machet, and—by fire. A growing company of farmers has moved faster and faster through the forest and then the farm bush, burning off the land on which to grow the rice and other crops. The farmers knew well that it was best to leave the land for at least seven years, preferably more, to recover from the burning and cropping. But the apparently undifferentiated bush is all marked out in ownerships, the claims as clear and distinct as if they were fenced; and gradually an increasing population has moved round and round its own area at ever shorter intervals. Where the land has been reduced to mere grass, the people have indeed migrated to find new and unappropriated bush. From the ruined—yet still mysteriously and mistily green—Panguma valley, the straitened farmers have moved north into Kono country, impelled as surely as if they were leaving a dust-bowl behind them.

This is the story which is unfolded at Njala—and has been set down in detail in the Report of the Soil Conservation Team which appeared in 1951. It is not a fresh discovery: books written before the First World War make uneasy reference to the rate at which forests were vanishing, farms climbed the hillsides, soil disappeared and the smoke of the burning bush lay across the land in the dry months. At Njala, a solution to the 'wasteful' native method of farming has long and earnestly been sought. But no sure rotation has been found that would dispense with the need to let cropped land go back to bush for regeneration. Under continuous cultivation, the land is exposed for too long to the rain, the sun and the scorching winds. No satisfactory fallow grasses have been found despite many—and continuing—experiments. Grasses—like napier grass—which to some extent regenerate the soil in the same way as bush growth, present as difficult a problem of cultivation as the bush itself, their tough roots impervious to the native hoe. Many rotations have been tried, but even the best fallow grasses, such crops as guinea grass, take a very long time to put back into the soil what a single crop of rice or cassava takes out. There is no local source of lime and no phosphatic rocks to redress the acidity of the soil and its lack of phosphate. You rarely see bones lying about in Sierra Leone as in other parts of Africa; they are too valuable a source of calcium phosphate and are quickly consumed.

For many years now the Agricultural Department has tried to stop the further dissipation of the land's fertility. The first and foremost need is to stop the growing of upland rice on slopes, and to lengthen the fallows where these are unduly short on level ground. The tribes of the north, Temnes and Lokos, have themselves shown the way by growing rice along the swampy banks of the rivers—so successfully, indeed, that a rice expert from Bengal could suggest no substantial improvements. The Agricultural Department has, in alliance with the District Commissioners, fought a long campaign to persuade the native farmers to make more use of the many swamps which exist in this heavily-watered country. It has done well; but still the cultivation of upland rice goes on. For in the eastern and north-eastern hills of the Kono and Yalunka country there are few swamps; and even where there are swamps, there are often not enough of them. The people aver that they prefer the sweet red upland rice, and will not offend their ancestors' spirits by any offerings of swamp rice. Moreover, the swamps are hard to cultivate by the native hoe. These are the difficulties which the Agricultural Department is now bringing in tractors to over-come. By tractor ploughing larger areas along the Scarcies rivers and the rivers of the south can be put down to rice; and with tractors many inland swamps can be ploughed, and thereafter sown and weeded by traditional methods—a woman bent double. If swamp rice production can be pushed up there may be a chance of slowing down the ceaseless destruction of the bush and the loss of soil.

Njala does not confine itself to rice; it experiments with every possible crop. It is concerned to introduce improved animal husbandry where it can, to develop the export crops—oil palm, cocoa, coffee, bananas, ginger, piassava, and many more—which will, by bringing more money into the cultivator's hand, permit him to buy rice where he should not grow it. But rice—subsistence farming—is the core of the tragedy which is being played out in Sierra Leone. To grow rice cheaply and plentifully where it should be grown, to grow much larger quantities of it to meet the needs of the increasing population, to use modern machinery and science to widen the areas suitable to it—this is the race against time in which Sierra Leone, basically, is engaged.

'... The main difficulties in the way of extending the cultivation and production of rice are economic and administrative. If these difficulties can be overcome, the path seems clear to a large increase in the local food supply and in the export trade of the Colony, both of which are highly desirable at the present time', wrote the Secretary of State for the Colonies in a Minute on the subject to the Sierra Leone Government. 'No time should therefore be lost in seeking a solution of the problems indicated; and I shall be glad if you will give immediate attention to this question and furnish me with your views and proposals at as early a date as possible.'

It was signed Winston S. Churchill, and dated April 24, 1922.

'Nomoli' prehistoric (?) steatite figure of the type dug up in Sierra Leone often placed in rice-fields to promote good crops and beaten if they fail to do so (see p. 161).

9. GEORGIC

The cassava saves the rice
MENDE SAYING

THE farmer can take only one year at a time. He may
notice that times are changing, that the six-year bush is harder
to find, that an acre which gave his uncle 750 to 1,000 lb. of
rice yields him only 300 lb., that grassland is moving southwards into the bush, that timber is hard to get, that the rivers
are browner, fuller and angrier than when his elders propitiated
their devils. The old men shake their heads and blame modern
impiety. But always there is the load of debt to be paid off, the
taxes to be found, the hungry children to be fed. January finds
him and his relatives, dressed in thick gowns of country cloth,
out in the bush cutting the shoots and saplings and branches
of the bigger trees with the cutlasses made by the local blacksmith. The medicine man sprinkles 'sawei' medicine over the
bush to drive out the witches which cause men to cut themselves and wounds to fester. The men work from first light to
dusk, with a pause at midday for food brought by the women,
in a temperature of up to 95 degrees in the shade—and as their
work goes on, the shade disappears. The Temnes call this month
'Pol pol', the month of the crack-crack of the brushwood as it
is cut down, or the crackle of burning grass. The Mendes call
it 'Pegbaa' or house-building time: houses are built with the
cut poles. The *combretum* is out in great trusses of crimson
flowers and waxy red fruits, while the pendant spikes of the
lovely Sierra Leonian laburnum, *pterocarpus erinances*, swing
golden-yellow to the drying wind from the Sahara. To the
sound of the cutlasses, the dea-dea sings its kroo-kroo note,
like the thud of a drum keeping time.

February is hotter than January, though a little rain may
fall in the south. The Temnes call this month 'Bankele', the
cursèd hot time, and the Mendes 'Vui', the tree-felling month
in which the 'Vui' wind blows. The cassias burst out in huge
yellow flowers. From Port Loko northwards the Lophira trees
put forth a mass of white flowers, so that you might think yourself in an endless cherry orchard in blossom. It is more exhausting

85

than ever to be out in the sun; but now the time has come to chop down the big trees which the previous month's brushing has left. The young corkwood and birch-like 'Hewei', with their feathery leaves, stand no chance as the axe is laid to their trunks; the teak and thorny 'sowuli' are brought down and set aside for building houses. Only the great cotton trees, often the dwellings of spirits, are protected, as well as the oil and raffia palms whose fruits or fronds will make money for the family—if they survive the coming ordeal by fire. To mark the boundaries of the crops a few great trees may be spared to wage an unsupported fight against the storms of summer.

When the brushwood is gathered into great heaps around the trunks of felled trees, the Mende farmer takes palm wine and medicine to the clearing, sprinkles the medicine over the ground with the words: 'I am sending rice into the farm', and offers wine to the ancestors to advise them that the brushwood will now be given to the flames. It is kindled on the windward side, before the smaller sticks become so dry under the sun's heat that they burn swiftly through without setting fire to the heavier wood. The burning is watched and controlled lest the sparks are carried down-wind to the dry thatch of a nearby village. The fire kills young palms, but the tall-trunked mature palms, though scorched, live through it. A good burning leaves no litter, save a fine ash which provides a top dressing of potash. Burning is sulphurous work in a sulphurous month, for the Temnes call March 'Gbapron', or the month in which to walk on the side of the roads that blister the feet. The Mendes call it 'Nyawolii', which also means intense heat.

After the burning, the ancestors should be thanked with offerings of rice cooked in red palm oil; and to show the land how to bear the rice abundantly, the farmer and his 'love wife', or courted favourite, may plant quick-growing bananas and paw-paw trees. A trap of burned sticks is set to catch any witches approaching the prepared land.

Now the critical month arrives, April, 'Befu' in Temne and 'Buwui' in Mende. In Temne it means 'have new', or plant; the month to plough and sow, or rather, to sow and then hoe in the time-tested manner. The appearance of the poisonous-footed centipedes, round reddish flexible creatures five or six inches long and familiarly known as 'Mende trains', and the flowering of the ground orchid in great purple spikes show that the soil is ready to be fertilized. But first the aid of the ancestors must be invoked lest it refuse to nourish the seed. The farmer and his hired men, all members of the Poro, build a little house or 'shimbeck' of sticks and palm leaves, in which the top of an ant-hill is placed, and a small-scale ploughing-in and sowing of rice is done in front of it. A hoe is broken and placed before the ant-hill. The farmer takes a cock and cuts its throat, scattering the blood and feathers before the shimbeck. Red rice is left as an offering. Thus again, the spirits of the dead are made partners in the enterprise of the living; invoked to help against the uncertain forces of nature disturbed by the presumption of husbandry and abuse of the potent earth by man.

The rites concluded, the farmer and his helpers gather, stripped to their loin-cloths. The section to be hoed by each is marked out. The farmer marches in front with his bag of seed, scattering it broadcast among the blackened stumps still left in the land. The men—perhaps helped by the women—follow him in a line of 10 or 12 abreast and hoe the exposed seed into the soil. They stand astride, and drive the hoe into the soil to a depth of two or three inches, bending double with each stroke, tearing out weeds and providing a seedbed for the seed, with which seeds of cotton, okra, green-green and sour-sour are mixed. There are no pure stands of anything; cassava cuttings and beans are thrust here and there into mounds and levelled ant-hills to grow amid the rice.

Ploughs? There are no ploughs, for to use a plough would require that the land should be stumped each year, which would be impossible, both because of the toil involved and also because the bush regenerates from the roots left after brushing and burning. The roots hold the soil, and the scratching of the hoes do not unduly powder it, so that when the rains fall in sheets the soil has some cohesion wherewith to resist their wash. And, in the south, there are few oxen to draw any ploughs, for even the indigenous 'Ndama' cattle, tolerant to 'tryps', hardly thrive, in this tsetse ridden country.

I asked a Temne chief in the north if he had ever thought of using a plough. He replied that he had one, but no longer used it. 'Did it break?' I asked. 'No, it was unbroken.' 'Then why give it up?' 'No reason—the hoe is better and we are used to it.' And on those rolling hills and rain-washed slopes it *is* better, though dangerous enough. Hard it is to drive into the baked earth even two inches, so that a man is quickly exhausted as he follows the sower. Wherefore a hill slope offers a certain relief, since gravity aids the pull of the hoe and the loosened earth is dragged a little downhill . . . where the rain finds it easy to push down further.[1]

Only in the level swamps, inland and along the rivers, a little later, in May and June, is the putt-putt-putt of the Government tractor increasingly heard.

And now, in May, there are other things to do: in the north the land is ready to plant groundnuts and yams, and in the south ginger. A rough shelter must be built near the sprouting rice to shield the weeding women from the rains that threaten from the cloud-loaded skies. As the first rains fall the bush bursts into life, a tremendous though not spectacular flowering. For the tropics are mainly a study in greens. Nearly everything flowers in delicate greens and greenish-whites, tiny bells and trumpets and lanterns throwing out a blended perfume that is unidentifiable but pervasive, and whose authors remain incognito except to the botanist with his dog-latin, or to the natives whose names, uncouth to our ears, are as suggestive as those of our own English wild flowers and herbs. The Temnes call this month 'Yantomi', 'the drop of the ripe fruit'. The Mendes, however, name it 'Golei' after a fish which now leaves the big rivers for the streams and is easily netted—a nice extra to the diet.

June is called 'Wofe' by the Temnes, meaning heap together from a dry measure—that is, the beginning of the hungry season. The Mendes call July the hungry time, 'Nanoi'. The old rice has nearly all been eaten; the young rice has not yet come up; and ready money is needed. Now it is time to harvest last season's plantings of cassava and eat that, unpalatable though it may be. Cassava is a great stand-by—but it is not rice. 'If you see a white man eating roast cassava, be sure his shop has gone bankrupt', declares the Susu proverb. But in June and July the white men's shops are full of rice, and the white men are wreathed in welcoming smiles. It is then that the family must collect the fruit of the oil palm, make the red

[1] The plough is used in the north, however. See p. 120.

palm oil and bring the residual nuts in sacks to the Syrian who is ready to buy—at his own price; or kola nuts which the Syrian knows how to ship profitably to the Colony and French Guinea. And if these things still will not feed the farmer and his family, then he must pledge himself to sell a part of the rice harvest in advance, at the Syrian's price. And the price of a future and uncertain harvest is far lower than that of a bag of rice in the shop; though it may not always be easy to say how much lower, for the shopkeeper cheerfully hands out kerosene, lamps and cloth as well as rice, and keeps his own account. He does not live on roast cassava. I have—when my chop-box ran out of tins, and rice late in June was unprocurable in the market.

July is called by the Temnes 'Anof abana', the big month, when planting is general. Meanwhile there are palm kernels to sell. The fruit of the oil palm is gathered and is prepared in various ways. The Limba people clean the fruit, and in February bury it in a hole near the house and plant sweet potatoes on top. The sweet potatoes are harvested in May or June, and then the fruit is dug up and made into a black, malodorous oil, which is used as a purge. The Temnes boil the fruit in five- or ten-gallon iron pots. Then the softened fruit is pounded in the mortar. After a thorough beating the pulp is emptied into iron pots half filled with water, which is then boiled. The Sherbros use a 50-gallon pot and raise its sides with poles interwoven with leaves to increase its capacity. A fire is made beneath and the fruit is cooked in steam from midday to dusk. The boiled fruit is then emptied into a chamber cut in the clayey soil, or into a dugout canoe, and then stamped out with feet, like a wine-press. The receptacle is then filled up with water which is poured from a height; this causes the oil to settle at the top, whence the women can skim it off. The inner nuts settle to the bottom, and are taken out and cracked with stones to extract the kernels. The palm fruit yields two oils: the red oil of the pericarp, the outer rind, which is eaten by the Africans as their fat, margarine and salad dressing in one; and the kernel which will only yield its valuable oil under mechanical pressure. The export of kernels is the main export of the country; and these the Syrian traders are ready to buy—as are the Syrian and other agents of the Produce Marketing Board if the amounts are large enough.

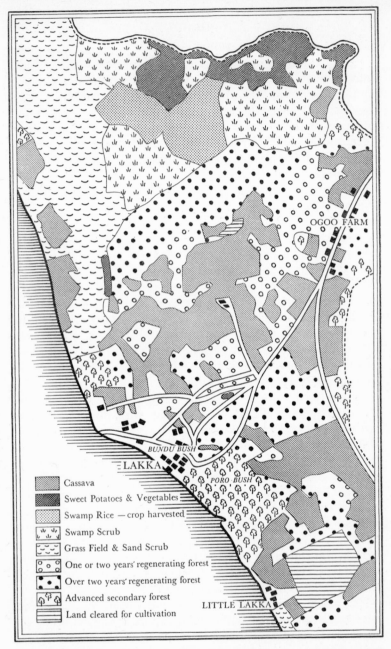

Legend:

- **Cassava**
- **Sweet Potatoes & Vegetables**
- **Swamp Rice — crop harvested**
- **Swamp Scrub**
- **Grass Field & Sand Scrub**
- **One or two years' regenerating forest**
- **Over two years' regenerating forest**
- **Advanced secondary forest**
- **Land cleared for cultivation**

Map labels: OGOO FARM, BUNDU BUSH, LAKKA, PORO BUSH, LITTLE LAKKA

Map to illustrate the method of 'shifting cultivation', or bush fallows, round a village. The actual areas under various crops in one year are shown, and the areas returning to 'bush'. 'Advanced secondary forest' is 'ripe' for cultivation next year, the cropped areas for abandonment to bush. Lakka is also a fishing village, and has swamp rice—cultivable every year.

In July the women go to the rice fields and weed the crop. The women pull up the weeds by hand from the two-foot rice stalks, helped by the children, and pile them in heaps. When the rice is three feet high it must be weeded again. Weeding is a long and arduous task, for germination and growth are far faster in the tropics than in northern climes. It may take to the end of August; a man with many wives has little or nothing to pay for outside help.

In August the rains are almost continuous; it is 'Dawii' in Mende, the month of river floods, and 'Paia' in the Temne language, the time of sickness. Men and women who labour in the fields in heavy rain are not exempt from rheumatism because their skins are black. The mosquitoes are breeding in their millions, and the flies which carry dysentery settle everywhere. But the work must go on: the weeds which steal the scanty nutrients in the soil must be pulled out, and the crop must also be protected from the thieves who reap where they sowed not. As the rice germinates it is attacked by rats and grasshoppers. The orange and black weaver birds, whose grass nests hanging like Christmas decorations in village palm trees are thought an omen of success, descend in flocks. Frogs chew the stems of the plants, and monkeys and the 'cutting-grass', a creature like a hare, attack the standing rice when it is four or more feet high. When the rice is almost dry, the bush buck and the wild pig come for their share.

It is the duty of the children to repel these invaders. They spear the frogs with pointed sticks and chase the monkeys from the crop. Boys with slings and piles of stones take up their positions on raised platforms and scare the birds with stones; sometimes by means of cans hanging from strings. Hunters with shotguns try to keep down the monkeys; and the 'monkey drive' is a standard service which may even be organized by the agricultural officer. The cry constantly goes up for more guns and cartridges. There is great pride in owning a licensed gun even if it does little execution.

In August there is more cassava root to be dug up, and in some areas the groundnuts are ready also; the maize funnels are swollen with the cobs and the millet is ready to be garnered in the north. In September the rains slacken off, especially in the north; the Temnes call the month 'Gbotko', the time of heavy raindrops, the Mendes 'Saa', the sound of the rain driven over the bush by the wind. Some rice is ready for harvest, but harvesting is generally delayed until October or November. Swamp rice is harvested later still. At the end of the rains there is a fresh flush of flowers in the bush, and the climate is clear and mild. Now is the time to build the rice store behind the farmer's house, if the old one is in disrepair. It is built like an ordinary house, but with platform raised above the ground upon which the rice can be left. The lower floor can be used to store farm implements.

Once again the farmer goes to the fields, now yellow with grain, to propitiate the ancestors. He prays to them, promising them a 'big pot'. He cuts rice from the first part of the land to be sowed, has it cooked in palm oil, and places it on flat stones for them, saying, 'Our rice is not big enough yet, but here is yours'. Then he cuts enough rice for a feast, with fowls and fish, and calls all those who have worked on the farm to join in the rejoicing. Everyone helps with the harvest in Sierra Leone, men, women and children, dependants and kinsfolk. Each harvester has his or her allotted task, depending on age, sex and strength; and those who come in from outside the family to help are given an agreed amount in return. They move through the crop, armed with short knives or sharpened pieces of bamboo, and cut the grain about five inches down the stalk. Bundles of cut rice are tied up and carried home on the heads of the harvesters, where they are placed on the drying platform in the store. Under the platform a slow fire is lit to dry the rice and preserve it from rot and insect pests. (Pepper may be mixed with it for this purpose.)

The Temnes call October 'Mufar', the mouldy month, when things must be dried. It is also sometimes called 'Sa Koma', the helping month, when relatives work together—and dance together. The Mendes merely name it after a mushroom, 'Galoi'.

'Ta rokane', the harvest month, the month in which the last of the rice is gathered in, is November. As the rice is gathered, there is music in the fields, and there is dancing and singing in the village at night. The weather is cool and lovely, and the tall grasses by the roadside and river banks are in flower. There are mists in the mornings, wherefore the Mendes call November

'Lugbu-yalui'. The season for gaiety and relaxation has arrived; meals are big, bellies full to bursting. For it is said that a woman and a bag of rice cannot live in the same house; the rice is consumed at breakneck speed. All day in the villages can be heard the thumping of the mortars as the rice is husked, and great mats are spread out to dry it after it has been parboiled in iron pots. The Syrian is paid back at 100 per cent interest, and the hungry months of the coming year are forgotten. The yams are ready, and so is the ginger and coffee; the cocoa farmer is fermenting and drying his beans. Begone, dull care! December is 'Tranantia', the marriage month, when still more feasting and dancing will enliven the sun-drenched days and warm, aromatic nights, sounding with the metallic whirr of the insects like a Lilliputian factory, and the berlinia trees are covered with huge white flowers.

But in December the new farming year starts; the site of next year's crop must be selected from the bush. The farmer rejects, if he can, bush of four years' growth or less—'Gboi yopoi' in Mende, 'Not strong yet'. He examines the earth with a knowing eye—its colour, the worm-casts, the depth of humus formed by fallen leaves and rubbish. He chooses the most promising, and if—because pockets of salts accumulate there after the rains—a hillside promises best, he decides to brush, burn and bare that land. It is his; and not all the pleas of the white forestry officer or the erosion-conscious D.C. will deflect him. Yet the deep wisdom of his own race may warn him. At Kailahun I was told a Mende story with a moral that grows more apt with the years:

'Once upon a time a farmer came to a town built below a hill which had never been farmed because it belonged to the spirits of the place. He swore that he would farm this hill, spirits or no spirits. The first day he went up the hill and made a start with brushing the hillside. The second day he went, and lo! all the rest of the hard work of brushing was completed. Boastfully he returned and told the people that the spirits were working for him. Then he went up the hill, and spent a day cutting the trees—and the next day he found all the remaining trees were felled for him. He then burnt the brush and trees, prepared his seed rice and went forth to sow. For a day he hoed in the rice, and the next day he found the whole farm had been hoed. His wife went to weed the farm; after one day's work, she found the whole farm had been weeded.

'At last, in this easy way, came the time for the harvest; and a magnificent harvest it promised to be. The man and his wife went up the hill and cut the rice all one day and returned that night with what they had cut. But when they went out the next morning they found that all the rest of the rice had been harvested too—and had disappeared.'

This is what comes of disrespect to the spirits—to the forces of nature which control seed-time and harvest alike. The hill-sides may provide easy farming for a time—but in the end the rain and the sun deprive them of any power to produce a harvest. Only a generation of farmers educated in some understanding of the living soil, the biology and chemistry of the land and climate, will grasp the modern interpretation of the parable. A D.C. said to me: 'I took them up the hillside and showed them the rock sticking through the soil, and asked them if that had been there even two years previously. They agreed that it had not, and returned in silence. But they farmed the hill just the same.'

10. SOUTH WEST

A big fish is caught with
a big bait
MENDE PROVERB

IN the swampy South-West Province of Sierra Leone the
Agricultural Department is making a bid to break through the
closed cycle of shifting cultivation, mortgaging of crops and
hungry seasons. The southern coast line is formed of the masses
of soil brought down by five great rivers, Moa, Sewa, Jong,
Waanje and Gbangbar. They have changed their courses often,
by depositing so much silt at their mouths that they blocked
their own outlets; and today the Waanje, for example, instead
of running southward into the sea, turns due west within five
miles of the shore and meanders along parallel with the coast
for 30 miles until it captures the waters of the Sewa, whereupon
the combined rivers run through a maze of channels beside the
coast till they flow into an estuary opposite Sherbro Island,
another 30 miles westward. It is said that their waters won't
mix, for there is ill will between them; if you pour water from
both rivers into a bottle, the bottle will burst.

It is a province of marsh and fenland, of waving sudd grasses
and islands of higher ground thick with forest trees and coconut
palms. Towards the estuaries, where the water becomes brackish
with the incoming tides, mangroves grow endlessly. Most of
the area is tidal. It is the haunt of water birds. Above the surface of the water, sidling along the banks, moves the head and
slender neck of the snake bird. Herons dart along the banks.
Cormorants poise on protruding stumps. The fish eagle, the
white leading edges to its wings conspicuous against the sky,
soars overhead. The kingfisher streaks blue along narrow inlets.
Brown and black divers abound, and I stared spellbound at
dwarf trees weighed down with flocks of pelicans. On shore,
through the grasses, move flocks of sacred ibis. The water teems
with fish, especially barracuda, tarpon, perch and mudfish. It
is only necessary to trail a line from the stern of one's launch
in these endless gently-moving waters. In the estuaries may be
caught the warm-blooded manatee, with breasts like a woman,

95

which screams like a human when killed in the bottom of your boat. It may or may not account for many native tales in which mermaids (or water devils) figure.

This region would grow plenty of swamp or tidal rice. Yet, in the past, Pujehun District was noted for its recurrent famines, and the great occupation of the Sherbro people is fishing, not rice cultivation. The land is lightly populated. Damp, steamy, highly malarial, the nights whine with several species of mosquito. But in the riverain grassland probably 60,000 acres would grow rice, and in the mangrove swamps—both those round the Sherbro and those of the Scarcies which are not yet occupied—another 120,000. This acreage would produce probably 140,000 tons of rice: enough to feed 450,000 people a year at the British intake of 3,000 calories a day.

With this rice available, the Government would be able to build up a reserve, lower prices, and improve nutrition; above all, in the process of developing its production, it would be able to draw some of the population from the eroded upland slopes to the more suitable swamps, while those who cultivate uplands, assured of an adequate supply of swamp rice at a reasonable price, could turn to the production of plantation crops, especially oil palm, cocoa, coffee, bananas, etc., which would keep the land in good heart. And where shifting cultivation continued to be practised, bush fallows could be longer and more scientific. There would be elbow room, too, to experiment with long grass fallows.

To convert the southern sedge lands into rich paddy-fields would have seemed a dream not long ago. The native hoe is a hopeless implement with which to cultivate land covered with tough elephant grass. The climate makes human exertion quickly unendurable. Bullock ploughing was out of the question, as animals sicken here quickly with 'tryps' and other diseases; insects make their lives a misery. Nor were suitable varieties of rice known. 'There were many stones, but few whetstones' in the Mende proverb—plenty of everything except the tool to do the work. That tool is now supplied by the modern tractor. Tractors can plough up the tough grass roots, and cut the grass in great swaths with a heavy disk harrow; once the land is cleared, tractor cultivation can keep it clean. In the rains the water level rises 10 to 15 feet over the swampy lands; but certain varieties of Indo-China rice grow rapidly and keep ahead of the water level. Thus the problem of population is partly solved, for mechanical cultivation does not require such a large number of cultivators either to hoe or to weed. The tractor cuts down the grass with heavy disk ploughs, the grass is gathered in heaps and burnt or left to rot, the seed is sown broadcast, and disked in. Once the grass has been cleared, moreover, it is merely a question of keeping germination down.

None the less to bring the potential area into cultivation would need a big increase in population. Some villages can be located on high land, and the cultivators can go by boat to their fields, but in other areas new villages would have to be located deeper in the swamps than the local people like—or migrants from the uplands could endure. The idea of living in a house raised on stilts above the marshy ground, for instance, horrifies natives unused to such ideas, and they will not tolerate it. Natives unused to sleeping under mosquito nets, too, have to be accustomed to the idea in these mosquito-ridden lands.

But the possibility beckons. I went with Paramount Chief the Hon. Jaia Kai Kai of Panga to see one 400-acre scheme in operation along the river banks at Gbundpi. He told me that it was enormously popular with his people, who were astonished to get yields of up to 2,000 lb. per acre. Tractor ploughing had for the first time made it possible for each family in the scheme to produce enough rice to eat all the year round—and have plenty to sell for cash also.

Gbundpi is, however, near to higher ground; along the banks of the Waanje, in the centre of the river area, rice is also being grown. Here the mechanics in charge of the tractors and ploughs must live in tents and depend on river transport entirely; labour must come by river and live in villages deep in the swamps. It will not be easy to expand these pilot schemes quickly, and the target for 1953 is only 4,000 acres; yet a big advance on the few hundred acres of a year ago. Running tractors and training tractor crews is hard and disheartening work; shortly before I paid my visit a driver tried to find out if there was petrol in his tank by the light of a match. There was.

In the past, the main crop of these fern-bearded swamps has been piassava. Piassava—which I confess I had not heard of until I reached Njala—is used for making brooms and large

H   97 brushes, such as the revolving brushes which are used in British towns to clean the streets. These tough, flexible bristles in fact nearly all come from Sherbro, which has a world monopoly of the best quality. 'Prime Sherbro' and 'Sulima' are unequalled anywhere in the world, and nylon is not likely to provide a substitute. The bristles are the prepared fibres extracted from the leaf stalks of the raffia palm, which grows over the whole area, but most thickly in Lake Kwarko and round the small port of Sulima.

The Lake-dwellers are skilled in methods of preparation; and to maintain quality the Government inspects the fibre and gives instruction. Only the lower four feet of the mature leaf stalk is used, since the fibres which represent the strength of the frond weaken above this height. The cut leaf stalks are trimmed and split lengthwise, and the strips are made into bundles and immersed in the water. After this 'retting', the softened bundles are taken from the water and hackled on spikes, and finally dried in the sun. The piassava makers' co-operative is the most successful in Sierra Leone. It has raised output by 150 per cent in four years.

Along the rivers and inlets grow thousands of coconut palms. In the 'twenties the Agricultural Department distributed over 125,000 seedling palms thoughout South-West Province, and now, fully grown, these form the nucleus of the industry. No doubt it would be larger than it is if the natives had been interested in propagating the palm. There is no copra industry. Sierra Leone is the nearest sterling source of coconuts to Britain, and supplies a million fresh nuts a year to the fairs and coconut-shies of the country; the f.o.b. price being ½d. to 1d. each. I paid 2d. each for mine, but they were absolutely fresh, the juice as cold as from an ice-box. I know no better drink.

On the coast and round Sherbro Island, however, the traditional industry is fishing. A country permanently short of animal protein in its diet is eager to buy fish. The fishermen of the south and western coasts are a hardy tribe, and, living mainly on fish with a little rice and vegetables, show no signs of malnutrition. Their fishing is primitive, and therefore demands the highest qualities of seamanship. For they go to sea in simple dugout canoes. The larger canoes, used for fishing with the cast net and seine, are manned by several men; but the small one- and two-man canoes go far out to sea. It is common to see a fisherman in such a cockleshell fishing with four lines, one in each hand and one held between the big and middle toes of each foot resting on the gunwale. Fishing with two lines, he paddles with his hands, so as not to scare the fish.

Inshore, the fishermen use various types of wall nets. A 50-foot net, distended by 40-inch sticks at intervals of nine feet, is dragged by two men through the water towards the beach, catching the fish in the trap so formed; the same type of net—sometimes larger—is fixed by sticks driven into the sand or mud at high tide to cordon off an area of sea, leaving the fish imprisoned as the tide goes down. The women's net, used inshore, is a sort of bag which is woven on to an extensible bamboo frame and kept in shape by a cord.

The fishery is as much a subsistence economy as is rice farming. A fisherman who makes a big catch will stay ashore until the proceeds are exhausted. The life is hard, and the catches generally not great; and indeed, round the coasts of Sherbro Island, the Tuntu Society enforces a baleful taboo against more capacious nets and more rapacious hunting down of fish; anything in the nature of a trawl, and indeed even cast and seine nets, are under interdict. It is said that the Tuntu Society is today more powerful than the Poro; its potent medicine, the Kontogi, rules the coast as far north as Shenge. The medicine resides in the devil bush in the old town of Dema, where on pain of death or madness no Court Messenger may appear in uniform, and Europeans must remove their shoes from off their feet. The medicine is supreme over the fish, and protects the chiefdom; it keeps its devotees safe from sharks and crocodiles. The Sherbro fishermen believe that if any nets but the simple ones in use were employed the fish would all migrate out to sea, and the fishery would perish. The medicine enforces this sole condition upon which the fish submit to be caught. An offence against the Tuntu Society is punishable by death. When the District Commissioner of Bonthe, in the interests of a more productive fishery, some years ago declared that the seine net might be used on part of the Turtle Islands off Sherbro, the paramount chief took it upon himself to obtain one, and died soon after.

This event enhanced the reputation of the Tuntu, thus visibly able to settle accounts with Government. The Turtle Islands remain aloof and mysterious, and the Assistant D.C. of Bonthe, who had recently visited them, described to me the sacred island in which is located an extraordinary deep fresh-water lake full of alligators and fish. It is rumoured that canni-balism still plays a part in the annual fertility rite, at which the dancers wear white, and four priests carry a piece of the potent medicine in one hand and a torch in the other, to demonstrate that while a dancer holds the medicine fire cannot harm him. I was told that owing to the vagaries of the tides, bodies and overturned canoes are always washed up on the shore; but once a year a fisherman disappears and no body is washed up. No doubt these dark but unverifiable rumours feed the medicine and keep it strong and potent.

It is the more remarkable that such a society flourishes, in that Bonthe is part of the Colony, and Sherbro, as well as part of the mainland opposite and 'Turner's Peninsula', the spit of land between the Waanje and the sea, were all acquired as British territory during the nineteenth century for the purpose of controlling a river traffic which largely consisted of slave-running. Then indeed the coast was prosperous; and after-wards, before the railway had been built or motor cars thought of, the rivers brought down a legitimate flow of trade to Bonthe, so that the virtuous Victorians could see the just hand of Provi-dence at work. In 1900 Bonthe did half the trade of the territory, and 5,000-ton steamers anchored up the estuary in view of the town. I arrived after nightfall. The lights of the town gave us our course for two hours after the fading of the gold and crim-son carpet which the sunset unrolls on these rippling, westering waters for the least distinguished visitor's approach. But my creole captain had to come up to the waterfront and quay in a wide circle, for otherwise even in a boat of 18-inch draught we should have run aground, so silted is the estuary today, so tortuous the navigable channels.

Bonthe, headquarters of a district which can only be visited by long launch trips, and recipient of as large a rainfall as Freetown, is regarded as the penitentiary for serving officials in the Colony. I can only say I found it charming—and it rained implacably much of the time I was there. Great mangoes, breadfruit, hewei trees and irregularly spaced and none-too-perpendicular lamp-posts, embossed with the word 'Paris', make a boulevard of its semi-Venetian waterfront, backed by the official residences of the D.C. and A.D.C., the Government offices, the Post Office, the rest-house, and the tin-roofed business houses of the great firms—U.A.C., Paterson Zochonis and the Cie Française de l'Afrique Occidentale, whose trading launches unload upon the sand their corded bales. Behind the waterfront stretches a tree-shaded little town of palm-thatched houses, each in its own small garden, murmurous with green doves, bright with alemanda and hibiscus, thriftily planted with paw-paw, pineapples and sweet potatoes, overflowing with children carrying smaller children on the hip. A stone-built church or mission stands in almost every street, muffled in bougainvilia and frangipani and other odours of the dear departed. Closer inspection showed that almost every house was a shop. Though the port has dwindled almost to nothing, Bonthe trades on, living by everyone taking in each other's washing, a rational process readily unravelled by economists, but somehow irritating to European critics of creole ways. Well, what else is there for them to do? I buy a large bar of soap with my shilling and cut it into 13 tablets at 1d. each; you buy with your shilling a 4-lb. lump of foo-foo and divide it into 13 foo-foo balls at 1d. each; and there is a possibility of trade between us and like-minded capitalists. Besides, a ripple of commerce still runs up the stagnant inlets of Sherbro. In the market a brisk trade was going on in fish, while on the opposite side market-mammies were selling fried sweet potato, kola nuts, pancakes of banana pulp and rice flour baked in palm oil, ovoid garden eggs and dark brown coco-yams, dried snails, crude looking and pungent ginger—and equally crude and pungent ginger-beer made from it. Apart from local produce, there were all the headcloths and cheap tin trays a woman could set her heart on.

Some traders felt as I do about Bonthe: an artistically-lettered sign read: 'Rogers from Liberia. For love of home I returned here. Now come and buy'. Bonthe is crumbling into the past like the gravestones of the Swiss and German pastors who laboured here sixty, seventy, eighty years ago, so sure they were building something on this spongy soil, under these ungainly breadfruit trees dropping unripe fruit like large green golf balls. Now the ironwork has been stolen from the graves, and many headstones are buried under the earthen skyscrapers of termites, who nourish their young stakhanovites and cultivate their fungus gardens in the broken skulls and paper-thin thigh-bones of those who wait their call to be refleshed on the day when we shall all of us be judged.

> *Der Tod zerriss die schönen Bände*
> *Zerstörte unseres Hauses Glück*
> *Und zu des Grabes dunklem Rande*
> *Schweist unser tranenschwerer Blick.*

I spent an afternoon talking with an American missionary who had first come to Bonthe in 1912, had left it about the time of the Great Depression, and was now revisiting it; he had found that while Mattru, on the mainland and connected by road to the railway, had grown out of recognition, Bonthe was little changed in appearance from the day he first came there to preach and teach, to tempt parents to give their daughters a Christian education by offering to take any boy at half price who brought his sister to school—she to be taught free. But the fight against 'impurity' was endless—endless as the mangrove swamps themselves, ramified, deep-rooted and tough, growing rapidly over the little clearing hacked in it by the machete of Christian teaching. It was a fight of Bible versus Bundu: 'I've spent hours with the girls here, brother, till my Bible was wet with tears; the Bible is the only way to save them'. I thought of him giving his youth with prodigal American generosity to the education of imitative boys and slim dark-eyed girls from the swamps and the impoverished back streets of the town, struggling with their elusive souls, bibling them up in a cocoon of Christian purity, his shirt soaked with exertion in the damp blanket of the lifeless air.

What of permanent good may fruit from such self-giving I cannot surmise; but all missionary work on this southern coast is, it seems to me, an act of repentance and restitution—it is the act itself that matters, not the results. For this coast has seen much evil done. The piracy perpetrated here for centuries taught the natives to call all white men rogues. It was one of the great slaving areas. I stood on the shore at Shenge[1] looking

[1] Pronounced, as it used to be spelt, 'Shaingay'.

towards the Plantain Islands, where the fantastic freebooter
John Plantain built in 1720 a fort whose loopholed walls still
remain, complete with dismounted cannon and slave barra-
coon. It was from this base of operations that he sailed to
Madagascar and became, at 30 years old, king of most of it;
there he lived in great splendour with a harem of native girls
to whom he gave names like Moll, Kate, Sue, Peg, and others
straight from the Beggar's Opera. The Plantain Islands are
still aromatic with descendants of the limes planted there by
John Newton 25 years later, when he was reduced to the status
of a castaway by his captain's black mistress and had to live
in the open, racked with rheumatism, feeding on berries and
gulls' eggs, and comforted only by a volume of Euclid which
he mastered to take his mind off his wretchedness. He escaped
and traded in slaves up and down the Sierra Leone coast, rising
to be the master of a ship, until he had a fit and repented his
wickedness, even to taking Holy Orders, as his biographical
memorial in St. Mary Woolnoth, London, bears witness:

> John Newton, Clerk,
> Once an infidel and libertine,
> A servant of slaves in Africa
> Was by the rich mercy of our Lord and Saviour, Jesus Christ,
> Preserved, restored, pardoned,
> And appointed to preach the faith
> He had long laboured to destroy,
> Near sixteen years at Olney, in Bucks,
> And . . . years in this church.

Newton's life seems almost a premonitory symbol of Britain's
mission in Sierra Leone.

Forts and slave factories dotted this coast from Sulima to
Shenge. Their activities are perpetuated in the names of many
leading African families in the South-West as well as in Freetown and the Colony. Thus Charles Rogers, Cleveland Caulker
and Abraham Tucker were cousins who came out to Sherbro
in the eighteenth century to trade in slaves, and set up in business in Sulima, Shenge and Bar Hall respectively. Rogers, at
Sulima, built up a big liquor business and was given a wife
from one of the ruling families; the children of this union maintained the English connection and, proud of their English blood,
sent their children to be educated at 'home'. They deliberately

cultivated some European ways, and become known as the 'krakas', or chair-sitters. At Shenge I called on Paramount Chief Caulker, whose family was one of the three ruling families to remain loyal to their treaties with Queen Victoria in 1898. Chief Caulker, who is 84, tall and upright as a forest tree, told me how the unbelievable news of the massacre of the white missionaries and their wives and daughters arrived on Sunday, May 3rd, and almost at once the Mende war-boys were reported to be making for Shenge to destroy the mission there. Immediately after the morning service, the missionaries were put in boats, Chief Caulker (not then the chief) practically using force to make the unwilling white men embark. They were taken to the Plantain Islands as a temporary refuge and later to Freetown. The mission boys and a few police opened fire as the Mendes advanced from the bush, irregular battles took place, during which Shenge was burned down. Chief Caulker's brother and cousin and other members of his family were killed before the arrival of regular troops restored order.

Today Shenge is a quiet fishing village, slumberous under palms and mango trees on the promontory facing the Plantain Islands, and drenched in the heavy odours given off by the *conofaringea*, a plant whose pendant biform fruit has earned for it an expressive if gross name in Mende.[1] Now that a motorable road has been built from Moyamba, the beauty of the place, the curving white beaches below the low cliffs overhung with palms, draws officials tired of the files and members of the Fourah Bay College staff wanting quiet for some serious reading. It is one of the most select holiday resorts in the whole world. But neither the tourist traffic nor the fishing makes it as prosperous as Chief Caulker would like it, or pay for the many improvements which the district development plan requires. He was pinning his hopes to the progress of a swamp rice scheme started with Government tractors near by, but was concerned at the traditional indifference of a fishing people to improving their standard of life. They *must* co-operate with the Agricultural Officer, he said, and promised to 'come down heavy' on them if they did not. Shenge at least will play its part in the effort to make Sherbro a granary of rice.

[1] Ngila boni.

11. SOUTH EAST

The snake that bites a Mende man gets
turned into soup for the Mende man
TEMNE PROVERB

UNTIL the railway probed to its vitals, the South-East Province of Sierra Leone was the most inaccessible region of the country; indeed, one of the most inaccessible in Africa. Today it is thought of as the richest. It produces nearly two-thirds of the palm kernels which are the mainstay of the country's exports. The feathery head-dresses of the palms top the low bush and high bush which grows where the forest stood dense and almost unbroken within living memory. In 1910, Commissioner Alldridge, maker of treaties with the Mende chiefs, published a congratulatory review of the area so recently pacified and brought under colonial administration, with the apt title *A Transformed Colony*. Mendeland has indeed been transformed, though the process was accelerated rather than set in motion by British rule and railways.

Travelling through Mendeland, it is still possible to nurse an illusion of the country as it once was, to catch the echo of its ancient seclusion and spiritual thrall. A wise ordinance now requires that the trees within 20 yards on either side of the roads may not be cut down to make farms; and the Forest Department is acquiring, with pain and patience, areas along the roads and nearby hillsides for complete reafforestation. Such segments of the indigenous forest as remain—and some bush that has gone back to forest—is found along these roads. The traveller drives much of the time through a green tunnel, some-times along lofty colonnades of cotton trees or, near Blama, rubber trees. When he reaches the river crossings, he bursts into the sunlight, but finds the barrier of dark, moving waters in front of him, closely overhung by forest; farming is rarely carried to the water's edge, and what are known as 'gallery forests' fringe the rivers. Nearly all river crossings are by ferry. As the wire ropes creak and the pontoons glide over the water, there is time to listen to the river and the country and the people.

Eastwards, the forest deepens. Even along the road sides, and all round Kenema, headquarters of the Forest Industries branch of the Forest Department, can be identified noble timber to rejoice the heart of the forester and woodworker. There is the Yairi, with its great rudder-shaped buttresses and digitate leaves, which seasons well and takes an exquisite finish. Hendui, which needs a century to reach maturity, is a termite-proof, saw-murdering wood, harder than greenheart, whose crown flushes red in the early rains: a perfect material for railway sleepers or wharf piles. Koondi stands on strange stilts, dense-crowned and short-boled, lovely for cabinet-making. Bodgei strikes the eye with its reddish-purple flaky bark. There are mahoganies, pearwoods, counter woods, sasswood and oaks; more species of wood are used in Sierra Leone than in any other West African territory.

Wild life is shy but abounds, moving easily from land attacked by the cutlass to land reclaimed by the bush or dwelling permanently in the forest and unusable wastes. Along the Liberian frontier roams the pigmy elephant; and, considered more dangerous and destructive, the dwarf buffalo, or bush cow. The pigmy hippo inhabits creeks, and sometimes, driving down the roads, you catch a glimpse of a bush buck or small antelope crossing your path, or a bush pig; often a snake, which touches off from a rooted instinct the reflex to accelerate and scotch it. The squirrel tribe is ubiquitous; most beautiful are the flying squirrels, and the side-striped ground squirrels. The forest conceals (at least from me) the giant booming squirrel, and the green squirrel also. The habits of the giant rat, three feet long, known locally as the ground-pig, provide the point of the Mende proverb: 'The ground-pig prevents the mind spreading'; or, intrigue destroys noble ventures and purposes. In the forest and high bush moves the leopard, that famous 'Bra Leppet' of native folk-lore, who is strong, fierce and wise, and is in West Africa the King of the Beasts. Bra Spider weaves his loathsome webs also; that equally famous Bra Spider whose plots defeat even Bra Leppet, and who is animated by a low cunning and selfish greed which luckily often defeats itself. I never could endure Bra Spider, either in life or legend; and my faint interest in the idea of climbing palm trees by means of a palm-rope cradle finally evaporated when I learned that a nine-inch diameter version of Bra Spider inhabits them.

The forest and bush is talkative with birds; that wonderful
thing the hornbill—destructive of all evolutionary logic—
flourishes around Segbwema.[1] The grey parrot is found in
Sierra Leone, as in West Africa generally, and is remarkably
educable; I heard of one which gives his master's formal callers
a polite if harsh 'Good morning', but salutes his habitués with
a cheery 'Hullo, you old b—!'

But there is nothing more exciting than the darting fire
finches, the paradise flycatchers, the bee-eaters with tails like
revolving fish-bait, and the red-headed lovebirds which in
those arboreal depths correspond to the coloured fish that swim
in clear tropical waters. Indeed fish as vivid are found in some
few limpid reaches of Sierra Leonian rivers: for a sign that the
water there is pure and undefiled. (But still, safer if boiled.)
The English swallow comes here. The red-headed woodpecker
is at work, making a monotonous sound different from that of
his workmanlike English counterpart. In the dark the honking
of owl and nightjar interrupts the frog chorus and the yearning
O! O! O! of the much-misunderstood fruit bat.

The creature which is most in evidence to the traveller is
the monkey. Monkeys have been increasing in recent years, as
the result of hunting Bra Leppet and Bra Cat for their pelts.
The monkeys destroy up to 50 per cent of the cocoa crop
annually. Their destructiveness is only matched by their abiding
charm and fascination; as an agricultural officer told me: 'They
have to be hunted. We shot them down in thousands on our last
drive. All the same—it was murder'. Many tribes of monkey
inhabit the forest. Great troops of the sooty mangabey are often
encountered under a chief, who leads them in raids on farms
and plantations. The black-and-ginger so-called putty-nosed
monkey, with its pointed white beard, moves in chattering
family parties of 15 or so. The handsome 'Diana's guerdon',
with his black beard and white eyebrows and chestnut
stomacher, is to be found only in the high forest; nor was I
lucky enough to meet the 'Court Messenger' monkey, with
his bright red tail and sides, yellow belly and white socks. The
silvery colobus vegetarian monkeys, equipped with modified

[1] Or 'Sei's town'. The word means 'Look at Sei!' and it is supposed that the
name commemorates a handsome chief and the gasps of admiration of love-struck
damsels.

stomachs to deal with large masses of foliage—a clear advantage which they enjoy over human vegetarians—are to be seen everywhere, industriously stuffing salad. Dog-faced baboons are also common; and in the south-eastern forest, under the authority of the primitive Freudian horde-father, move little groups of chimpanzees. Moved by the Cassandra-complex, the older horde-fathers, sometimes standing five feet in height, occasionally attack human beings; but young chimpanzees make delightful and all-too-human pets. When I went down to the Moa river crossing to visit French Guinea, I was kindly guided by Joe, the young chimpanzee who complicates the life of Mr. Turberville, the assistant D.C. at Kailahun. When we ventured into a canoe, he declined the channel crossing and set up a to-do; and when we returned he had vanished and indeed stayed out all night in disgust at our flirtation with French frivolity. He returned next day, however, and dined ceremonially with us at the house of Mr. Atkinson (the D.C.).

Into this forest environment migrated, perhaps 400 years ago, the ancestors of the present Mende inhabitants. They probably came from North Guinea, and perhaps were forced into the forest depths by pressures from other tribes from still further north. They came as settlers or hunters, at first mainly peaceably, and mingled to some extent with the existing inhabitants, the Bulloms or Sherbros, who now inhabit only the coastal strips. But after a time, warriors arrived from the north—perhaps men trained in fighting other invaders—and reorganized Mende society on a war chiefdom basis. The earlier hunting and farming settlements were converted into walled towns, and the young men conscripted as war-boys for fighting the chief's battles with neighbouring chiefs. While agriculture remained the economic basis of life, slave-raiding became of economic importance, because the slaves could be made to do the hard work of brushing and burning off the forest to make farms, while the war-boys pursued their military careers; when the European slavers along the coast created a slave market, the economic importance of slaving was enhanced. The successful chief was the man who could not only lead his men to victory but, with the slaves captured, maintain his food supplies and obtain guns and gunpowder to equip his forces. Quite large confederacies were built up by war and exaction of tribute, but none seem to have been very stable. The basic rule was all versus all: might was right. The free man fought to preserve his freedom; to gain the power necessary for this object, he fought to enslave his fellows.

When the British treaty-makers began to penetrate into the forests of the south-east from about 1875 onwards, they found this pattern of society fully developed. The country was traversed only by the narrowest bush paths, the terrain of ambush warfare. The towns were defended by concentric rings of walls and ditches. The walls were made of mud and thatched with piassava, which rustled and betrayed a stealthy attack. Outside was a ring of wooden stakes and a ditch, then a fingari of cotton trees growing freely or pollarded. The great rings of cotton trees round towns like Musaia (in the north) are the remains of these former fortifications. The defences were pierced with gates flanked by watchtowers. Within the walls, the circular houses were set close together so that a force which pierced the defence got lost or dispersed and could not find the defending H.Q., while the defenders could flash the alarm easily. Even today, in Mende towns of 200 houses it is easy to get lost, unless the town planner has been at work. The object of warfare was to capture the enemy's town, loot his stored grain and standing crops, capture his menfolk and slaves, and make his women into wives; and slaughter all those not required. Elaborate espionage preceded attack, which was both sudden and treacherous. War, however, was also a ritual with its dances, art and medicine. The Mendes, like the Ancient Greeks, also observed certain conventions, based on their common racial beliefs. Thus, young men and women being initiated in the Poro bush or Bundu bush were never seized or molested; inviolate by their medicine, to interfere with them would have been more fatal to the war-boys than the spears and muskets of their parents. As the initiation period was then often a year or more, this convention to some extent helped to preserve the race.

None the less, warfare and slave exports kept the population small. The Rev. Max Gorvie, himself a Mende, wrote: 'Whole countries were devastated. In some country towns in the Sherbro-Gallinas district, it was a common sight to see a few overgrown rice farms strewed with putrefying bodies; and many bleached skulls ready to tell their own doleful story. . . . Men lived in constant fear and were afraid to cultivate their farms to any large extent. Whether one planted rice or grain, there was no knowing in advance whether one would enjoy one's labour.' Alldridge saw the skulls littering the fields in the 'eighties and 'nineties. Memories are short in Africa. I have talked to elderly men who spoke of 'the first days', and the fighting and stockaded towns which they heard their elders speak of when they were boys; inquiry soon shows that they are speaking of events in the mid-nineteenth century, at earliest. At Kailahun I heard the tale of Kai Lundo, after whom the town is named, and his epic struggle with Ndawa, the warrior-chief of Wende.

Kai Lundo was born in 1844, and Alldridge met him towards the end of the century. He was typical of a series of such chiefs of genius who cleared by hard fighting an area of invaders and slavers, only to have their work obliterated a few years later. Named after a famous fighter, he was trained as a war-boy. In alliance with Ndawa he drove Chief Benya of Blama out of Luawa and Wende, then turned on his quarrelsome ally and drove his war-boys out of Luawa, of which he was made over-lord by a grateful people. Mende schoolchildren read of Kai Lundo's famous attack on the town of Ngeihu where Ndawa was entrenched. As Kai Lundo climbed the walls and jumped down inside, he cried: 'I am Kai Lundo. I have jumped down'. His enemy Ndawa rushed on him crying: 'I am Ndawa. You have now met me.' The former friends fought in hate, Ndawa first wounding Kai Lundo on his sword hand. Kai Lundo trans-ferred his sword to his other hand and slashed Ndawa across the forehead. Ndawa, stunned, dropped his sword; Kai Lundo chivalrously threw his away also and closed with his opponent. Throwing him, he cried: 'Come, comrades, I have cornered the fox'. Ndawa was captured, but allowed honourably to go in peace, on the understanding that he would leave Luawa in peace. Kai Lundo fought most of the warrior chiefs round him, and his empire stretched from French Guinea to Liberia, whence he brought back captives who turned in disgust from bananas and sighed for human flesh. The Mende instinct for ambush warfare was put to modern uses when the West African Division was fighting in Burma in 1944–5.

The best fighters are traditionally the Kpaa-Mende, who

inhabit the country round Moyamba and early came into collision with the Colony-protected chiefdoms. The middle-Mende, who speak the language in its purest form, live round the river Sewa; the eastern Mende, whose land stretches from Kenema ('the town in a clearing') into Liberia, have been influenced by the Kissis and other races. Luawa itself was originally to have become part of Liberia, but it was administered for a time by the British, and ultimately at its own request remained part of the Protectorate, a tongue of land projecting into French and Liberian territory at the tip of which, in the village of Koindu, is held every Sunday morning the famous international market. From early dawn the roads are noisy with lorries converging on the village from both sides of the river, booths are set up, and a varied and multilingual host gathers to haggle. French, English, Krio, Mende, Kissi and all the variants of the Mande speech can be heard. Though transactions are normally conducted in West African or French currency, the famous Kissi pennies are still sometimes in evidence —iron bars about two feet long, the only native currency in this part of Africa. Pegged to fixed quantities of rice or cassava their value fluctuates with the white man's money; a case of the 'commodity standard'.

At Koindu, might-have-beens would sadden one's reflections, were it not for the *soignée* charm of young French Mandingo ladies. This is the furthest point of British territory, thanks to the Parliamentary Select Committee of 1865. Yet, though the roads are still poor, it drains trade into Sierra Leone. 'The French', noisy and cheerful, bring quantities of palm kernels to swell Sierra Leone's exports, as well as not inconsiderable consignments of cognac and Parisian perfume. The British traders fill their stalls with cottons and Brummagem goods. Kola nuts are also in keen demand on the French side, for their stimulating properties and ritual uses. Still more important is coffee, for which the French were prepared to pay famine prices recently, and which was therefore exported despite the ban put on it by the Department of Commerce and Trade, which was trying to fulfil contracts with Britain at a much lower price. Possibly diamonds slip over the frontier at Koindu, too. To refresh traders in the intervals of such serious business, every variety of native dish and sweetmeat is on sale.

With Liberia, contacts are few. No road from Koindu or Buedu runs into the great forests which stretch beyond the frontier, and in which, only 20 years ago, the crack of rifles and sound of warfare could be heard at times from the British side. Bush paths lead into Liberia, and up them go missionaries who cannot reach their missions from Monrovia for lack of roads, and down them come the more potent bad medicines, such as the Borfima which, compounded from parts of the human body, cannot now be had really fresh in Sierra Leone.

But Liberia has the trees, whereas in much of Mende territory bush fallows are down to five years. Peace and the suppression of slavery changed the direction of Mende energies. They began to farm without fear, and more extensively to provide food for growing numbers. The need to pay taxes turned rice partly into a cash crop, and when taxes were paid the experience of handling cash taught people the pleasures of trade. The railway and roads brought in new products, and farms were still further increased. When the domestic slaves were liberated more farmland in waste places or on steeper hillsides had to be found for them. The Forest Department stepped in, and in the years before the First World War reserved what forest remained to conserve a supply of timber; now the object of the Government is to conserve what fertility is left in the soil. Indeed the fertility is in the vegetation rather than in the soil itself.

The South-East Province should not be used for arable farming at all, apart from swamp rice in the swamps and vegetable crops on level ground round towns and villages. It is tree country, and where it is not reafforested should be used for tree crops. It should grow more oil palm, coffee and cocoa, for which it has an almost ideal climate. Cocoa, for instance, could be grown under a canopy of forest trees in a wide area from Pujehun to Kailahun, and enjoy much the same conditions as in the Gold Coast. Coffee trees would flourish in an even wider area, untroubled by the drought months which occur farther north. Oil palms flourish, but could certainly be grown more scientifically as a plantation crop if trees were planted in large numbers, bad palm wine tapping was stopped, and improved high-yielding varieties were used. Even rubber would grow well, if it could be made economic. When Malaya fell in the last war, the remains of old plantations which had failed in the

First World War were tapped—indeed, the Serabu Catholic Mission was largely kept going on rubber in those years.

This is now the object of production planning and land use—of the Childs Plan. But it requires a big reversal of the tendencies of recent years. The palm kernels shipped from the South-East Province in 1948 declined by nearly a third compared with 1936. The failure of the efforts to establish the rubber industry are still remembered—as is the earlier failure to establish (in a rainfall of 150 inches!) cotton plantations. Coffee and cocoa prices are high, certainly—but to put down big plantations where rice has been grown for food argues a great faith in world economic stability by a people who have no idea of the world, but an incorrigible suspicion of Government. Besides, rice prices are high too. And life is based on rice farming. To produce adequate supplies of rice is as inevitable a way of life to the Mende as work in office or factory is to the Briton. A meal without rice, whatever it consists of, leaves a man hungry. The ancestors require rice sacrifices. The movement of dances is based on rice-farming operations. The division of family labour is based on rice farming. The women understand rice.

Mendeland is a battlefield between the forces of tradition and modernity—between the old wisdom and the new wisdom. The new wisdom has a big job. Not only is a whole people to be persuaded to change its way of life, but it is to be *persuaded*. A forestry officer ruefully told me how, after he had managed with the utmost difficulty to get a native administration to set a few acres of eroded hillside apart for forest reserve, he had heard that the French Guinea government, alarmed at the rising floodwaters, had issued a fiat reserving for reafforestation thousands of square miles of the watershed of the Niger. In Sierra Leone, good husbandry and scientific agriculture must come through resolutions passed in inexperienced district councils, by 'hanging heads' in chiefdom barris, through co-operative societies, as an exercise in democracy. Can it be done? How can it be done? It was in pursuit of some understanding of the difficulties that I plodded, notebook in hand, pockets bulging with district development schemes, a doubtless foolish figure, along the narrow paths through the bush, sweet-smelling after the rain—a smell that I found absurdly redolent of a newly-opened tin of condensed milk.

12. THE NORTH

> Know that every Muslim is the brother
> of every other Muslim. All of you are
> on the same equality: ye are one
> brotherhood
>
> MAHOMMED'S LAST SPEECH

AS you drive north from Mendeland, whether into the hills of the watershed, where the rivers have their source and the roads gradually cease even to be jeepable tracks and the Kono and Yalunka folk pursue their ancient ways, or diverge into the heart of Temne territory through Port Loko or that bustling centre, Makeni, the land changes its dress and aspect. No longer are the roads overhung with high bush, monkey-apple, mahogany and musanga. North of Bumpe one traverses the last great belt of oil palm. The land becomes more open, and the vista extends—on high ground it widens out for miles. The trees are less tall and sparser; a few species predominate, especially Lophira with white flowers and Parkia with yellow. Their trunks are carbon black—for they endure a yearly ordeal by fire. Between them grow a profusion of grasses—napier, star-grass, elephant grass, tall and short, clumpy and creeping; some with tassled heads and some with razor-sharp blades. *Andropogons* and *pennisetums*, their Latin names are legion and nondescript. Bright green in September, flowering before Christmas, when in January and February the dry winds blow and what trees there are have captured most of the moisture in the soil, the grass carpet turns brown and tindery. A spark sets it in a roar of flame and smoke, racing downwind, a death-dealing battle line, driving the wild creatures before it and converting any sapless tree into a torch. Behind it the land is black and scorched, so scorched that the thin humus itself may be calcined to lifelessness, whereupon, as soon as it is cool, men scatter their seed and entreat it with charms and verses of the Koran to yield bountifully.

On the roads leading to historic Kabala, ensconced in its cradle of great hills, one encounters herds of dwarf cattle moving southwards driven by tall, rangy men in Muslim caps.

These are the native Ndama cattle which can survive in tsetse infested country, and of which the northern tribes possess perhaps 50,000 head. They give little milk but what they give is rich in butterfat. It is to provide their feed as well as to prepare a tilth to grow rice and corn that the land is burnt every year. Early in the rains, a proportion of the herd is driven south to Freetown for meat or trade, being replaced by beasts from Futa Jallon in French Guinea, where still better pastures are. But the grass spreads steadily southwards, as more and more trees are burnt to death and young shoots fail to establish themselves. The bush shrinks back from the burning, and only annual grasses can survive. When the grass is burnt, the rains, which in the north are mainly concentrated in the few 'rainy months', smash down on the dry soil, carry it downhill and leach the goodness from what is left. Yet the land looks, still, green and wooded enough; when the rain has fallen the grass tastes sweet, even though it may not fatten the cattle as well as that which grew where trees were denser. The white man may worry—but there is a saying from the Vai people of the south: 'The falling of a single hair will not spoil my head'.

It is a country of amazing variety and beauty. Where the Scarcies rivers drain it into the sea in the west, the big African elephant still roams, the crocodile, taking its toll of riverside dwellers, infests the swamp, the hippopotamus churns the muddy water, and below the surface the turtle glides, a saucer-shaped submarine. Northwards, the flocks of white cattle egrets move among the legs of grazing cows and bulls, ridding them of torturing flies and other insects; the leopard, bush cat and the bush cow hunt the undergrowth while overhead circle vultures and kites. Round the weathered rock-faces of the Guinea hills hover the eagles; and the bustard, weighing 20 lb. or more, is here. The scaly ant-eater, that should be such a friend to man, follows its diet in its own circumspect fashion; for if you tether it to an ant-hill, as often as not the ants seem to eat it. The tortoise *runs* in Sierra Leone, positively scuttles about; one absurd variety possesses a sort of retractable ramp to protect its head. Dry as seems the land in the days of the Harmattan, when the nose bleeds easily, the nerves seem overstrung, and the sun goes down in a chiaroscuro of scarlet and madder and rose, innumerable swamps lace the hollows and will grow rice excellently—if they are protected by a fence of shrubs from seep of sterile sands that seem to threaten them more as the years pass. And in the wet months, the thirsty soil is forced to swallow up to 100 inches of rain. Maize and millet grow well, though the climate is on the damp side for their health; groundnuts, the stuff of wonderful soups and the gravy of superlative stews, here flourish; better still, they have been shown to regenerate tired soils in a most useful fashion. It is a land where the naturalist can still find new species, or, at any rate, sub-species, with which to immortalize his Latinized name; but quite apart from appearing as *Smithii* or *Jonesii* in Kew's capacious catalogue, agricultural officers have told me with conviction that they would not work in any other part of the world for choice.

It is, too, a land of many peoples. The Bullom race has been driven to the shoreline, and successive waves of invading people have warred themselves into territories of uneven shapes, like folds in the rocks. The Mandingo tribes, remnants or offshoots of the Mandingo Empire which was disintegrating under Berber attacks, entered the country from the north and east, the Susus and the Limba on one side, the Konos and Korankos from the other; while the Mendes, under the name of Lokos (Mende is a European term), thrust up from the south. Upon these tribes, early in the sixteenth century, there descended the Temnes, who like the Kissis spring from Bantu stock and speak a tongue allied to Swahili. The Temnes came south after the break-up of the Sonhai empire under Arab attack. Led by Bai Farama, they conquered and enslaved the Susus, Limbas and Lokos, who were expelled from their trading capital, Port Loko. Temne traditions recall that in those days the Temnes had no guns, but duly got them, and 'destroyed all that country', including the white men. These were some of the first Portuguese traders and missionaries. The Temnes created a strong state which straddled the trade route from Port Loko to the Sudan and Niger, and derived much of their prosperity from slave-trading with the Europeans. They sold Hawkins 300 slaves in 1562, but three years later drove him off with a fleet of war canoes.

The Cross was on the Coast before the Crescent; but the Cross was accompanied by the slavers, whereas the Crescent had shed the full iniquities which attended its south-westward drive through Africa. The succession of Christian Temne kings ended in the seventeenth century. The Susus, converted by a Mahommedan native trader called Mahadee, revolted against the Temnes and set up their own state on the Scarcies rivers. They in turn thus became overlords of the Temnes, who absorbed from them the new fighting religion, with the Muslim system of crowning kings, even as they had previously absorbed from the Bullom people the Poro and Sande secret societies for the initiation and training of the young. In the nineteenth century, Muslim kings in Port Loko refused to allow the Church Missionary Society to have a settlement there.

Meanwhile, in the north-west the Futu Jallon state was also organized on Islamic and theocratic lines; it lived by the destruction and enslavement of the unbelievers. The Fulas of this state, a mixed race of Fulas, Susus and others, struck south into Yalunka country, and made slaves of the people. In the end the slaves revolted under a more successful Spartacus, Sorie Manga by name, threw off their masters and built the walled town of Falaba, which is to this day circled with great cotton trees that were quick stakes at the end of the eighteenth century. Falaba means 'palaver' town: the town of many troubles and battles. The enraged Fulas attacked it fanatically again and again, but never took it. Sorie Manga became the chief of the freed people, and his line ruled till the 1890's. North-east of the Fula kingdom, however, the country of the Sofa, ruled by Alikali Samodu, was sending forth raiding parties into Koranko country. Samodu received visits from British agents, who might have extended British control over him as early as the 'seventies; but getting little satisfaction, he concluded treaties with the French. These he later denounced. In 1892, 'the horsemen', as the Sofas were called, turned against the Yalunkas and tried their luck against Falaba. But the town, under its heroic chief Manga Sewa, drove them off at first with heavy losses. However, when the Sofas invested the place with large forces, Manga Sewa, seeing his people dying of starvation, retired with his wives and a barrel of gunpowder into his hut and blew the royal line to bits. The town fell, and the Yalunkas were slaughtered or made into war-boys for the Sofa army, with which reinforcement Samodu now asserted his independence against the French. A British force was also sent against him to punish his invasion of what was—by 1893—regarded as important border territory. Samodu had the pleasure, at least, of hearing that the two European powers had fought each other under the impression that they were at grips with one of his detachments. For the French attacked the British force, of whose operations they were ignorant, one dark night at Waiima in Kono country. There was a fine set-to, with rifles versus rifles for a change, and before the European officers realized that something was unaccountably wrong, in view of the disciplined and accurate fire of the opposing force, the French commander and most of the British officers were dead or wounded . . . A melancholy affair.

Thus the endless warfare along the fringe of the great rain forests petered out at last, and the tribes settled down in some degree of amity. Kabala, a town half Koranko and half Yalunka, became the administrative centre, and the railway, which had been projected through Kabala to Timbuktu in the 'eighties, in fact crept up to Kamabai, whence it was necessary to make a four-day trek by bush path. But now roads have been built through Kabala and Falaba, and begin to probe into the rice and cattle lands beyond. Bendugu has been reached and will ultimately be linked up with Yengema in Kono country.

Kabala lies between two great hills, on one of which the D.C.'s house stands, a wonderfully located spot, surrounded by jackfruit trees and flamboyants. The rock faces in the north are oppressive in their steepness, and inevitably the haunt of spirits. On the road from Musaia to Bafodia is Kakoia Hill, a 2,000-foot face of rock weathered into buttresses and bastions, and there, in a cave high up where a white slab of rock appears like a door, the guardian spirit or Krifi of the Limba people dwells. When a Limba chief dies, weird moans issue from it. Limbas can hear the dead man being brought to Kumba the Krifi, and those possessed of the Four Eyes can see it—a squat figure with woman's breasts. When the road was being built it made rapid progress past the honeycombed hills hereabouts; the labourers—Limbas and others—were anxious to get past the place. A similar, though smaller, hill faces the bungalow of the General Manager of the Yengema Diamond Mines, Kwi Kongo in the Kono tongue, or Leopard Hill. Every year in the old days all male Konos met at the slope of the hill and sacrificed a cow and a sheep. When the Kono people were being pursued and slaughtered by the Mendes, led by Kai Lundo and other warrior kings, the remnants of the Kono race found safety in its caves. The white birds on the hill belong to the Krifi and are sacred. Dead Konos can be seen climbing the hill with their bundles, and sometimes the hill utters terrible and ominous noises—the last was in 1939.

The Fulas, who had in the past often ravaged the country from their own empire of Futa Jallon, and to whom the sons of Temne kings were sometimes sent to be instructed in the Islamic faith, found themselves landless men. They had herds; but the Temnes, Korankos and Konos had the grassland. A system grew up under which the Fulas hired the grazing by payment of an agreed number of cattle, which were desired by local chiefs for prestige purposes, for feasts and for the purchase of wives—the value of which is still calculated in cows (the current rate being 8 cows = 1 woman). But the chief's herds are usually put under Fula herdsmen, since men of other tribes do not understand cattle. Cattle are an investment—a way of banking one's profits from agriculture or court fines. But as the bank account is reckoned simply in head of cattle, and the herdsman is remunerated solely by the milk, these herds are not particularly meritorious.

The cattle whose lowing can be heard round the northern hills mainly belong to nomads, many of whom migrated from French Guinea. They continually bring new animals from over the border to replenish losses. Since they move their herds as pasture offers and local chiefs strike a bargain with them, pastures are often grazed to destruction. The animals, of course, subsist on grazing alone. No roots are fed to them. Sometimes, in sparsely populated areas, the herdsmen settle down and farm; and though the cattle remain their chief interest and their visible wealth they often make good farmers. They are not, of course, mixed farmers as we know mixed farming. Thus manure is not returned to the soil: it is valued rather as a weatherproofing finish for the walls of houses, or for flooring. Nor do they realize the possible uses of their cattle. Those that they drive south are the minimum required to earn money to pay taxes or raise a little needful cash. For the most part, the herds are, as in many other parts of Africa, a mere burden on the land. They offer the eye an illusion of wealth and good husbandry; in fact, the burning of the grass to provide grazing reduces fertility and accelerates erosion. To counteract this, agricultural officers are persuading farmers to burn the land earlier, before the grass gets so dry. Burnt in November while it still has sap, it burns less hotly, doesn't kill the soil or trees, and produces a better growth of new grass.

Yet mixed farming in these areas is far from impossible if it could be taught, and if those who own and understand the cattle could be made one and the same with those who own the land and understand the crops. I was assured in the Government Experimental Cattle Station at Musaia—a sort of miniature Australian range—that Ndama cows and bulls could survive even in the south if properly fed and looked after, so that their tolerance to 'tryps' and other cattle afflictions in this climate is maintained by keeping up their vitality. At present, cattle are camped in 'warris' or fenced enclosures during the rains. As new warris are made, crops are grown on the sites of old warris where the soil has been enriched by concentrated manuring. In swamp areas in the Mabole valley a small group of farmers has been successfully ploughing with oxen since 1928, the year in which they lost their slaves. There they could grow cassava and groundnuts with cattle, and thus dispense with bush fallowing. Here is the spark of an agricultural revolution: can it be fanned?

It will require a new generation of educated African farmers to adjust new ideas of husbandry to traditional lore. It would be a mistake to presume that African farmers are incapable of striking out on a new line: on the contrary, the growing of rice in the tidal swamps at the mouth of the Scarcies rivers is (like the Gold Coast cocoa plantations) an African enterprise. There are many indigenous rice grasses in Sierra Leone, but the better strains may have been introduced by the Portuguese. The Africans of Sierra Leone experimented with them and indeed have many names for them—'bone in the grain' rice, 'elephant dung' rice, 'great axe' rice, slow ripeners, quick-droppers, and so on. A new rice may be called 'Padeecee' if 'Pa D.C.' recommends it. About 70 years ago, some landless men came down to the swamps and began to cut down the mangrove trees and grow rice; and the swamps have produced rice since

Self government and self help: a district council meets under the chairmanship of the D.C. to plan the new roads which will bring trade and 'copper' to up-country markets, of which Koindu (below) is the biggest.

Two pictures epitomize the destruction of soil fertility in the tropics: after heavy rains the leached salts appear as white froth on a hillside which has been bared by burning for cultivation

Loss of fertility can only be stopped by fallows, rotation of crops, selection of crops and the encouragement of animal husbandry and manuring: at Njala Agricultural College the farmers of the future learn to keep the land in heart

'Prime Sherbro': villagers bringing in piassava
cut from the swamps; after the day's work, the
evening meal and gossip in the barri (right)

The White Man's Grave—but modern medicine has gradually conquered the climate for white and black alike . . . though the witch doctor still flourishes, an African medical faculty is transforming by science African life and health

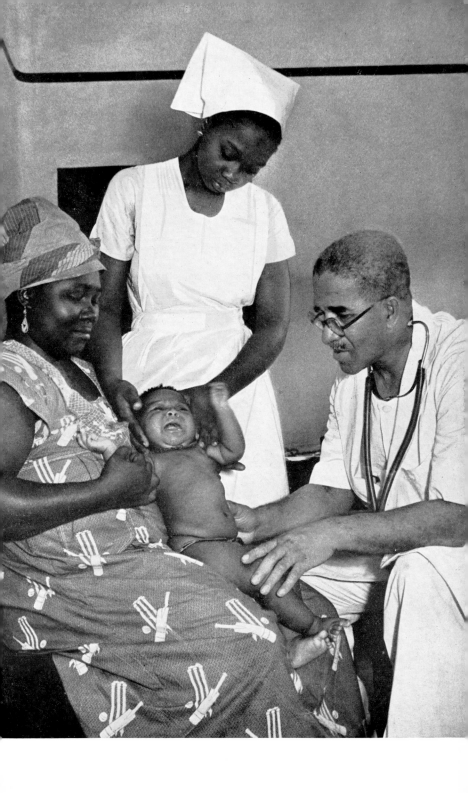

Industrial development pays for social welfare, and brings the African in touch with technology whether in iron ore mining (above) or woodworking and joinery (below). But it substitutes wage-earning for tribal life and farming . . .

then, year after year, maintaining the yields, which may reach 2,000 lb. per acre.

It is perhaps not surprising that the area cleared has there-fore steadily grown. Conditions are almost ideal. In the dry season, the rivers fall, and the salt water flows inland to flood the low paddy-fields and to poison the weeds. Then come the rains and the rivers are in spate again; so great a flood pours down that the water is fresh at all stages of the tide, and even in the estuary. The rice grown in nurseries on higher ground is then transplanted. Near the sea this must be a variety which matures quickly, because as the flood slackens the tides bring back the salt water which would kill the rice; farther up the river the rice can take its time to mature—but may suffer from weeds which the salt water will not have succeeded in destroy-ing. Meanwhile the flood every year spreads over the land a thin layer of the most fertile silt, contributed by the top-soil eroded from the slopes of the upland rice-growing farmers in the hinterland.

When the Sierra Leone Government arranged for a Bengal expert on paddy rice, a Mr. Pillai, to report on tidal rice-growing in the Scarcies, he could offer no suggestion for improving methods, indeed he admitted that the Indian culti-vator would be glad to have such lands and such yields. How-ever, better rice varieties are possible, and are being supplied; further, swamp rice farmers are being urged to protect their river bank by letting a fringe of mangroves remain to defend them from wash. To the mangrove the farmer owes that entire silt terri-tory, arrested and woven by the tough roots against the sea. The best land has been taken up and cleared, but in less acces-sible places, even in the Scarcies, there is still much land to be cleared and planted; this the Agricultural Department is doing, using tractors. To use tractors in such country is more than agriculture—it is a mixture of an assault course, big game hunt-ing and small boat navigation. For the tractors have to be brought round by sea in second-hand landing craft, about the time of year when storms are sudden and the sea rises rapidly. Next the tractor has to be landed on a slippery mud bank when the tide is just right. Then it has to be operated in remote country, approximately 15 hours by launch from the nearest town—and Heaven knows how long from the nearest spare part. In the course of operating it, there may well be an argument with bush cow or elephant.

In the Scarcies, as in the swamps of the south, tractors can be used to clear and cultivate land where there is no population to bring hand methods to bear. Large areas of land, to be made into paddy fields, await heavy capital investment. Near the coast it will be necessary to build walls and dykes to keep the salt water out of the land most of the year if the salt is not to poison the soil. Where the Rhizophora mangrove grows, curiously enough, the soil is less porous and badly drained land retains the sea salt and will not grow rice. Experiment alone will determine how such areas can be made productive.

At the Rice Research Station at Rokupr that kind of problem, as well as those of the southern riceland development, are being studied. More rice from the Scarcies and the inland swamps of the north would ease the need to grow rice on the uplands, and enable farmers to think of other crops—and of cattle. Rice mills—like the one already operating at Mambolo —will parboil and husk the rice brought in for sale, and send it down by sea or up-country by launch or lorry. Those who make money out of rice will buy from those who want to make money out of meat. The scalped hills of Tonkalili will no longer be needed for food production, and the people there will let the Forest Department reforest them. Early burning will keep the trees alive in the grassland and cattle will be fat and healthy far to the south. It is simply a matter of getting the people to understand—Temne and Susu farmers knee-deep in floodwater; Limba and Temne farmers setting fire to the grass after the feasting of the Marrying Month; Fula cattle-men moving from one worn-out, grazed-out hill slope to pastures new; Konos and Korankos remote and still beyond the reach of roads. The map of a richer future, entitled *Proposed Zones of Production*, has been produced following a thorough survey by the Soil Conservation and Land Use Team. It is just a question of explaining what has to be done. But explaining is not easy.

13. BORBOH

The small boy has nothing,
he pierces my ear
MENDE PROVERB

N O; it is not easy to explain.

It is not easy to explain why, though European ideas of tropical agriculture were highly unsound in 1902, they are pretty reliable in 1952. It is not easy to explain that though a petrol tractor has sparking-plugs, a diesel tractor has not. It is not easy to explain why one kind of cup should be used to serve Missis tea, while another kind should be used to serve Missis coffee. It is not easy, either, to explain why it is not easy to explain, but that is the most important explanation of all in Sierra Leone—or in Africa.

Everyone meets at the ferries. On either side of the river the red road plunges steeply into the water where a thousand iridescent butterflies congregate. The lorries queue for their turn to cross. Women in variously tied and variously hued lappas discuss matters of importance; men in gowns, men in shirts and shorts, men in collars and ties, discuss. The drivers exchange professional comments. The children stand about, watching with large eyes, behind which their thoughts move invisibly as fish under the brown surface of the river. But when I smile at a 12-year-old and mop my brow in comic despair she ripples with laughter—her whole body atremble with fun, her teeth agleam, her soul agleam. Oh! That infectious bubbling merriment of the Negress: how it made me long to cross the unbridged barrier of language. Impossible not to envy a man like Tom Harris, who could take me into a household of Mende women at nightfall and sit with me there, the centre of a fusillade of chaff, of trilling, rippling laughter, so that the men gathered at the doors to join in the badinage, the children squeezed between the legs of their elders, and the firelight danced on twinkling eyes and teeth like pearls.

A round house, with a circumference of perhaps 30 feet and no partitions; no ceiling, and the conical roof of thatch a cap of darkness from which stalactites of soot depend; the wooden

shutters closed; nine beds disposed around the walls, each wit
its small canopy and challa matting curtains which can l
lowered to make a cubicle; chests and boxes disposed in r
order on the floor to sit on and put scraps of personal proper
in; sacks and bundles head-high among the tie-beams; the ba;
of food hanging within reach on palm-fibre cords; the bones ⸱
a chicken on a string over the door to appease an offende
ancestor; three tiny fires smouldering between burned ston⸱
on which pots rest; a single smoky hurricane lamp to illumir
the fingers of an old woman spinning; a hardened mud floo
and crouching women, some young, some old, all with fing⸱
nails worn to the quick from weeding the rice . . . To such a scer
the African child of the hinterland, Borboh or 'little boy', fir
opens his eyes, and from it first learns to adjust his focus, 1
understand the depth and the shape of things: first learns 1
know his mother and his family.

Slowly little Borboh learns about the world; absorbs it int
his awakening soul. First his mother, who feeds him wheneve
he feels hungry, at a single cry, first with her milk, then b
thrusting cassava pap down his throat even despite his protes·
that he has had enough, that he is choking with food. Strappe
to her back he goes forth into the village, into the farms beyonc
He may hardly set foot to ground until he is two. When he ca
stand he joins a gang of other children, brothers, sister
cousins, nearly all kindred at some remove. They have no s⸱
routine of life. They play as they will; share their food, slee
when they desire. On moonlight nights in a village, the childre
will be up and about at midnight or later.

Little Borboh knows his mother; but he has many hal
mothers, his own mother's mates. He calls them all mother, ⸱
grandmother. They may show him affection, or they may no·
if they do not, his real mother will be cautious of demonstratin·
her love for him. If the family is rent with quarrels, little Borbo·
may find, also, that his father, who lives in another house in th·
village, will be sparing of caresses. He belongs not to his moth·
and father, as one side of a triangle, but to his mother and h·
mother's people; and he is looked after by quite a number ⸱
motherly or auntish women. He may be the centre of a comple
family tug-of-war to gain possession of him. He may have nigh·
mares about his parents being driven away from him by h·

aunts and uncles. There are, of course, families in which a child lives with his father and mother, especially if they are poor, and life is lived lean-ribbed and close to the earth. But in the main, whether Borboh is a pagan or a Muslim, he is part of a Mawe, or household of many people scattered in several houses—for houses to Africans are much what rooms are to Europeans, each having its purpose. Little Borboh must know and respect personages of importance, as well as grown-ups generally—his uncles, especially, and his father's head wife, whether she is his mother or not, the village elders, among whom his father may or may not be numbered. Gradually he begins to understand the ramifications of his family in the town, in other towns round about, or even far off. He will soon realize that there are few strangers who are not of his kin at some remove.

Probably he wears no clothes, but he will certainly wear a charm against witches, concerning whom he will early acquire knowledge, and also as a prophylactic against bad medicine, for it is likely enough that someone with a grudge against his mother or father will seek to take it out on little Borboh. His little sisters and brothers and cousins die, often before his eyes, presumably for this reason. They go sick, and they are dead before a medicine man can perform all the things needed to save them. Their little bodies are wrapped in leaves and buried in rubbish heaps.

Borboh gets a wash perhaps once a day; but he is pretty well covered with healthy dirt. He is taught to relieve himself in the bush, which does not smell pleasant before the rains fall, especially near a biggish town. He has no toys, though he might, once in a way, be given a live bird on a string: it soon dies. He will learn to play various games of the 'cat's-cradle' variety; a game of African draughts exists—*warri*—but is mainly played by his elders, for high stakes. He follows the men and watches them at work while his sisters follow the women and carry a calabash on their heads even if it is empty. He begins to learn the names of all the trees and living things; the powers of the tools the grown-ups work with, axe, adze, hoe, bow, gun, pottery, loom, blacksmith's bellows, knife, and so on. He eats with the men when he can, and imitates them. He goes out with them on fishing expeditions, or to the farms, or to build the road because the chief has ordered it.

He may be sent away to another town to be brought up by relatives entirely when he is seven or eight; his parents may fear he will be spoiled, or killed in spite, if he stays at home. But the new people, and the new surroundings, will be a replica of the old. There will be the same easy affection from all, the same sense of belonging to the place and people; he will neither lose nor gain intensities of love. He is never alone. All tasks, all actions of life, are done in company. He gains, as he grows older, a sense of responsibility, of duties to be done, partly for his household, but in general for the community, for everybody. He begins by collecting firewood for the house, trapping small animals, then scaring birds or monkeys on the farms. Small boys can always be found plenty to do; so can small girls. He sets his fine-boned shoulder to the great work of keeping alive as a group, his pot-belly shrinks and his muscles harden as he uses stick and sling and canoe-paddle.

He learns the names of the days, months and seasons, of the farming and fishing operations. He learns to count: one is a finger; five is a hand; the intervening numeration is supplied. Six is a hand and one finger; ten is two hands. Twenty is a man —two hands of five, two feet of five. The Mende or Mandingo lad learns perhaps that his village has houses three men finished, ten on top, two on top: 72 houses. When the town grows, he says it has a *hondo* houses, a useful word the white men brought with them. Larger numbers are for boys who go to school. He has no word for half; he says 'give me the piece' when something is shared—but few things in the high forest or the grassland *can* be exactly halved. Fair shares, however, whether of a cooked chicken, a fish, or a red rice stew, are perfectly comprehended; and so are black eyes. 'Take two each', in a soothing tone, is expressed literally, 'Take them, two, two'.

Borboh learns all things from his elders; and he must be polite to them. From them alone can he find out what is done, and what is not done, on any occasion. Through them, he learns to respect the ancestors, those who have gone before, and are powerful in the world of spirits. They may be approached at graves, hills, river banks, trees and sacred stones. He sees the ceremonies done to enlist their aid, at every farming season, and on all other occasions. He sees how those that die are helped over to join the majority. The older people know these things:

they know what was done in the old days, and if they were not there to report precedent, knowledge would die.

From Grandmother or Grandfather, Borboh learns how the world was made, and why men are here. A Mende Borboh will learn, perhaps,[1] that once upon a time a spirit lived in a cave. He created animals to prevent himself getting lonely and gave them all they wanted: on one condition—they must not touch his food. But one day an animal was overcome with temptation and ate some of it. But the spirit divined his guilt and threw him out of the cave, saying: 'From now on, your name is cow'. One by one the animals disobediently tasted the wonderful food and were thrown out, last of all the men. Men still wander round the world dissatisfied with it and hungry for the magic food. The spirit is Ngewo, who has gone up above and is sitting watching who will eat his food. His name means Gone Up: from a disobedient world. Only the ancestors can intercede with him, except in moments of frightful emergency, when he may hear a short prayer from a full heart and come to the rescue of a worthy man. A Temne Borboh (if not a Muslim, which nearly all are) will learn that this is the second world made by the Great Spirit —whose name also in Temne is Sky or Up—and the second race of men, and that it will end presently, and then he will make another. The present world was made on the head of a giant; all things that grow are his hair, all things that move are the lice of his hair. The giant turns all the time, but so smoothly that people don't notice it; when he doesn't, there is an earthquake.

The Great Spirit made a man and a woman, and gave them all that they wanted: but every time he gave them something, they wanted more, first food, then fire, then animals, then tools, then medicines. Then they wanted to increase and multiply. So God prepared eight pills. By the hands of a servant (or angel) he administered two to the woman that she might have the greatest desire, the remaining six were then equally divided. But then God sent them clothes, and put modesty on the woman with her strong desire, and boldness on the man with his weaker desire. They had children, two pairs of boys and girls, one white, one black. God sent them to live separately, and make different nations: only he made the white pair cleverer. At first

[1] Unless instructed according to Bible or Koran, or according to another account which is also current.

men did not die, God only sent his servant to bring living peop
to him when their time was up. But one man refused to com
though asked politely several times. So God sent Mr. Sickness
get hold of him, so that he cried: 'Mr. Sickness has got me, b
I don't see him', and could not move. Next day God se
Mr. Death to bring the man pinioned by Mr. Sickness, so
died and was buried.

Thus Borboh learns of that First Disobedience and its fru
which brought death into our world and all its woe. Thus
accustoms himself to the strange powers that make things ha
pen as they do. Elders and ancestors, the one to become t
other, can alone help him to follow his path through a host
world: animals and reptiles that kill, sorcery that produces sic
ness, malevolent grifi or spirits that cause the crops to fa
However, with proper care, things can be made to go right; a
life is jolly with dancing, singing, and the telling of tales a
legends of Kai Lundo, Ndawa and other heroes. The tales pr
vide a reason for everything, and the proverbs are a store
wisdom and precept. Conversation in Mende and Temne, as
other Sierra Leone languages, indeed, is often a subtle bandyi
of proverbs, much as men in the nineteenth century bandi
biblical texts, or schoolmen bandied syllogisms. Tales expla
the animal world: the original Just So Stories come out
Africa. The nature of every animal, fierce or gentle or subtle,
explored and explained. There are, too, a multitude of stori
about men and women, or perhaps one should say about t
vices and virtues personified, rather than about person
character. An old gentleman in Mateboi told me a moral ta
(which any Borboh may hear) which may serve as an exampl
it was explained to me as the conflict of cleverness and vanity.

Once there lived in a certain chiefdom a brainy boy call
Timpe, who always had the best of every argument and made
fool of anyone who tried to get the better of him. At last an o
man decided to put the boy in his place once and for all. I
dressed up with great care, and went with his friends to the bc
'I hear you make a fool of everyone, my lad', he said. 'We
now, just you try to make a fool of me.' Timpe answere
'I have fooled everyone else, but I can't even try to fool *you*, Pa
The old man, puffed up by his easy victory, smiled and ask
him why. 'Why,' said the boy, 'you are so finely dressed th

you completely overawe me. Your wonderful hat, for example.'
'Well, well,' said the old man, 'if you think you can make a
fool of me without my hat, you're welcome to try.' And he took
his hat off. 'That's a bit better', said the boy. 'But then, look at
your wonderful gown, Pa. I cannot fool you in that.' 'Oh, all
right', said the old man, and divested himself of his gown. The
boy then went into raptures about the old man's shirt, and the
old man smilingly removed it; but no, even then the boy could
not try to fool him while he had such a magnificent pair of
trousers on. The old man took them off. 'See,' said the boy,
'I have made a fool of many people—but this naked old fool is
the silliest of the lot.' There are plenty of tales to redress the
balance on the side of age and experience.

Borboh will know a good deal about the Poro before he is
initiated into the secret society, the 'Purrah' of early travellers
who were impressed by its mystery and power. Every season the
throb of the Poro drums can be heard in the bush, and senior
members of the society come to take boys away to be initiated;
they leave as Borboh's playmates, and return as serious young
men. After Borboh has been circumcised, his time comes. The
Poro Devil groans in the town, and Borboh is marched out to
the Poro bush, which is now out of bounds to everyone else, and
especially to women, who must clap their hands if they come
near it. Borboh has been coached; at the first entrance he is
asked: 'Could you bring water in a basket?' and answers 'Yes'.
At the main entrance he makes a show of resistance but allows
himself to be pulled into the bush—a clearing in which temporary huts have been erected. The harsh note of the Poro horn
is heard, first in one place, then another in the bush. Borboh and
his fellow neophytes are then thrown to the ground, naked, and
scarred with special marks with a razor or other instrument; the
drums roar to drown his cries of pain. The spirit has now bitten
him; in the bush he has been swallowed and from the bush he
will emerge reborn—as a man.

Dressed in special Poro clothes, he will now pass through a
Spartan training in the bush. When boys were trained in the
Poro bush to be warriors (and hence by the Europeans were
called, at first, 'Poro boys') they often remained in the forest
for years, and learned farming, tracking, hunting, and all the
arts of ambush warfare and the noiseless scaling of stockades.

K

Today the period is much shorter—for townee lads it may be little more than a day. A boy who stays in longer—and may perhaps rise later in the Poro degrees—learns useful arts: farming, fishing, basket-making, weaving, pottery and so on. He receives, also, sexual instruction—advanced theory, one is inclined to presume. But especially his knowledge of wood lore is greatly extended by experienced teachers. If Borboh is a Mende he learns more of the traditions of the Mende race, for the Poro is in a sense the Mende national council, a spiritual authority which rises superior to the temporal divisions of the land into chiefdoms. Borboh also learns drumming, singing and acrobatics; above all, he learns comradeship with his fellow initiates and with the society's officials. He is expected to stick a good deal of hardship—the remnants of military training—and is often deliberately asked to do impossible things, so that he may be unjustly beaten and learn to bear beatings and injustice —both of which he may expect in full measure during a man's life. He and his companions may be required to find most of their own food, by stealing if need be, though their parents are expected to 'feed the devil'.

The education in the bush comes to an end with three important ceremonies. In the first, Borboh and the rest of the Poro camp dance round the town with the Poro Devil, impersonated in leopard skins and other finery and blowing his horn. He is given presents of rice and palm oil by grateful parents. Back in the bush a fowl is sacrificed, and the death of the fowl is a 'warning' to the boys of their fate if they divulge the secrets they have learned. A week later, a feast is prepared in the town, collected and brought into the bush by the boys; again the warning is given. Finally the boys are 'pulled' from the bush in a ceremony known as 'Ngafa gohu lewe lei', or beating the spirit's belly. The spirit is unwilling to give birth to the boys he has swallowed, and he has to be constrained by a time-honoured native midwives' practice in breach cases. All the equipment of the camp, and everything worn by the boys, must be destroyed, for women must not see it; then the whole camp dances in the town. This is a night of ordeal for the boys, for if they sleep the spirit will not emit them, and they will die. Their parents send them kola nuts to keep them awake. The spirit groans and a basket filled with the boys' initiation clothes is dragged round the town and belaboured with sticks. At dawn, no boy having slept, the spirit leaves the town, and the boys are now told the final secrets—that is, the secrets of the first degree. They receive their new names, for each boy a fowl is killed, and he is sprinkled with its blood. Borboh, with the rest, is then ceremonially shaved, given rice to eat while he is sworn in, and dipped in the river and washed clean. Then he polishes his new-born body with palm oil, and wearing a new gown and head-scarf, returns to the town, where he and his class-mates are feasted and given palm wine and honoured in the barri. Finally, the head-scarf is ceremonially removed from Borboh's shaved head—a libation of wine is poured, and the Poro session is over.

Borboh is now named, for example, Ansumana. He is a man; his sex is sharply differentiated; he has seen rites and been told secrets no woman must ever know. He is also a citizen: he guards Mende secrets no outsider may ever know. He realizes that there are men of higher degrees to be respected, and still more secret secrets. He is trained: he can both cultivate the soil and perform the ceremonies which alone will ensure that his seeds will sprout. It is perhaps not very important what the secrets are. The Poro arcana confer no special powers or wonderful knowledge—except the inestimable honour and knowledge of being found worthy, of being able to keep secrets, of being able to play the man. Swami Vivekananda used to say that no one should believe that there was any 'secret doctrine' in yoga; everything that could be said, had been said: what was mysterious—the actual practice—could only be learned by personal effort, and *that*, so learned, was incommunicable. Talk of secrets was the advertisement of quackery. Howbeit, in the degrees of Poro, secrets are communicated, as in European Freemasonry, and they are not told—even Europeans who have entered the first degree of Poro (and there have been quite a number) think it good taste not to blab them.

Although what Borboh actually hears that is untellable cannot be defined, he graduates from Poro with a sense of valuable possession. More important, he understands the meaning of the saying 'Mende man helps Mende man'.

Northern boys do not go through Poro, for this institution only exists among the Mende, Sherbro, Vai, and some of the Konos and Temnes. Muslims have no such society; but all tribes have the comparable women's society, the Sande, under some comparable name. The northern Borboh learns Arabic prayers, which he does not usually understand, but serve him for charms and secrets pretty well. Especially he is taught the meaning of brotherhood among Muslims—the essential doctrine of Poro, which helps similarly to guide his later conduct.

'Crocodile' mask used in dances of the Poro secret society

14. BORBOH GROWN UP

To respect a man is better than
to feed him without caring
TEMNE PROVERB

BORBOH is now a man—but his status is junior. Until he is married he will still be called a 'boy': indeed, until he achieves the dignity of two or three wives he can hardly become the head of a household.

Something, of course, depends on his family connections; and something on fortune. If he belongs to one of the two or three ruling families in the chiefdom his chance of early marriage and promotion are fair; he may even be in the running for the office of section chief, or for such lucrative posts as chief's 'speaker'. But if he is descended from a family which was enslaved until the British Government abolished slavery in the Protectorate in 1928, a long period as a simple labourer on his father's or uncle's farm lies before him. If his family has large claims to bush, and some wealth, connections perhaps in trade, relatives in salaried employ under the white man, daughters that can be advantageously married off for a large bride-price, then, again, Borboh's future becomes correspondingly more hopeful.

In the ordinary course of events Ansumana must expect to become a fisherman or farmer on his family's farm. He cannot own land except by inheriting it, and if he wants his father's he will have to contest his uncles' claims to it when his father dies: for theirs is the traditional claim. As a member of the family he has only a right to live off the family farm in return for working on it. When, if ever, he inherits the farm along with the headship of the family, he in his turn must concede to his sons and nephews the right to work on, and live off, the farm. In any case he will need their labour to brush and burn; and his father and uncles will now want the aid of his muscles to keep the family farm going. As a helper, therefore, he enters the farming cycle (as described in Chapter 9). He helps to brush and burn, he follows the sower with the hoe, he joins the harvest throng with a larger 'stint' suited to his grown strength. He also helps to gather kola nuts, and palm fruit for the women to boil into oil;

he may crack nuts and carry kernels on his head to the nearest Syrian trader. He will hunt and fish, listen to village discussions in the barri, and he will live with Poro classmates in a small bachelor establishment. He may earn good wages helping to make his neighbours' farms when he has finished brushing his family's, and he may be allowed to keep the proceeds of the palm nuts which he collects and cracks. With this cash he will pay his share of the hut tax, buy clothes and entertainment—or save up the bride-price of a wife.

Ansumana has other tasks. He must find money to pay dues to the chief, or (in remoter areas) work on his farm unpaid. There is always much porterage to be done. Nowadays he will be paid for the work which the chief orders him to do on the road—though possibly not the legal price for it. It is well to oblige the chief and his officers. In the village, everything has to be kept in repair—farm implements, tools, fishing nets and, above all, the houses. From the moment a house is put up to shelter man against nature, the elements combine to pull it down. The rain attacks it with fury, battering and soaking the thatch, washing away the mud walls, rising through the mud floor. Termites attack the structure of the poles as soon as the sap has dried in them. Rats burrow in the mud of the walls; birds go for the thatch. The structure thus weakened, the winds of the stormy season will bring it down. Therefore, after the farm has been brushed and the poles are ready, Ansumana will help repair houses and build new ones.

Houses used to be built in the traditional way: a circle of poles round a central pillar, made from a stout tree trunk; the poles woven together with light sticks and tied with palm fibre cords; the interstices filled in with mud-balls and finished off with mud cement; the roof of palm-leaf thatch. Borboh was taught these simple processes of joinery and thatching. Except in remoter areas, houses are becoming more elaborate, espe- cially under the watchful eye of the Health Department. Ansumana will help to build either rectangular houses with two or three rooms, the roof carried by girders of poles, or houses more of the old type, but divided into two semicircles with a large square room in between. Rafters carry tiles made of palm- leaf thatch; the walls may be finished with cow dung and decor- ated with designs of flowers, or possibly cartoons of the white man's silvery birds that hum overhead from time to time, with windows and engine nacelles exactly observed.

In such a house, one has to choose between keeping dry and free of insects, and an atmosphere of smoke and soot. Smoke from an open hearth preserves the thatch. Thatch on a house with an open fire lasts four years, as against one year on a house in which no fire is lit, or which has a chimney. The hot sun will shrink the thatch, which will not swell again and become watertight until it has been thoroughly soaked. In native houses I have woken to find my bed a sodden mass, have put on my overcoat with the expectation of a sleepless night, only to find that, having once wetted me and my belongings, the thatch thereafter turns the rain. The smoke not only preserves the thatch, it kills off the mosquitoes and possibly the bugs; the mud floor, however, harbours jiggers, an insect which buries a sack of eggs, for preference under the human skin. This must be dug out with a thorn if one is not to be infested with worms. But there are so many species of worms that Ansumana is certain to be sharing his vitality with several.

In this house Ansumana will nurse his ambitions, dream his dreams; and to such a house ultimately conduct his wife. He will have no illusions about the picturesque quality of thatch, and will regard the corrugated iron roof of the chief's compound, the Syrians' shops and the D.C.'s bungalow as the mark of a really high and desirable standard of living—along with concrete or mud-block walls and well-carpentered door jambs and shutters. The rusting tin roofs of Freetown, or, for example, of rich villages in Ashanti, would seem to him (if he ever thinks along such lines) the goal of social welfare.

His eyes will be upon the slender girls who walk with willowy grace beneath the headweight of a calabash, girls fresh from Sande, demure yet coquettish; but alas! they will rarely be his to take. A network of barriers lies between him and them, however hugger-mugger the thatched houses of his village stand with the nostalgic-scented wood smoke blue about their tips. Whom he may and may not yearn to love is first the business of the Humoi Society, which is the censor of sexual behaviour and the guardian of the prohibited degrees. These are very extensive, and to cross them is to commit *Simongama*, an heinous offence against decency and the ancestors, only to be purged by heavy

SIERRA LEONE

fines and complex rituals—possibly by flogging as wel
Ansumana must not only observe such taboos as are printed i
the prayer book for Christians, but a great many more
Marriage or love-affairs with one's paternal first cousins is pro
hibited, and even with second cousins is discouraged. If h
brother, or half-brother, has had an affair with any woman, sh
becomes out of bounds to Ansumana. It will seem natural fo
him to walk circumspectly, since he has been taught that it is
disgusting thing even to sit on his sister's bed; and when h
marries, he must not even shake hands with his mother-in-law

In a community in which relationships, formal and informa
are of a rich complexity, some such society is necessary to pre
serve the decencies; in fact it supervises a good many matte
which among the white people are considered entirely privat
Ansumana will have to consult the Society or its head, often th
chief's wife, before he takes any decisions about his affection
But even then he will find marriageable girls hard to get. Ric
men, heads of households, with two or three wives to wee
their farms, snap them up under Ansumana's eyes. The hea
wife of a rich man will slip round to make the proposal to th
girl's parents after he has hinted: 'I like Fatmattah. Let us mal
a larger farm next year'. He will get a weeder, and she a han
maiden. The parents will get a good money payment and
permanent connection with a steady supply of rice and cassav
and palm kernels. What can Ansumana offer? Indeed, old m
engage Fatmattah before she goes to Sande, by paying h
finishing-school fees and giving her parents presents. If the g
is good-looking, the parents are glad to send her to the chief
section-chief to join his seraglio, because even though he pa
a mere nominal shilling to make the marriage legal, if she is h
wife they can 'beg' him, whenever they are in need of help
influence. It is said: 'A chief does not get his wives for nothing

Ansumana will have to save hard to make up a sum, and a
assured future, to meet such competition. In fact, he w
probably have to wait until he has risen in the household cou
cils before he can offer a good present to the girl's parents at
an advantageous union. The marriage is an alliance betwe
the families, not an individual contract. It is her parents, not t
girl, whom he holds to the bargain; and his children belong n
wholly to him but to his family. In former times he would n

expect to marry until he was 35—for he was a warrior, and warriors must refrain from self-indulgence and household distractions—wherefore children were not too many for the farms to feed. But today Ansumana can perhaps marry younger, say at 28.

However, it is not easy to save; for he will not be denied feminine company before he marries—if he can pay for it. Among the wives of rich elderly men he may hope to find one, or more than one, who is discontented with the time her husband can give her, or even dissatisfied with his embraces. Even the girl who thought she loved, and married, can find that she was wrong, and that young Ansumana, lithe, smooth-skinned, jet, is her adored. True, opportunity will not be as easy as it appears—for it would be a heinous sin to perform the sex act in the bush; this would injure the fertility of the land. But lovers find trysting places. She will break the rules for him; and perhaps sing the old Mandingo song:

> Quarrels end
> But words once spoken die not.
>
> Lovers may part
> And still belief remains.
>
> Marriage may break
> But still respect survives.
>
> To leave your mother's keeping
> For your father's company
> Why should this be
> Unless through changing love?
>
> And when from father's house
> A maid goes to her man
> It is the same, we see—
> It comes through changing love.
>
> When she slips out at night
> To seek her lover's arms
> The same old rule applies
> 'Inconstant love'!
>
> My darling one!
> My chief!
> Today's a festal day!

She will seek Ansumana's arms, but he may find it an expensive business if they are found out. He will be brought before the chief's court and tried for 'woman damage'. If convicted he will be fined, and if the fine is beyond his means, he may (at least, in the remoter areas) have to work it out on the aggrieved husband's farm. Husbands with plenty of wives, but short of male labour, arrange matters that way; their polygamous households are lubricious webs to catch farm labour. Once caught, it is fatally easy for Ansumana to settle down as a permanent lover to another man's wife, working on his farm for a small wage or none at all. Fines from woman damage can be heavy, and it sometimes happens that a town loses much of its youth as the result of spirited young men preferring to run away rather than be reduced to serfage.

It is also rather easy to be caught. Inconstant love may change once again; and if any suspicion arises, the suspected woman may be 'sworn'. A medicine is brought, and the husband sacrifices a fowl, saying: 'God come down, I have brought you your fowl: as this woman has lied against me, she it is I am swearing now. If she is to blame, let it fall on her. Hold her hands, her feet, her heart, her intestines, hold her sleeping-place, hold her resting-place, let her not be saved at all. Let her die quickly'. If the medicine is strong, few women will risk their lives by withholding the names of their lovers; the husband can then 'pull the swear': 'You medicine, now lying here in this place, loosen her hands, loosen her feet, loosen her heart, her intestines, let her be saved'. The man himself will be sworn if he does not pay up.

Indeed Ansumana moves continually in danger of having a bad medicine put upon him by rivals in love, aggrieved husbands, ill-wishers of all sorts. Nasty things can be done to him: *Yeke yekei*, for example, causes syphilis; *Konde wopoi*, a kind of snail shell, makes it impossible to break off sexual intercourse; *tilei* merely causes the nose to rot away. If a man is convinced that a bad medicine has been put upon him, he must pay a large sum to a medicine man to get a suitable antidote. If a man steals from a farm which is defended by a medicine, naturally he expects to be in trouble; but an entirely blameless man can be persecuted by witches. The sign of a witch is an enlarged spleen —which means, in a malarious land, that there is plenty of evidence for witchcraft. A man was recently convicted of murder for killing another quite suddenly in the bush with a cutlass. His explanation was that this man had come to stay with him, and had overstayed his welcome. When invited, at first tactfully, then repeatedly and frankly, to go, he refused, saying: 'No; I like it here'. His distraught and impecunious host one day invited him to take a walk into the bush and cut him down. He opened the body and found a large spleen. Q.E.D.

When at last Ansumana has the money or gets from his family the money to obtain a wife, the ceremony is simple. He may put a girl through Sande, and marry her afterwards, or he may take a girl who has been through Sande. In the first case he ties a rope round the girl's wrist, pays her and her parents sums of cash (up to £1) and when she is initiated pays her fees, perhaps £5. He must make many gifts in cash and kind to her parents and to the Sande officials; and finally he must pay the bridewealth in cash, cloth and perhaps other goods. (The girl must give her consent to the marriage; if she does not, the money must all be given back—and Borboh will have kept an itemized account, if he is a true Mende.) The mother then spits on the girl's forehead and blesses her; she is taken dancing to her husband's house. She must now serve him; and it is the responsibility of her parents that she does.

If Ansumana has not enough money he may be able to commute part of the bridewealth by working on the farm of his bride's parents. Or he may contract a form of marriage with a husbandless woman—a woman who has run away from illtreatment (which is the usual way to arrange a divorce without having to pay bridewealth back), or with a widow. But no marriage is legal unless the woman's parents have agreed. If the marriage is not legal the husband has no right to the children, which then belong to the woman's parents. He will prefer, normally, an alliance with a rich or influential family.

Once he has a wife, Ansumana can make a small farm, he doing the brushing and burning, she the weeding; by working on other farms, or collecting palm fruit and kola or other fruits, and possibly by weaving or other craftwork, they can raise the money necessary to hire extra help. If Ansumana desires a larger farm, however, and if his wife wants domestic service, he must marry again; she then becomes a big wife, and he is on the

way to found a proper household. He farms in the family bus
area, with permission of his father or uncles, but, under mode
conditions, he may gradually come to think of his farm as h
own. He may be go-ahead and do well, perhaps planting coffe
cocoa, ginger or some other cash crop; perhaps, in the nortl
keeping cattle with skill. He will then marry again and agai
his household increasing with labourers and children.

On the other hand, as his wealth increases so will the dang
of witchcraft from jealous men; and so, too, will increase tl
exactions of the chief, who will probably judge Ansumana a
just the right person to billet strangers on, or to perform onerou
and expensive duties for the chiefdom, such as erecting a re
house. The danger of being fined will increase, and the numb
of presents he will have to give to the secret societies will al
increase. His wives' relatives will expect him to look aft
them.

Ansumana's promotion to head of the household may, on tl
other hand, come from his inheritance of his father's or h
brothers' bush, or from a share in their wealth. But it is like
enough that he will never get rich, never acquire more than on
or two wives, and those when his first youth has passed, hov
ever well he farms. The hazards are great: sickness, court case
fines, trouble with relatives, with the chief, even with tl
Government; losses from gambling, from thieves, from pest
from the strange changes in the prices Syrians pay, and whic
they say are dictated by the witchcraft of men over the seas. H
may despair of becoming independent and himself resort t
magic. He may be content to wear a leopard's tooth to obtai
good luck; he may merely redouble his sacrifices to his ancestor
laying rice on stones and by the river, and making sure next da
that it has been eaten (by the birds, for the ancestors). He ma
fear that he has unwittingly transgressed the rules of the Hum
Society, or the Njayei Society, and go through purificatio
ceremonies. In the Gpaa-Mende country he may join a socie
largely devoted to changing a man's luck, the Wunde. Membe
are taught to be expert in politics and finance; it has a mo
potent devil who lives in a cave protected by bees and it is sai
to remove inconsiderate persons who stand in the way of i
members' careers. Its officials defend it on the grounds that it
simply a helpful get-together of business men, comparable wit

the white man's joint-stock companies or Rotary. He may even resort to the Keepers of the Heart of the Medicine and try to get inconvenient persons out of the way. Decoctions of the heads of poisonous snakes, chameleons, scorpions, tarantulas, centipedes and parts of the skins of human beings are said to have great power to achieve such wicked ends. Ansumana will nowadays probably not go beyond a good 'swear' against those he thinks are wronging him—but one way and another he will probably spend quite a lot of his money on medicines and sorcery.

At last his time comes to die, to become one of the ancestors. The son whom he named, spitting on his forehead and saying: 'Resemble me in all ways, being named after me', now gazes on his dead body, gaunt with living and toiling and fearing and scheming. In Mendeland, an incision will be made in his back and his spleen removed to see if, after all, he was possessed by a witch—and if it is enlarged, then he was a witch, and the neighbours mock his relatives come to mourn him. But if, in spite of having chronic malaria, Ansumana escapes this revelation of his true nature, he is wailed for, and his wife sits apart. His feet are washed, and then the family stand round him and one by one mention all his offences against them, and declare: 'We have now no bad in our hearts against you; Ngewo, let him reach the white sands of Heaven'. The grave is dug, perhaps in the compound (though the authorities discourage this now), leaves and sticks are laid to protect his body from the earth that is now filled in. The drums rumble, and the family dances over the grave. But Ansumana is still with them for three days, probably watching their grief from the body of a bird. On the third day the family gathers round his grave again and makes him a sacrifice of red rice and pours him out a drink of water to refresh him on his journey. 'We are leaving you now', they tell him, 'as we have finished your last ceremony. We want you henceforth to look after your family.' So he crosses the river, and for Ansumana too (why not?) the trumpets sound upon the other side.

Ansumana is Everyman in the Protectorate. The pattern of his working life will vary if he is a Muslim, if he lives in swamps, or with cattle, or with the treacherous sea. But the quality of his surroundings, and the influences upon him, will, very broadly, be the same. When things have to be explained, whether it is a matter of taking his bush for forest, or of growing rice in the swamps, or of burning grass in Mufar instead of Pol Pol, or of growing cocoa instead of rice, or of keeping pigs and feeding them better than himself in the hungry season, or of voting for a member of a tribal authority, or of sending his son to school, or of building a pioneer mill for his palm fruit, or of using expensive fertilizer, or . . . all must, in the end, be explained to Ansumana.

Earlier simple type of 'Bundu' mask. This one sports a hat which may be nineteenth-century sailor's straw or may represent a top-hat which in late nineteenth century had become the symbol of authority both in Sierra Leone and Nigeria. Brought back by Alldridge at the beginning of the century.

15. MARIAMA

The sweet rice is eaten quickly
KORANKO PROVERB

BORBOH'S sister, Nyalui, early learns to help with house-hold tasks. She sweeps out the house, cleans the kitchen and cooking pots, helps to wash clothes with her mothers and grand-mothers by soaping them with palm-oil soap and banging them on rocks in mid-stream. She fetches and carries, learns how to buy food in the market, and how to sell. She learns how to scrape the rind off the cassava root, how to husk the rice in the mortar and winnow it by pouring it on a windy day from shoulder height upon a mat. She looks after her baby brothers and sisters, and defers to her older brothers. She goes with her mothers and aunts to the farm in the rainy weather and helps to weed the rice. A good girl is hardly ever seen without a calabash on her head or a tot on her hip.

She listens to the story-telling in the evening with Borboh and the other children, and probably hears other tales as well when she is helping the older women to cook or do their hair. Her questions are always answered by a story. Why is an African's hair so short and fuzzy? 'Once upon a time' (comes the answer) 'there lived in Moyamba ("Yamba's town") a woman with beautiful long straight black hair; it stretched from Moyamba to Mano ("town of the folk who persist in fighting"). Her husband was rich and had the largest farm in the world, so she called her son Yamba. Doing her hair was a terrible business, beautiful as it was, and so she decided to shorten it. She told Yamba to go to Mano and set fire to it, and not to tell anyone what he was doing. Yamba went to Mano and set fire to his mother's hair; it blazed up and people came to ask about the approaching fire. But the woman brushed her hair and sang:

O Pa ka Yamba	(O father of Yamba,
Korr kama toi!	They are burning off your farm!
O Pa ka Yamba	O father of Yamba!
Kum belem belem	Fizz! Crackle! Crackle!
Kushe kelelu! Kushe kelelu!	Brush, brush, brush,
Ngau!	Now it has burnt.)

143

So the people went away satisfied; but when the flames came within a few miles of Moyamba they came again, and again the woman sang as she brushed her hair; and again they were satisfied. But the woman did not realize how fast the fire was moving, and suddenly felt it tingling next her scalp (Kushe, kelelu!) and put it out with water (Ngau!). Ever since then, hair has been frizzy and short.' In these wonderful stories, of which there are thousands and thousands, handed down from mother to daughter, songs, nonsense verses, miming and hyperbole are all employed to increase the entertainment. 'Her mouth was so small that the water had to be pounded in the mortar before she could drink it' is said of one dainty heroine, who reminds one of the princess who could feel a split pea under a dozen mattresses.

This Temne tale recalls the House that Jack Built:

'Once a boy caught a bird, and his mother ate it. He said: "Mother, give me my bird which I found under the root by the waterfall". His mother gave him some maize instead, but the termites ate it. The boy said: "Termites, give me my maize which my mother gave me in exchange for my bird which she ate which I found under the root by the waterfall". The termites made him an earthen pot instead, but the cataract broke it. The boy said: "Cataract, give me my earthen pot which the termites made me in exchange for the maize which they ate which my mother gave me in exchange for my bird which she ate which I found under the root by the waterfall". The cataract gave him a fish instead, but the hawk swooped down and carried it off. The boy cried: "Hawk, give me my fish which the cataract gave me in exchange for my pot which it broke which the termites made me in exchange for my maize which they ate which my mother gave me in exchange for my bird which she ate which I found under the root by the waterfall". The hawk gave him a feather instead, but the wind took it. The boy cried: "Wind, give me my feather which the hawk gave me in exchange for my fish which he took which the cataract gave me in exchange for my pot which it broke which the termites made me in exchange for my maize which they ate which my mother gave me in exchange for my bird which she ate which I found under the root by the waterfall". The wind shook down some beans for him instead, but a baboon grabbed and ate them. The boy said: "Baboon, give me my country beans which the

wind shook down for me in exchange for my feather which he
took which the hawk gave me in exchange for my fish which
he seized which the cataract gave me in exchange for my pot
which it broke which the termites made for me in exchange
for my maize which they ate which my mother gave me
in exchange for my bird which she ate which I found under
the root by the waterfall ". But the baboon had nothing to give
in exchange for the beans, so the boy put a rope round his neck,
and took him to market and sold him.'

Childhood, however, is short for Nyalui. Even before she
enters Sande she may be betrothed and know her destiny. Her
husband will bring her parents and relatives presents; she will,
perhaps, realize that she must serve his 'big wife'. At 13 or 14,
her parents receive a small piece of tobacco, indicating that the
Sande session is about to commence. She and the other girls of
her age are whitened all over with clay by their parents, dressed
in local cloth dyed in blue patterns with Gara, and go to the
Bundu bush, where women of seniority in the society receive and
instruct them. They are taught weaving, basket-making and
domestic science generally; they are taught the ceremonial
dances suitable for all occasions; they are also taught obedience,
cheerfulness and respect to elders—a respect that must be trans-
ferred to the middle-aged and elderly husbands awaiting their
graduation. Chores are done with a song; the evenings are spent
in dancing. No man must see the girls; cries warn males to turn
aside if any Sande girls move outside the Bundu enclosure.

The Bundu Devil is present at many of the ritual dances, in
some of which hypnotism is employed. The anaesthetizing
powers of hypnotism are also employed to deaden the pain of
the operation performed on the girls—clitorectomy. The origin
of female circumcision is not clearly known. Europeans suppose
that its intention is to reduce sexual desire in women and make
them more faithful to their husbands; if so, in Sierra Leone its
purpose is frustrated by the effects of polygamy. It does, however, symbolize the change from girlhood into womanhood, the
pains of defloration and childbirth, the suffering of a woman's
lot. The drums thunder to drown Nyalui's cries. In exchange
for this agony, she obtains from the Sande women with higher
degrees certain priceless womanly secrets. Indeed, if the Sande
school through which she passes has been modernized, under

145

L

the influence of such African specialists as Dr. Margai (now minister for health and agriculture), she may learn some useful physiological and gynaecological facts, and the operation will be performed under reasonably hygienic conditions.

There can be no question of the power of the Bundu Devil, whom it is said the women first discovered, but failed to keep as a secret, so that it was appropriated by the men and used for the Poro. In the north, where there is no Poro society, the women's society exists: it is necessary. 'An irresponsible child goes into the Bundu', it has been said. 'In a month out comes a woman, modest and well-demeanoured.' The fees for this finishing-school course may be quite high for there are schools and schools, and a girl who has been through a good one can expect a better husband. Families spend a lot of money putting girls through Sande, and the Sande officials do well out of the institution; nor does a western education weaken that feminine insistence upon being perfectly *au fait* which a girl in Sierra Leone only feels if she has her Sande degree. Fashion, everywhere, is inexorable, however painful. Women accept the symbolical values of inconvenience whether it be tight shoes, tight lacing or permanent waving. Nearly all girls, even a few of the Christians, go through Sande; the drums throb in Freetown during the school holidays.

Nyalui emerges from the Bundu bush as Mariama, her skin glistening with oil, dressed in a party frock, bedizened with finery and jewelry—and possibly even wedge-heels—provided by her loving family. A throne awaits her at home, where she sits to be admired. The society puts on dances, where she shows her prowess; the spirits dance under their masks and canopies of leaves and raffia; the chief may ask the newly initiated girls to dance at a funeral—or to honour a visiting Opoto or Pootah (i.e. a Portuguese, or an Englishman). Her childish name is discarded; she is a woman fit for marriage.

Mariama is soon claimed by her husband, the final instalments of the bridewealth are paid, and she goes to his house. If she is his first wife she can look forward to consequence at an early date, when she has 'mates' under her authority in the *pewa*, or woman's house; more likely, she takes her place as second, third or even fourth wife to a much-married man. Until she becomes pregnant she enjoys little consideration—unless she

146

is a great favourite with her husband, and is clever enough to manage his senior wives by means of, or in spite of, this tribute to youth, beauty and personality. As the chief's favourite, she has power. But for most Mariamas, their first child is the great moment in their lives. Ardently they long for children, both for the status their production confers and the insurance which they represent for a possibly widowed and loveless old age. Married to a considerably older man, and sharing his embraces perhaps with several other women, she may not quickly have a child; and when she has one she may easily lose it (and her own life) in childbirth. Even if a Mission hospital lies only twenty bumpy miles away by lorry, she will probably be deterred from going to it by the older women. They know what to do, they say; if there is difficulty, a witch has got her, and must be expelled: beating her belly, or dragging her round the hut till her back is lacerated with cuts, may do the trick. It may; or the hypnotism of the Sande instructress may. If, however, the Bundu operation has scarred her badly, it may go ill with her.

When she has the child, she faces the danger of witches. She will buy spells and charms. For two years, while nursing the child, she must have no sexual relations with her husband; this is prohibited by the Humoi Society. If he has other wives, this will not matter much; if he has not, he may decide to take another. Mariama is willing, for it means help with the baby, company, less weeding, and a contented husband. She will bear children at three-year intervals as long as she can.

Her married life will be supervised by the community. It is public; nothing can be hidden. A severe quarrel with her husband will bring his and her relatives to the house to discuss matters. A noisy altercation with her co-wives may well cause her husband to be hauled before the native court and fined by the chief. He is responsible for her social behaviour, and a bed of nettles she can make his life if need be. Need will be, when she wants a new lappa. She is subordinate to him, and cannot escape her duties, childbearing, cooking, the boiling of palm fruit and parboiling of rice, and weeding, weeding, weeding. But she will know how to spend his money, and how to insist on her marital rights.

If her husband does not appreciate her—well, there is a friend of Borboh's youth, some Lahai, Musa or Vande, waiting till she can slip out to him at night. If her husband cannot, Musa at least can give her the longed-for child. Musa is youth, balm for loneliness and neglect, sympathetic listener for the recital of wrongs and slights. He wants her—he at last is love. There is, in Mende or Temne, but one word for love and lust and mating; but every human tongue can separate the shades of emotion. She is his *mbeta* at first, his sister-in-law, the girl he winks at; then his *baté*, his sweetheart, and in those charged moments when they are alone together he calls her *sewa ka mi*, loved one, and she calls him *han ka mi*, sigh of mine.

> If I beat up cassava leaf
> And mix it with green-green
> And eat my fill of it,
> And then take my drum
> And beat it with a will,
> Ah! then my mind goes back
> And I remember your caresses
> Ah! How sweet it was—
> In that little room—
> Where we first told our love!
> Breathe it to no one!

If Temne can express feeling with such delicacy, it is flexible enough for art, if not for technology.

Mariama can, of course, run away with a man she loves. It will probably cost him a lot of money if he is caught with her, even in another chiefdom. Alternatively, she can visit relations for extended periods, thus making it possible for them to stay with her for comparable periods. One way and another, she will find means of spicing life with variety, however complete may be her subjection to her husband and his big wife.

Between domesticity and the bush farms, the years slip away from Mariama. Her breasts fall; she puts on weight with wisdom. Children come and children die in their terrifyingly sudden and inexplicable way, but if she does not offend the spirits she sees two or three grow to manhood and womanhood. For them she contrives. If money be short, to put the girl through Sande she toils out into the bush and gathers palm fruit, makes more palm oil and cracks kernels till her arms are weary; carries the product of her labour miles to the Syrian to collect the extra shillings. For the boy's education she scrapes, and pinches, and saves, and goes to the Mission people and begs. She will take additional degrees in Sande to widen her influence and acquire friends, if she can afford it. She will set up a little stall in the nearest market and sell whatever the farm will yield—cassava balls, ginger root, groundnut patties. If she has acquired the lore from her own mother, she will gather leaves and make simples, and cry their virtues. The good housewife is always selling something, making something, carrying something.

Widowhood may come to Mariama comparatively early in life, if her husband should be fifteen or twenty years older than she. At his funeral obsequies she must perform some special ceremonies. She may not live with another man, or marry again, until she has been purified and washed of the dead man's hold on her. The water used to wash her dead husband's feet is poured on the ground and made into a mud paste by an old woman who specializes in these matters. She drags the newly made widow about by her hair, smears her with the mud; she is dressed in rags so that her husband will no longer desire her. She must sleep with other women, lest he return to her before he crosses the river. At last she washes the mud from her—the last touch of her husband. She now finds that she is free of him—but may pass to the keeping of his brother. She may marry again, if she is still desirable and can do farm work. Or she may, while remaining part of her male kinsfolk's household, live on her own, by trade, or even by farming on her own, if she inherits claims to bush.

There are many possibilities for her in the work of the societies. There are still palm kernels to be cracked and kola nuts to be picked and peddled. A vegetable garden yields okra, pineapples and sweet potatoes which may be sold. The children come to hear the stories of Bra Spider and Bra Leppet (Leopard). If Mariama is a wise woman she may have skill by now in the divination of dreams: she can advise a man who has dreamed that a dog bit him that a snake will bite him if he goes into the bush, or predict to a man who dreams that his front tooth came out that he will soon lose his father or mother. It will cost him something to be thus forewarned.

Old age brings Mariama respect, but not necessarily any comfort. If she has sons and daughters they will care for her, but despite the complex ties of kinship, if she finds herself without close relations she will probably suffer increasingly from neglect. A woman of personality, a leading Sande official, possibly an official in the Humoi or Njayei societies also, an authority on herbs and genealogy, a repository of family history, a living fund of witty stories and acid comment, will make enough money or elicit enough gifts to provide herself with all the necessities of life, among the most important of which is a niece or great-niece to fetch things for her, to help her with her bath, to do her housework, to provide a target for grumbles and an object to receive her last flushes of affection. She may then attain a ripe old age, and watch a younger generation die, according to the Temne proverb: 'The rice that has flowered has been harvested, leaving the rice that has still to be harvested'. A cracked pitcher lasts long.

But if Mariama has no such claims on the younger generation, and if her close kin have died or gone away, her lot will be hard. Who will mend the thin roof, give a new lappa to replace the one torn beyond repair on a thorn bush, fetch firing, help her rise up when rheumatism weighs her down? What if a cataract films her eyes, or arthritis chains her to the shelf she calls her bed? Invalids do not live long in the little round mud-and-wattle houses with thatched roofs, where there is no light, no sanitation, and no bell. While you can stagger out into the sun, life lasts; when your legs fail, it is best to slip away quickly.

16. MODERN TIMES AND MISSIONARY INFLUENCES

> One takes the elephant for a friend,
> to help one on one's way
> VAI PROVERB

BUT Ansumana, and even Mariama, may break from the traditional cycle of living from season to season—living patiently from brushing to harvest, from the *'ndogboe hinti*, the bush ripe for burning, to the *'mba woma*, the bush worn out with cropping. There are jobs, more and more jobs, in the mines, in the Firms, in trade. There are more and more lorries to be driven and repaired—tractors, too. If Borboh can attend school, then in season Ansumana may attain the dignities of a Government job. His chances of schooling are one in twenty, and Mariama's are less—but they are growing. In even remote villages more and more Mariamas and Fatmattahs toss their heads at the prospect of a lifetime of hoeing and weeding, dream of clerks and mechanics for husbands, and murmur: 'We don't want to marry farmers who earn only by the year'. Their preference in husbands puts the young men on the road to find the jobs that bring in a steady wage, and a wife with it.

The railway drove a wedge of cash-register values through the country, standardizing the customary dues in kind for services rendered in terms of shillings and copper. Along the railway, *individuals* could make money by collecting and selling palm kernels, ginger, kola. The ramifying road system has extended the process of change to remote villages. Up the roads come men and women who live by profit and loss, and snap their fingers at authority. Up the roads come hints of a wider, more expansive life. Why should Mariama put up with a neglectful husband, or submit to the tyranny of his Big Wife? Why should Ansumana submit to the chief's fines? The road beckons.

It was always possible for a few to change their allegiance. A man could join the army, and perhaps after his service return to his village in Court Messenger's uniform, a man of authority with a pension ahead of him. Now that the army offers technical training, men of the tribes present themselves at the recruiting centre at Daru as if it were a college. Or a boy could go to a Mission school—ruling families, of course, often sent children to school in Freetown. Education meant then, as it means now, a break with tribal life. The teaching and medicine offered by the Missions were intended to bring children under Christian influences. The convert had the chance of a Government clerkship, ordination, or a teacher's post under Mission patronage. These were considerable inducements—and, besides, they did not prevent the taking of degrees in Poro. The educated tribal lad became to some extent a creole—perhaps married into a creole family.

Education was the frontier between the old tribal and new westernized, creolized life, which brought to him who crossed it new associates, new ideas, new clothes, new personal ambitions. As a Christian he was to have but one wife; as a clerk he could probably only afford one. As a Christian he was to consider himself freed from the web of witchcraft. His brave new world was a divinely organized system of causes and effects, not an anarchy of spiritual thrones and powers. To the extent that he could live up to his belief, the Mission boy was Europeanized. He was in transition: a creole.

With the farmers the Missions, though they laboured and still labour earnestly, had less success. The missionaries encouraged plantations and experimented with new crops, but they did not succeed in changing the basis of farming. They exhorted the Christian to confine himself to one wife, but did not explain how his weeding was to get done. Individual farming and cash payment for labour increased the advantage of extra wives, while families felt that in sending a girl to the chief's compound they were ensuring some pull with the all-powerful white government. The Missions explained the meaning of Christian fellowship; but as an insurance policy it looked flimsier than the system of family alliances and social obligations under existing native law, which Government upheld. 'I am a Christian. I am prominent in our local Church circles', an African trader told me with pride, but added sadly, in reply to a later question: 'Oh, yes, I have three wives. You see, it is a matter of poor relations. In Africa we have so many temptations'.

So presumably he sinned—but he fed 39 mouths from his little shop and vegetable garden.

What strength Christianity had in the Protectorate derived from the fact that it was the religion mainly of the middle and governing classes in the larger towns; of those who had thrown in their lot with the white English and the creole English. Today, education, though still very largely in mission hands, comes also directly from a secular Government. It is now possible to imbibe western thought and influences without being Christianized, let alone converted. The Missions still struggle with the problem of getting their message to the farmers. Social change is now working in their favour; women are more independent, and polygamy, except among the chiefs and very wealthy, is now tending to decline. The transition to cash crops, especially plantation crops, and away from upland rice farming might help. Co-operation, missionaries think, would help more, by enabling family groups to do each other's weeding and other women's traditional tasks without the need for polygamy.

Missionaries say that the old customs are crumbling. The sanctions of the Humoi Society, for example, are much less powerful; not only are the once innumerable minor restrictions relaxed, but the forbidden degrees are increasingly trespassed upon. The authority of heads of households is weaker; nor can the chief impose his will, or fine offenders hauled before the court, as he used to do. The young men work on their own, or leave to find work at a regular wage. Girls who quarrel with their husbands run away, and contract another marriage else-where, or live even less morally but quite prosperously. Those that remain still take lovers, but the lovers can no longer be so usefully forced to labour on the husband's farm. So unsatis-factory is the modern girl that her parents fear to accept her bride price, lest they have to pay it back at an inconvenient moment. Money is everywhere a solvent, loosening all ties and weakening all obligations. A woman is free to run away—but she may find it harder, too, to find anyone to look after her in her old age.

The old beliefs are weakening also. Witchcraft remains a basic article of faith, but the balanced system of ancestor-wor-ship, the lore that lies behind it, the stories that spring from it,

the art that vivified it, are losing their hold. It is necessary t
talk with the elderly to gain any real understanding of it. 'Ou
medicines are not as strong as they were', they say wistfully, a
the mammy-lorries rattle down the village street bearing thei
trading names—'In God We Trust'—'Why Worry'—or, 'Tak
It Easy'. Poro and Sande remain, with most of the other secre
societies, but in some places initiation of boys is performed in
couple of days, of girls in a week.

The Missions hope that Christianity will fill the void create
by the disintegrating effect of western ways. Missionaries, a
least the informed and thoughtful among them, perfectly realiz
the strength of the society that is now beginning to break up
They cannot deny that the general increase in 'immorality' i
the result of the changes caused by the western impact. The
see that while many of the reassuring features of the old belie:
are disappearing, the fear of witchcraft, of bad medicine, a
well as of petty malice and tyranny, of extortion and endles
bribery, remains; possibly grows stronger. Christianity *shoul*
cast out such fears, *should* reform such abuses: therefore th
missionary hopes that the African will turn to it. Many missior
aries feel that Poro and Sande must stay, as institutions necessar
to give Africans a sense of allegiance and kinship during th
period when the other ties break down, and until Christia
fellowship becomes a reality.

Most Missions exert their influence through doctoring, edu
cation, personal example and the general prestige of Europea
values and technology. Some missionaries feel that Christianit
and western technology should be presented to the African a
different things, and that certainly Christianity must dissociat
itself from modern western materialism. However that may be
the Mission with its schools and European teachers still ofte
lies on the road towards the technical training or technic
education which more and more young Africans crave. Missior
located deep in the bush nowadays take an extremely practic
line. At Serabu, which was started by the Fathers of the Hol
Cross in 1906, sand is recovered from the bed of a river som
miles from the town, and the Mission buildings, which include
clinic, hospital, schools and church, are constructed of concret
blocks. In view of the steady exhaustion of good timber, Missior
are pioneering new building methods, persuading the people t

make mud block buildings, for example. Most have their carpentry and woodworking shops. Some set an example in mixed farming, demonstrating the proper conditions for keeping cows, pigs and Rhode Island poultry. Many missionaries teach with their lives as well as with their textbooks and examination successes.

In the effort to expand education rapidly in recent years, the Government has leant heavily on the Missions; indeed, there are signs that natives prefer Mission schools to Government schools —perhaps less because of the religious instruction given than because of the well-qualified white teachers which Mission schools possess, and which only a few Government secondary schools, paying secular salaries, can afford. Yet in Government, and especially in European business circles, a good deal of criticism of the Missions is to be heard. They are supposed to 'spoil' the African mentality, to set Borboh and Mariama on the wrong track. They are accused of not realizing that their conversions are mere sycophancy, that the Christianity they spread goes hardly skin-deep, and is certainly no substitute for the old beliefs; that, if anything, they send out a semi-educated product which is far crookeder than the illiterate 'bush native'. I was told that Islam is in any case far more suited to the African mentality than Christianity. It was hinted that some missionaries were not very good influences, or very efficient teachers.

I found no missionaries in Sierra Leone who were under any illusions as to the difficulty of their central task of making Christians, although I was assured that they were being overcome. In the first generation of converts backsliding is expected, and St. Paul's epistle to the Thessalonians has a literal application; it is the second generation, the development of children in Christian homes, in which some deeper rooting of Christian doctrine is expected. It is less rare than it was to see an indignant Christian mammy chase an affrighted mendicant 'devil' down the village street with blows from brush and tongue.

It is, however, instructive to consider the divisions of Christendom as they are reproduced in miniature in Sierra Leone. The missionaries, in fact, much prefer the native ethic and the seclusion of bush life that is passing away, the time when the chief possessed authority and obligation was understood as a word and respected as a reality. They criticize the changes effected by the materialism of the modern state and of modern business—yet without the wealth these bring, unrelieved poverty and ignorance would make their task impossible. District Commissioners still feel that they are the guardians of the people's rights against exploitation and interference, religious or commercial, yet Government control and the *pax Britannica* constitute the largest interference with tribal life that can be imagined. And what the point of such interference is, if not to promote wealth through commerce or better agriculture, and happiness through spiritual advance, the official would be hard put to say. The commercial man quarrels with the sentimentality of the missionary, and demands technical education and sound secular administration from the Government, but he never ceases to complain of dishonesty in his workers and is the first to squeal if a materialistic younger generation demands that he should be more severely taxed, or whispers the word 'nationalization'. Yet all of these, in their several and legitimate ways, represent the civilization with which Britain desires to endow West Africa.

Islam is extending its influence. Its leaders speak with quiet confidence of its progress southwards. It offers some solutions which are forbidden to Christianity. It permits plurality of wives. Its teaching on the restraint and chastity of women falls upon grateful ears of polygamists who, if they cannot secure 'woman damage', at least wish to curb the favours distributed gratis by their wives. Islam teaches a practical sort of fellowship, understandable by those who have been initiated in Poro. On the floor of the mosque, it observes a simple democracy which appeals to African susceptibilities. Above all, the Muslim missionary is an African, often a trader, who, after he has discussed business and eaten with his customers and friends in the African style, discourses eloquently on the Faith, its modernity, simplicity, practicality and holiness. From the foundation of the 'Christian Institution' (later Fourah Bay College) in 1827, the Church Missionary Society has sought to build a purely African ministry to carry the Gospels from the free settlement of Sierra Leone into the interior. And indeed it has trained, in over 100 years, some fine men who have done just that. But its work today is less impressive than the steady advance of Islam through its informal teachers; somehow the African pastor brings with him

a religion of the white man, a religion against which racial prejudice works in proportion as it assists the Muslim proselytizer.
It is uphill work, which may explain the view in some Church
circles that the African Ministry of the Church of England has
failed to develop the zeal and recruit the numbers which the
Christianizing of Africans by Africans requires.

Influenced by Somerset Maugham, and perhaps by my lay
readings in general anthropology, I went to Sierra Leone prepared to disapprove of missionaries and their influence. I
stayed to admire them. But for their work and personal devotion, the people of the Protectorate would have received an
impression of a purely administrative and commercial—a neo-
Roman—Empire. Thanks to them, Africans can hardly separate the idea of education for self-development or self-government
from the idea of Christianity, nor western medicine from the
devotion of Christian doctors; and most of what is known of
African language and culture and society has been rescued and
recorded by missionary interest in the African concept of God-
head and revelation. If the visitor wants to get to know the
people of Sierra Leone it will not be long before he gratefully
accepts Mission hospitality. Of course missionaries vary in
quality, like officials. One Mission does nothing but preach, at
fixed times in the day, salvation by the Book and hell-fire for the
rest—and a horrid thorn in his flesh the local D.C. finds it. Some
Missions' appurtenances are almost more an advertisement for
American technological prowess than for an apostolate first
founded in poverty. While I was at Bonthe, a 'Mission', consisting
of two apparently quite untrained, if undenominational, enthusiasts in a motor boat, dropped anchor.

But when I think of the pride of the people of Serabu in 'our
Mission', the 350 children attending school, the cool groves of
citrus and rubber, the neat houses and gardens, the indefati-
gable interest of the Fathers in wells, sanitation, girder construction, sulpha drugs, co-operative farming, the teaching of
civics and political economy in schools, dancing and the un-
questioned virtues of Large Whites; when I think of Bunumbu,
where Church and Dissent have come together under the bunui
trees in a common effort to train Africans to teach their fellows
and shape for their use the tools of western thought; when I
think of the schools and hospitals of the Methodist Mission at

Segbwema, and the apparently inexhaustible store of knowled
of Mende life and tradition which flows from the Rev. T. Harr
when I recall that American Christianity supports nearly ha
the mission schools in the country; then I know which side
am on in this argument. It may not be the winning side. It m
be, as Christian ladies and gentlemen assured me in Freetow
that Islam is 'more suitable' for the African. But there's som
thing about the morale of the troops in the front line that g
to the heart.

Protectorate people are now reacting against creole cultu
which may be an added drawback for the Missions, since cre
culture is Christian. *Malgré lui*, the tribal African becom
creolized; he takes to western dress and ideas, he becomes a
ministrative and political in outlook, he wants furniture in l
house, cigarettes, gadgets. He insists that he is African, b
whether he likes it or not, he loses contact with tribal cultu
Only—he is now in better shape to get the jobs in the Prot
torate which Colony-born creoles once monopolized: teache
posts, clerkships, and Government positions, as well as the jo
of running the new native administrations. Mende and Tem
girls take still more readily to creole dress and creole indepe
dence, to the comfort of a house with a tin roof and a pip
water supply. Missionaries have told me that they take read
to Christian monogamy also. There are cases of girls refusi
to marry the man who courted them by presents to their pare
while they were at school and claimed them when they ca
out of Sande—and of continuing to refuse after sound thrashir
and every imaginable family pressure. I heard of an incide
during a discussion at Fourah Bay on British family life, whe
Mende girl student cried out: 'Don't you realize how fright
it is for *us* to hear you talk of love and these things when
know we must go back to our families and be married to so
filthy old man we hate?'

Ansumana wants a job; Mariama wants to marry a man wi
a job; both want the knowledge, training, capability a
diplomas to entitle them to employment. The Government, t
Mines, the Railway, the Firms, the teaching, medical a
nursing professions, all want skilled personnel; the Agricultu
Department wants the farmers to learn to change their tin
honoured ways, and the D.C.s are trying to educate a generati

of ratepayers and local government voters and officers. The missions are earnestly endeavouring to supply everyone with a bit of everything. But it isn't easy. The educated do not return to the farms; children returning from school are still often mocked as 'white men' by a jealous elder generation. The school which Chief A, by threats and cozenings, filled with children stands half empty under his successor, Chief B. There is jealousy of the creoles; intrigue by the creoles who feel their position undermined. 'Paddle here, paddle there, the canoe stays still', runs the proverb. In fact the canoe is moving fast; but do the rowers propel it, or is it in the grip of rising winds and racing tides?

'Bundu' girls dancing. These are the girl novices of the 'Sande' (pronounced 'Sanday') women's secret society.

17. ART—AND ARTS AND CRAFTS

An orange never bears a lime
TEMNE PROVERB

I HAVE been told that a chapter on art in Sierra Leone would be as short as a chapter on snakes in Ireland. Certainly when a culture breaks up, and especially when a more primitive culture is submerged by a less primitive one, the inspiration often goes out of art. 'Art?', said a paramount chief when I asked him, 'I'm afraid there isn't any now. There's no market, so there's nothing for an artist to live on.' I assured him that Sierra Leone in this development was ahead—but only a little —of England.

When art is intimately bound up with the religious life of a people it suffers in proportion as that religion sickens. Sierra Leonian visual art—especially Mende—finds its most typical expression in the mask worn by those who impersonate devils at festivals. Commonest is the Bundu mask, worn on the head of the 'Nome', the second-degree official of the Sande. These masks are made from cotton-tree wood and resemble a Greek helmet in shape; the mask fits over the head and eye-slits are cut to enable the wearer to see through it. Some are exquisitely carved (with knife only) with intricate arrangements of the hair, and decorations which embody fertility and motherhood motives—mice, snakes, ferns, lizards and so forth. A mask actually used is sanctified and concealed when not used.

African masks are abstract expressions of the features and corporeal embodiment of spirit-deities. These spirits and their activities were needed to explain the many otherwise inexplicable occurrences of nature and human life. Most Mende masks confirm man's belief that he is made after a simian image of God; but with differences. A supernatural face is a face, but not a human one, or even a burlesque of a human one; deity must possess a countenance to out-face his worshippers with. Some masks, or perhaps I should say some devil-dresses, are provided with amalgamations of animal features. They are remarkable in themselves, but live with an eerie animation when they move with the special movements ascribed to the particular devil.

They have a specifically non-human mode of progression, with a zig-zag movement, sudden sideways leaps, and a gait which suggests sometimes one leg, sometimes three.

Carving for aesthetic pleasure, apart from religious significance, is rare, nor is decorative carving a part of the Sierra Leonian architectural tradition. Animals carved in wood, and well observed, are sometimes to be found, and occasionally elaborate pieces such as the representation of a chief, or a white man, being carried in a hammock. Staffs for chiefs, or chiefdom officials, are sometimes beautifully carved with the Hippocratic emblem, and in addition to the snake, near the knob, often carved as a lizard's head, there is sometimes an imprisoned, free-moving ball in the shaft. Carved wooden bowls and spoons are decorated by burned designs; carved figures of men and women, which may be mistaken for dolls but have ritual significance, do exist but seem to be rare: there are several in Bo school museum. The carver's art has naturally found an outlet in the provision of a worthy casket for a powerful medicine: designs of fishes and birds are used. Small soapstone figures of men and animals called Nomoli, which are found only in Sierra Leone, are not the artistic productions of any existing tribe, though they are greatly valued as bringers of good luck and fertility; at the time of planting rice they are whipped to make them 'work'. They are, apparently, the handiwork of an earlier bush culture and are found in the gravel of rivers or in the bush. They have, however, been convincingly counterfeited by Mende craftsmen for European collectors.

Painting is not an indigenous art; and although some domestic decoration is to be found, it is unusual. Representational drawings on the mud walls of houses are crude. A tradition could not evolve because nothing could be preserved against the erosion of rain, wind and 'bug-bug'. Neither in Temne nor Mende are there words to express any range of colouring. There are words for black and white (meaning clean). Black includes dark blue and dark green. Red includes yellow, scarlet and brown. Green is simply the word for ripe. And that is all. Africans have no idea what a white man sees when he gazes at a sunset.

Drawing-paper and modern pigments are now being introduced to African students and children. The results are not

161

M

impressive, but their fascination with painting and colours m
be. It is interesting to see the attempts of teachers in rem
primary schools with paintbox and paper to visualize for th
pupils trains, ships, or simply crowds of people in the streets
Freetown. The art critic, comparing the inspiration of t
Bundu mask with these poor little daubs, would perhaps fi
here the most horrifying examples of the destructiveness of
alien culture. But painting and drawing are means to a n
form of observation of nature which is alien to the African, l
which he must acquire if his ambitions are ever to be fulfill
The culture which inspired the spiritual perception of t
Bundu mask did not enable the African to realize, for examp
that the caterpillar and the butterfly were one insect.

Native pottery is not shaped on the wheel, for the wheel w
unknown until the Europeans came. Cloth is woven only
narrow strips, which must be sewn together to make up bla
kets or garments of any size. The loom consists simply of t
shafts, or heddles, carrying oil-palm fibre pedals suspended fr
the roof of the hut or the apex of a tripod of sticks, with t
foot-pedals to give the up-and-down motion. The tension in
warp is provided by drawing it tight between two fixed points
the opposite ends of the building or verandah, and as the we
ing proceeds and the cloth develops, the tripod suspending
healds is moved forward. When the weaver has completed
length of the verandah the cloth is tied up in a roll at one e
and more warp is released from the ball at the other end
continue the process. The shuttle is passed from hand to ha
through the shed made in the warp by the up-and-down acti
of the healds. Most cloth is therefore one up-and-down pla
weave. Some simply patterned cloth, in designs of great char
is produced, but most of it is striped. Cloth or thread is dy
with camwood or gara, excellent fast vegetable dyes, the secr
of their preparation and application being passed down fr
mother to daughter. Dyed patterns are produced by systems
tying the cloth in knots, or in loops by bits of palm-fibre stri
so that white areas of varying size and shape, but regula
distributed, are left in the blue ground.

The import of fabrics and a dearth of home-grown cotton h
reduced the production of 'country cloths', which are still
demand for 'bush gowns', worn when entering thorny places

cut down the bush, and for ceremonial purposes. Prices have accordingly risen; even so, there are fewer weavers than formerly.

If the peoples of Sierra Leone produce less impressive art than other territories in Africa, it is with reason. The rain forests of the west coast are out of the main stream of migration and of cultural influences coming south from the Nile Valley. They were, on the contrary, refuges for survivors, refuges whose very fastness imposed limitations on life. Cattle could not be kept, ploughing was impossible, wheeled vehicles useless. Man could barely survive in the struggle to wrest a living from fecund, overmastering nature, and to defend his living from the rapacity of other men.

Incentive to build to last, or to store possessions, was lacking. The only demand upon the craftsman was for tools, utensils, palisades and boats—and for the choreography of dances to invoke the spirit-deities, masks, costumes and musical instruments. Art was utilitarian, limited: intimately related to the needs of the whole people—one into which the community could enter. It was based not on the observance and representation of nature (like the Greek) but upon an intuition of the threshold-world inhabited by mankind, half in nature, half in the spirit land—an intuition that nature itself was the outward manifestation of a communion of spirits: of dominions, potentates and powers which could only be controlled by sympathetic magic.

The dance is therefore the principal medium of folk art; it is one which European influences are least likely to affect. There are dances for every occasion, and for every age and both sexes. There is every variety of drum to dance to. There is the rhythm of the rattles—stones in a calabash—the clap of hands, and in the north the Korankos have their typical xylophone, the *balangi*. In Sierra Leone the variety of tribes is matched by the variety of dances. In one short evening's entertainment I witnessed a dozen. The dance of happiness, the *buyan*, was a sort of adagio danced by two teen-age girls dressed in what looked like white jodhpurs, knitted vests and white hats, making play with red kerchiefs. The *kabadia*, danced by a small girl in blue, seemed to owe something to the effect of yaws; the step was a complex one danced mainly on the outside edge of the feet, the knees bowed. The *Ferenke* was danced by two young boys, heel and toe, waving black scarves; applause was shown by spectators rushing into the ring and throwing the boy lightly over the shoulder and gently returning him to the ground. The sword dance, or warriors' play dance, was perhaps derivative, but the lightning evolutions of the sword, thrown up in the air from time to time and caught by the hilt and by the blade, were sufficiently impressive. *Tongojama* was a devil dance; a humorous devil, who teased and wooed the audience. The Fula dances were different, more acrobatic and comic; sometimes the dancers danced while continuously blowing a whistle; sometimes they performed athletic feats on the roof and portico of the chief's compound where the performance was being staged.

Dancing and singing go together. At big festivals, whether such Muslim fêtes as Eid-ul-Fitri, the termination of Poro or Sande, or funerals of chiefs, the whole village community dances together, led by their leaders, drums and soloists. While tribal life survives this art will exert its power. And even when tribal life disintegrates it may live on, the symbol, at least, of Africa's particular form of consciousness. You see Zulus practising their ancient war-dances on vacant lots in Johannesburg. In the dance, Africa holds to the past, to man's forgotten hundred-thousand years; perhaps Africa will hold it to some purpose for the future, even for the febrile, cerebral men and women of the West.

18. THE WHITE MAN'S GRAVE

If you catch yaws,
it will sharpen your wits
MENDE PROVERB

THE common people of Sierra Leone, the people who have
to cut the bush, plant and weed the rice, bring in the harvest,
and carry the loads; the people who have to be out in the sun,
be drenched by the rain, be muddied up in the swamps—these
people firmly believe that to conserve one's health one should
expose oneself to such exertions and weather as little as possible.
They think that hard work makes you ill. They admire and
respect the superior European and office-worker for his ability
to achieve a livelihood which involves no real work at all. The
office-worker, European or African, does not take quite this view
of the situation as it is represented to be, out of doors or indoors.
There is a limit to what you can do, even under a fan, when the
temperature is 80 degrees and the humidity is 75. Not everybody, indeed, thinks it advisable or incumbent to work up to
that limit.

Between 1814 and 1885, five Governors and seven acting
Governors died at their posts or on the ship home. The country
had a sinister reputation. Rankin, in 1847, called his Sierra
Leone travelogue *The White Man's Grave*. Lethbridge Banbury
used the phrase as the sub-title of his book in 1889, and recorded
the heavy pleasantries which attended his departure: 'One kind
friend, more facetious than the rest, observed that, inasmuch as
I was bound for such a deadly place, it would only be judicious
to include a coffin in my equipment, since it might come in
handy at an early date'. It needs but a wood-engraving and an
italicized stage direction—*Total Collapse of Intending Empire
Builder*—to be good enough for *Punch* of that date.

Yet all travellers to Sierra Leone have denied its unhealthi-
ness. Mrs. Fauconbridge, who visited the mismanaged settlement in the first years of its struggles, records that: 'It is quite
customary of a morning to ask "How many died last night?"';
but after a harrowing account of the colonists without huts or
bedsteads, wanting almost every comfort of life and exposed to

165

putrid stenches produced by stinking provisions, she ask
'Would you, under such circumstances, expect to keep y
health or even live a month in the healthiest part of the worl
She kept very fit herself, and recorded, in the most casual m
ner, the demise of her husband, the Sierra Leone Company's ag

Rankin, in fact, produced figures to prove that the Col
was actually healthy, though he did not deny the prevalenc
fever and commended a medical project for sterilizing
putrid miasmata, which were thought to be the cause of mala
by discharges of carbonic acid gas from lime-kilns erected in
mangrove swamps. Bishop Ingham, in 1894, breezily obser
that the climate was carried about in a black bottle, and c
lined an abstemious regimen which would keep a missionar
occasionally below par, none the less in sufficient health to
'excellent work' in implanting 'peace and happiness, truth a
righteousness, religion and piety'.

Freetown never experienced the cholera outbreaks wh
frightened London. But malaria was endemic and undermi
Victorian constitutions, however hardened. Woollen und
clothing and flannel next the skin failed to stop the chills on
liver which led to dysentery. Recurrent epidemics of yel
fever killed Europeans in scores. In the first 25 years of missi
ary operations, the C.M.S. lost 109 missionaries. In Janu
1859 a party of six Catholic Fathers arrived; by June all w
dead. As late as the 'nineties, every European who died
given a slap-up military funeral; as the band began to play,
creole children came running with the cry: 'Soldiers! soldi
White man dead!'

In these circumstances the creoles created a qualified med
profession. Africans studied in London and Edinburgh and w
appointed medical officers to the Government. It was, howe
Florence Nightingale and Sir Ronald Ross who dispelled
country's reputation; the establishment of the Board of Hea
in 1867 arose out of Florence Nightingale's pioneer work
sanitation, and it was Ross who discovered that mosquit
not miasmata, transmitted malaria. He visited Freetown
condemned the way in which stagnant water lay abou
puddles, old calabashes and other receptacles. His was
recommendation that, in the interests of more vigorous admi
tration by healthy colonial servants, the colonial officials sho

be moved up to a new residential quarter in the hills, Hill
Station. In a dispatch to the Colonial Office urging its construction and a railway to link it with Freetown, Sir Charles
King-Harmon reported that he was 'impressed with the fact
that the sinister reputation which attaches to Sierra Leone,
which is impeding its advancement and causing it to be regarded as a blot on the Empire instead of the Bright Jewel of the
Crown for which its material wealth and capabilities befit it,
can be wholly removed' by the adoption of the Hill Station and
mountain railway project. So Hill Station was built, and the
officials began to move up; and in 1902 the creole doctors (who
stayed down, with their patients) were relegated to inferior
positions in the new West African medical service. This measure
also provided a prophylactic against the appointment of an
African doctor as Governor—as had happened when the
Governorship passed in 1847 to Fergusson, a creole who, in the
words of a traveller of the time, 'said and did everything
without vanity and pride . . . the manly bearing, inseparable
from and belonging to those only who have followed for years
the military profession, gave to his whole appearance the stamp
of a superior man'. There were, however, no Hill Stations in the
Protectorate (except, perhaps, Kabala): notwithstanding, the
District Commissioners, with the aid of quinine and chlorodine,
carried on creditably.

The great majority of Africans remained untouched by the
scientific medicine and sanitation which have made Sierra
Leone a healthy climate for Europeans. Outside Freetown, the
majority is still untouched by them. The state of native medicine remains much as it was described by Dr. Winterbottom in
1803: 'The practice of medicine and the art of making gree
grees and fetiches, in other words amulets, to resist the effects of
witchcraft or the malicious attempts of evil spirits, is generally
the province of the same person. . . . The powers of witchcraft
continually excite the apprehension of the natives and frequently destroy their peace of mind'. Africans make a clearer
distinction, however, between physiological and magical medicine than Dr. Winterbottom gave them credit for. Skill in
medicine runs in families or in secret societies: it includes a lore
as ancient, and perhaps not less efficacious, than that contained
in the old Saxon herbals. In Sierra Leone, to become a medicine

167

man is, literally, 'to go and learn the leaves'; and it is
pity that so far no qualified African doctor has taken his lice
tiate in the bush and recorded from expert knowledge the nati
pharmacopoeia. The virtues of every plant in the bush a
known, and the skill of some witch doctors in healing sk
diseases, for example, cannot be denied.

Considerable reliance is placed by the native medic
faculty—as in England in Dr. Winterbottom's day—in purge
the African, Europeans find, is profoundly interested in 1
bowels. It is not only necessary that they should move, but th
they should move adequately, and the right number of times
day. If a man feels ill, his first instinct is to open his bowels. It
not uncommon for a mother to bring her baby to hospital ar
complain that his bowels don't open enough; on one occasio
a doctor told me, he asked a mother how many times her bal
had opened its bowels that day. The reply was three times. T
surprised doctor asked her how many times she thought w
necessary. Six, was the answer. Some herbal remedies are goe
enough purges taken in the proper dose; but a worried Africa
is liable to take dose after dose when nothing happens, and er
by killing himself.

Whatever virtues the leaves possess, many of the practitione
are quacks, charging high fees to kill or maim the patient. Th
will put lime juice and red pepper in the eye of a patient suffe
ing from mild conjunctivitis, and get a man's friends to stamp o
his strangulated hernia. The midwives are as ignorant: t
Reverend Mother in charge of the lying-in ward at Seral
clinic told me how, when she was dealing with a difficult birt
the patient's female relatives marched smiling into the labo
room armed with heavy sticks to help deliver the child, ar
were flabbergasted when all the response they got to their offe
of expert assistance was to be bundled out of the door.

Inevitably the witch doctor leans heavily on psychologic
medicine, well knowing that dread of witchcraft, as Dr. Winte
bottom observed, 'may properly be considered as a ment
disease'. Physical symptoms are the result of spirits. There a
authenticated tales of the apparent power of witch docto
over organic ailments: a man with pneumonia confessed th
he had injured his dead brother; the doctor prescribed a visit
the dead man's grave, confession, sacrifices and an appeal f

168

Bringing rice and fish and palm oil to Freetown, the 'Bullom boats' are the same as the Portuguese taught the Africans to build in 1500. From the boats trade surges up the slave steps into the city . . .

The Deserted Village: its garden overgrown, the mission is closed. The people
are scattered, the land decays

The shores of the Colony: tropic greenery pressing down on beach after beach of silver sand. Two views from Kent

One of the most select holiday resorts in the world: Shenge, now noted for its fishery, where pirates once lived in splendour and mingled English blood in the genealogies of African kings

Bonthe, dreaming under breadfruit and mango trees of a Victorian past in which African traders chartered steamers from all over the world

'Ta Rokane', gathering-in month: the women winnow the new-harvested rice

The women's trade—boiling the oil palm fruit in cauldrons, expressing the pericarp oil and separating kernels for sale. . . . And the smith's trade—shaping the hoe from old iron in a charcoal fire blown by foot bellows

Ricelands to be: cutting down the mangroves

forgiveness. He recovered in a week. But in general the power of native medicine is to induce or remove hysterical symptoms. A man was blind although his eyes were undamaged: he had dreamed that his dead father had come to him and thrust a nail through his eyes as a punishment for neglecting to give him a proper 'crossing the river' ceremony. If a man knows a medicine has been put on him, he usually sickens. The whole atmosphere of Sierra Leone is impregnated with swear and counter-swear, with witchcraft and antidote. Europeans are not considered wholly immune. Rankin records the death of a Governor after a swear had been put on him from the gallows. I was told of a certain D.C. some years ago who arrested a man for forgery and put him in prison. Next day, to the affright of the onlookers, he had vanished from his cell and was found coolly sitting in the barri to be tried. The D.C., however, soon found that a terrorized Court Messenger had merely unlocked the door of the cell in the night, a circumstance that made the Briton not only send the man to gaol, but, which was worse, scarify him with his tongue in public. 'You will regret this,' yelled the enraged sorcerer-counterfeiter; 'you will *feel my weight.*' Africans shook their heads when, some time after, the D.C. was invalided home. In Africa *post hoc* is invariably *propter hoc*, a reflection which may have comforted the other D.C. who, some years ago, completely lost his temper with a prevaricating and perjured witness in Court, and shouted: 'I've had enough of you. I've a jolly good mind to put a big medicine on you, you rotter. Now get out'. The man died three weeks later.

These things are said to be dying out. But a doctor told me that a few months previously he had examined a woman, the wife of a chief, brought into hospital secretly by friends. There was nothing organically wrong with her, but she seemed half paralysed, muscularly uncoordinated and mentally apathetic. He was told that she had committed adultery, and the chief, being unusually jealous, had put a juju on her to kill her. ('*You medicine, hold her hands, hold her feet, hold her heart, hold her intestines, hold her sleeping place, let her die quickly . . .*') The doctor got to work on her, and told her that he would save her as his medicine was far stronger—in fact, he gave her a standard tonic. He talked to her and persuaded her that her own mind, with his aid, could drive back the shadow creeping across her life.

She began to get better. Then one day he heard that the chief was trying to visit her in hospital. He asked the woman if she wished to see him. She begged to be left alone in hospital; the doctor therefore gave strict orders that the chief was to be refused admittance. Soon after, doing his rounds of the wards, he found a huge crowd round the woman's bed, with the chief, her husband, at her side. He ordered the nurses, Africans, to throw the visitors out. They shrank back. They knew what was afoot. As the chief departed with dignity he told the doctor contemptuously that the woman was going to die; and that he wanted her to die in her own home. In spite of all the doctor could do, he found that he could not keep his patient; she was discharged and died soon after.

'So many things happen in this country', the very nurses in the hospitals say; they are more fearful of medicine than of hospital discipline, which in any case is powerless to prevent their charging patients 1d. for the use of the bedpan. It is one thing to build hospitals, as the Government and the Missions are doing as fast as roads are constructed to give access to them (a hospital served by bush paths stays empty); it is another thing to engender confidence in western medicine. 'Hospital?' said a witch doctor to a missionary not long ago—'Who do you think sends the people to your hospital? I do. Otherwise they would not go.' Every doctor has cases of patients demanding to be discharged because they are sure that their typhoid is caused by a witch possessing them, and they want the witch 'pulled' in the bush. But there are cases on the other side too; like the man who had a strong medicine put on him by a rival to make his arm wither in a week. When the week was over he bashed his rival's face with the 'withered' arm—and was not taken to court in the matter.

The people gain confidence in certain cures and certain medicines rather than in the hospital as a whole, in remoter districts. Castor oil and aspirin are in keen demand; but above all the African puts his faith in injections. He may even decline to discuss his symptoms with the doctor, reiterating: 'I want injection'. Hospital is now recognized as a better resort for hernia cases than the bush doctor—besides being a great deal cheaper. All kinds of ulcers, tumours and goitres, though traditionally the sign of 'bad medicine', are brought to hospital; perhaps the most extraordinary cases being those of elephantiasis, the result of an infection with filarial worms, which block the lymph vessels and produce outsize swellings, especially in the external organs, the breasts or testicles. A scrotum weighing 106 lb. has been successfully amputated in a Freetown hospital. Such cases are fairly common; in more than one hospital I saw several sick-eyed patients awaiting release from these outrageous burdens. Leprosy is common enough, too; European children running about on bare feet have occasionally been known to develop it years later. Cow-dung floors, in particular, harbour jiggers and tetanus.

The hookworm hatches in damp ground and waits patiently for a bare human foot to tread on it. It then bores into a vein and gets carried by the blood stream to the heart, whence it is pumped to the trachea, finds its way into the oesophagus, descends to the stomach and gut, and there gets a grip on the lining, and sucks blood in enormous quantities. The female lays eggs in the gut, and these are excreted; where they fall they hatch and duly take up their position to find their host. Nearly all Sierra Leonians share their blood with a large population of worms. They develop a degree of tolerance: the worms apparently realize that something must be left over for the human being to keep alive on. But people with insufficient blood tire easily, long for their hammocks, are averse to undertakings involving much labour—however lucidly the Agricultural Officer explains the advantages.

Up the rivers live certain water snails. They harbour a worm which floats down the current looking for a human being. It enters the body and produces the condition known as bilharzia. It drains the body of energy; intermittent fever, continual sense of being out of sorts, periods of utter lethargy, are among the symptoms.

A man gets an ulcer; ulcers are very common when you have to cut thorny bush to make your farm. It heals; they mostly do. Then little red and yellow bumps appear all over the body—by then the subject knows what he is in for. He is the victim of cut-nose medicine. He hurries off to the nearest medicine man to buy an antidote and arrange sacrifices to the offended ancestors. He also scours his body and breaks off the nodules, leaving raw patches. However, this treatment rarely does any good. Before long he has searing pains in his joints. The skin on the soles of his feet hardens and cracks. They become agony to walk on. A man who has yaws badly walks with bowed legs, so as to bring only the outside edges of his feet into contact with the ground. He walks with extreme care, thinking out every step in advance —every step that he must make during the day, for every step means pain. 'If you catch yaws, it will sharpen your wits.' Yaws is a spirochete, but it is not venereal. It is acquired by contact with an infected surface. About 12 per cent of the people of the north are thought to have yaws. Nobody with yaws wants to do much. People with yaws like to put their feet up.

The tsetse fly is endemic over most of Sierra Leone. It does not like the dark, as the mosquito does, and is inactive at night. But it likes shade, and it waits in the bush till a human being comes within range of a hundred yards or so, and then attacks with the speed of a dive bomber. Tsetse can be found waiting for people on the shady side of the road. The odds are that once in 2,000 bites the victim will have the sleeping-sickness parasite injected into his blood stream. He will then gradually feel more and more unwell, with indefinable body pains, occasional fever, swollen glands on his neck. Then he will tend to fall asleep in the day time, though he will remain wretchedly wakeful at night. At the end of two years, if he has it badly, he will fall into an almost continuous coma and die. In the 1940's, tax returns showed that some parts of Sierra Leone, especially Kono and Kissy country and Luawa, seemed to be losing population. Investigation revealed whole villages denuded of people. It was a sleeping-sickness epidemic, such as has ravaged this part of Africa periodically. It spreads; the tsetse can only get the virus from an infected human, and the more people have it the more get it. Then the population goes down, the tsetse itself acquires the virus less frequently, and the epidemic is over. The bush reclaims the deserted farmland and renews the fertility of the soil, and after a time the people, armed with axe, cutlass and fire, return.

To bring modern science to bear upon these debilitating sicknesses, the Endemic Diseases Control Unit was set up with the aid of Colonial Development and Welfare funds over ten years ago. It can beat yaws with arsenic and bismuth injections, sleeping-sickness with penthamylene. Bilharzia can only be destroyed by putting a poison in the water where the snails live—it kills the fish, too, but not the mosquito larvae. Hookworm can only be controlled by better water supplies—hard work in building concrete wells, proper latrines, decent living conditions.

Apart from malaria, these diseases are yielding to science. (Of malaria an African doctor said to me: 'Not too much prophylaxis, please! Our hard-earned immunity is valuable. Don't take away our nice enlarged spleens—we need 'em!') Except in Sherbro Island, 'Sleeping-sickness is fully controlled at a very low or negligible incidence', in the words of the 1950 Annual Medical Report—a dry phrase which gives no hint of what was involved: of doctors and dispensers toiling through the bush, forest or swamps in darkness to catch a village at dawn, and even then perhaps finding half of it running in terror into the bush; of rounding up the reluctant people, taking their names and relationships and finding who is away and where, of setting up a treatment centre, soothing superstitious fears, injecting, injecting, injecting . . .

Superimpose this picture of disease upon the farm routine, upon the lives of Ansumana and Mariama, upon the little railway failing to pay its way, upon the lack of schools, upon the frustration of the European, trader, official or missionary—and the portrait of Sierra Leone may gain a little more perspective. It becomes easier to understand, too, why the population seems to increase so slowly over the years—according to the official figures only from 1,800,000 in 1931 to 1,900,000 in 1948. But it is not merely endemic disease which keeps the rate of increase down to less than 100,000 per decade. Polygamy leads to infertility and to the spread of venereal disease. But the biggest cause is infant mortality. For the Colony it is given officially as 148·4 per thousand in 1950 as against 208 per thousand in 1946. Nobody knows what it is in the Protectorate, but doctors have told me that it is in the region of 500 per thousand for the first year of life. Some said 600. In a Freetown hospital dealing with creole and tribal native cases, figures showed that mortality in the first five years of life was 52 per cent.

Every African you meet in Sierra Leone is a survivor; naturally selected for resistance in a fully Darwinian ecology. It is for this reason, perhaps, that they further survive hookworm, yaws, sleeping-sickness and so forth as well as they do; though, once stricken with a serious illness, they often show little resistance, which doctors ascribe to malnutrition and avitaminosis in childhood. Even if the official figures are unreliable, being based on taxation assessments which everyone tries to minimize, it is incontestable that the population is, steadily if slowly, increasing. It was thought to be 1,323,151 in 1911. It is thought to be 1,900,000 in 1948. And now the Endemic Diseases Control Unit has tasted blood; it has seen what modern drugs will do against disease. Sheer professional pride prompts men like these to see what modern medical science can do against an infantile mortality rate of 500 per thousand.

Drugs alone, of course, are not the answer. It is strictly forbidden by the Humoi Society, for example, that a woman who has not had a child should see one being born; that would lead to madness and the production of monsters. The answer—as the medical man and the administrator sees it—is education. It is roads, it is hospitals, it is trained midwives, dispensers, nurses, infant welfare clinics, it is Africans by the dozen walking the wards of Mary's and Guy's. Today 60 qualified doctors serve Sierra Leone's population of close on 2,000,000. Two hundred is considered the proper number. Mission doctors consider that a hospital should be located within eight miles of each village. In fact there are a bare dozen for the whole Protectorate: nearly all small hospitals, with three or four wards of 10 or 20 beds. Yet their influence is growing, and the chiefs are beginning to ask for more.

Health and sickness are an important factor in the complex equation that is Sierra Leone. A healthier population means better farming, more labour for roads, construction, public works, more crops for export, more food at home. But to achieve it more money must be spent on medicine and on education— money that can only come from more export crops. A healthier population means a more rapidly growing population, which requires more food, and so more bush-burning and more soil erosion, unless the Agricultural Department's recommendations about swamp rice farming and plantation crops are acted upon quickly. But to speed up the Agricultural Department's plans means more staff, more instructors, more machines, and more education. And this means more money, which can only come out of export crops, which can only come out of a healthier, more active population . . .

It is a difficult equation to solve; but most Africans think it can be solved in only one way—by more and better education. Even beyond health, they cry for education. They cannot begin to understand the problem, any problem, they say, unless they have the intellectual tools. If there were schools enough, teachers enough, literacy enough, then the difficulties could be tackled; until then, one continues to wrestle inconclusively with a vast inertia, with a delicately-stepping, sceptical, tradition-bound race of bush farmers, who grudge any extra effort that has to be paid for from one's slender stock of health and vitality.

19. CHILDREN AND TEACHERS

Elifant ed no to pickin lod
An elephant's head is no load for a child

CREOLE PROVERB

THE blueprint for education is, indeed, impressive. Sylla-buses are being overhauled, teachers paid more, more teachers being trained, reports being written. District Commissioners are chivvying native administrations. Native administrations are building schools. Paramount chiefs are coming out strongly for education for girls. Some handsome schools have been built with impressive façades; the Freetown Secondary School for Girls, the creation of the late Mrs. Benka-Coker, would grace any British county town. In the Protectorate large sums are being spent in the rebuilding of the famous Bo School with girders and concrete, mahogany floors, a theatre, laboratories with tiered seating, and houses designed to house boys, house-master, and *esprit de corps* in surroundings as different from the villages of mud huts, first erected to make sons of chiefs feel at home, as can well be imagined. At Magburaka ('the town of the uninitiated') a complete education centre is going up, including a Central School with verandahs so long, so clean, so guarded with shining metal rails that they are inevitably compared to the promenade decks of the *Queen Mary*. Fourah Bay College is being turned into something like a University, and the fibre-board walls of the Principal's office are decorated with archi-tectural drawings of the noble buildings which will one day crown Mount Aureol and visually justify Freetown's former proud claim to be the Athens of the West Coast.

Some Freetown schoolboys and schoolgirls now do their lessons in spacious, airy classrooms; some boarders at Protec-torate schools are pulling plugs and turning taps for the first time (and perhaps the only time) in their lives; and there is something solid to show the British taxpayer for his contribution to the educational development which is the prerequisite for self-government—a contribution which, between 1947 and 1950, amounted to about £240,000 through Colonial Develop-ment and Welfare funds. Schools remain, however, which are 'so bad as to be, in all probability, physically harmful to the pupils', in the words of an official Report into Educational Development. Mr. Nichols, Headmaster of St. Helen's School, Exeter, who was called in to survey the secondary schools, reported in 1950: 'Of the state of their buildings I need only say here that, with the exception of the new Harford School for Girls, they are in a doleful condition. Some are dilapidated or even dangerous and should be rebuilt, all need extension'. Some *are* being rebuilt, others continue to crumble.

But buildings are externals; education is a matter of children and teachers. In terms of quantity, about 20,000 young people attend schools and colleges of all kinds in the Colony, and about 21,000 in the Protectorate. About 55 out of every 100 children of school age in the Colony do, in fact, go to school, and about five in every 100 children of the Mende, Temne and other tribes. The schools are of every kind, private schools, Government schools and native authority schools—but Mission schools predominate. It was the Missions who brought primary and secondary education to Sierra Leone, and they are still responsible for the best of it.

The quality of this education is not high. It is strongly criticized in Government reports. It is positively denounced in private gatherings, whether of informed educationists or of those ladies and gentlemen, European or African, who smart from the results of it. One is told that things are not much better than the state of affairs described by a visitor over 100 years ago: 'These girls read very well, pronouncing the most difficult English words with perfect fluency. Yet it is astonishing to me that they understand so little of the meaning of the simplest sentence. I try to make them comprehend what they read, by explaining its sense in the broken language used by themselves'. Blame is thrown about lavishly. The Government is blamed for not spending enough money, the Missions are blamed for putting souls before syntax, the parents are blamed for taking their children away from school too soon or sending them much too late, the teachers are blamed for their apathy and ignorance, and the children are blamed for their lack of intelligence. No doubt all the parties share the responsibility in some degree; but there are extenuating circumstances. Education is for living in a particular way, and when the way is changing and

177

N

purposes are uncertain, education itself lacks direction. And, basically, education in Sierra Leone is for an *alien* culture.

Poro and Sande trained boys and girls for tribal life. Literacy leads—whatever it does or does not do for tribal life incidentally —to contact with, and some absorption of, western ideals, customs and forms of thought. Whatever soothing remarks the syllabus may make about the vernacular languages, whatever warnings the syllabus may instil about falsely assuming superiority merely on the grounds of knowledge of English, the central aim of education in Sierra Leone is to supply English as the basic tool of thought. Possession of English means access to western civilization, literature and technology. English is much more than a superior medium of communication: it is the civilization which Britain is undertaking to give, the Africans to assimilate.

Even in the Colony, English has to be learned at school. For Krio is adequate for little more than traditional African needs. Krio provides the Colony child in primary school, certainly, with a vocabulary of nouns, adjectives and verb roots common to English; but everything else has to be learned, and is almost as strange to the descendant of Africans liberated in the early nineteenth century as to the Mende or Temne child. The grammar is different; there is the passive voice to master, relative clauses, complexities of expression through the use of prepositions and adverbs, a different order of words, a wider vocabulary—above all, a new attitude to thought, an abstracting capacity.[1] In learning, the child stumbles over expressions which arise out of everyday experience in temperate climates and scientifically minded countries, but have no meaning for an African of the rain forest—Spring is a simple example.

In Freetown, the creole child at least has a working model of the material environment of written and spoken English. The Temne and Mende child has no such advantage, still less the Kono or Koranko child. In infant classes, tribal children must first learn in their own language the preliminaries of school life —orderliness, punctuality, cleanliness of clothes and person, posture at the desk, the use of pencils and paper and books, and so on. The child begins to think in Mende and Temne about

---

[1] To give an example of the breakdown of ideas in English and Krio: 'Take the third street on your right' would be rendered, as an intelligible instruction: 'Yu falla yu rit an, yu go trait, yu conte de treet, de wan way mak tree na im dat'.

178

his familiar surroundings not merely in a more orderly way but in a new way. A new and remoter idea of causality enters his life, and new ways of understanding behaviour—or it should. He begins 'nature study' as an English child does, with instructions to find a chrysalis and put it in a pot and watch it, not as his illiterate friends do, by being told the names and lurking places of insects, especially the edible and the dangerous varieties. The child in school begins to measure objects with that astounding instrument, a graded ruler. He begins to count in the European way before he or she knows English.

English then comes to the child as a tongue completely new in structure, vocabulary and thought. The Mende child is not in the position of the English child learning French or even Latin; the parallel is more with the English child learning mathematics. He can learn a little—in which case he gets a close substitute for his own language: Pidgin or Krio. But he soon finds himself wrestling with mental concepts as outlandish as the Greek optative appears to the English schoolboy: with this difference, that if the child is to become fully literate, to pass examinations, to be able to read, he must completely master these new forms of expression. Mende has no 'if' or conditional clause, but one preposition (and a few postpositions), no relative clauses, few adjectives, few adverbs. The Mende child, for example, has no equivalent in his mind for such an English concept as 'without'. He has to say: 'Trousers, none on him' for 'without trousers'. 'Behind' in Mende is the noun meaning 'back'; 'before', meaning 'in front of', is the noun meaning 'eyes'. To use the same word ('before') to express priority in time, as well as position in space, seems extraordinary to the Mende child, especially as he has little idea of priority; he expresses time by a succession of sentences. To convey the idea 'Do this before you go', he has to say: 'You this do first, you not go'. The Mende or Temne child is forced in school to jump centuries of complex language-making based on complex thought-making. To aid him he has only his imagination, his intelligence, and a capacity for memorizing photographically what he is told, whether he knows what it means or not.

From the beginning he learns to write, as well as to translate from his own tongue, this new language. Even the idea of writing is new to most children in the remoter parts of the country. To help him, the child has primers of reading and writing; and these are much better than they were, thanks to educational efforts by teachers in many parts of Africa. But the interpretation of the smudgy drawings presents difficulties, not only because they contain objects, such as two-storey brick houses, which are incomprehensible to many village children, but also because the western conventions of perspective in flat drawing are unfamiliar. However, the child gradually recognizes hens and hats, ants and asses, along with the letters for them, even though asses are a rarity in Sierra Leone, and indeed children are not always sure, from reciting English nursery rhymes, whether a horse has four legs or two.

However good the teaching, the tribal child, even the creole child, is struggling with ideas which have little or no relevance to its own home life. Few children can share their school experiences with their parents, though it is pleasant to read in the *Bo School Magazine* that boys 'stage annual concerts in their provincial towns, thereby demonstrating to their illiterate parents the sort of things they learn at school'. But even at the primary level the world of school is divorced from that of the mawe and bush farm. A slight change in the family balance of power may lead to the child being withdrawn after a year or two's schooling to go to work on the land. Fees are ten shillings a year, and the child has to be properly clothed—especially if it goes to a Mission school. Parents know, as well as does the official syllabus, the inebriating effects of gaining a command of English: the child will think itself too good for the hoe and cutlass. In the village, and even in the Colony, the hope of a white-collar job, on the other hand, is dim and far. Even if children persist with their lessons for a few years, the older educational institutions may reclaim them irrevocably. When a girl has graduated from Sande she feels a woman, apt for wifehood and motherhood, and often finds that she no longer wants to be a schoolgirl, even in a glorious mauve uniform and green beret. Even the most perfunctory Poro initiation makes a tribal boy feel a man, and renders school discipline a derogation in status.

In the Protectorate, the influence of the chief is often all-important; if he feels that you should stay at school, well, your family too will think it best for you to persevere. If the chief is indifferent, the teacher or mission find it hard to keep up or increase their numbers. Nearly a quarter of the children who enrol on school registers only complete the first year at school; another 15 per cent give up after the second year; after the third year another 13 per cent of the original total fall out, and at the beginning of the fifth year barely 40 per cent remain. It probably takes fully five years for a child to get even a modest grip on the reading and writing of English. The full primary course takes six years at the least, and perhaps a quarter of the children complete it.

Other entanglements make difficult the path of learning. According to the 1950 Education Report, the commoner ailments of children at school are yaws, scabies, ringworm, ulcers, nose and ear discharges, occasional conjunctivitis and debility ascribed to the presence of intestinal and other parasites; 'the problems of malnutrition and avitaminosis have not yet been the subject of serious investigation in Protectorate schools, but it is probable that they contribute to, if they do not largely occasion, a high degree of unresponsiveness to instruction on the part of scholars'. They are serious enough, even in the Colony, for Mr. Nichols, in his report on secondary schools, to recommend that physical education should only be developed with the greatest care, for fear of over-straining the children.

It is no easy thing to do schoolwork in another language under these conditions. And however hard the children try, what they will achieve depends on the teacher's quality. Except for a tiny minority, Sierra Leone children learn English and the rest of their culture from an African who has himself learned from an African. The teachers are simply those children who have been able to complete the educational course, despite all the hazards. Indeed, most of the teachers, even in Government-assisted schools, have *not* completed it—nearly half are not only without any teacher-training but have not finished the secondary school course, which means that they are barely equipped to teach infants. Another third, though they have not completed the secondary school course, have had some teacher-training. Out of 1,100 teachers, only 71 were trained and had a full secondary education; only 61 had university qualifications of *any* kind.

The secondary education available to those Africans who wish to pass on the torch of learning is very variable in quality. It is liable, if not to quench, at least to dim the torch.

Mr. Nichols found it based on the ideas of the English grammar school as they were in England 50 years ago. 'Bookish' is the modern English headmaster's word for it. 'The teachers, industrious and painstaking as they are, are so eager to cram too much into too many heads in too short a time that they forget that real understanding must be based on pupils' own experiences and active investigation.' Mr. Nichols found that even botany in Sierra Leone was being learned out of books, and that chemistry was the memorizing of formulae; three schools had science laboratories, and one other kept its lab. in a box. 'All they do is learn from books what others have discovered . . . the information they gain thus may be important but they get no scientific training in acquiring it.'

English is a dull grind of grammar and prescribed texts for the school certificate; there is little other reading, for there are hardly any school libraries. History is usually a matter of things called Periods: one Period is a family of chiefs called Tudors who did well, followed by a family called Stuarts against whose exactions the English people rebelled, as the Mendes do against their chiefs; another Period is the wars between tribes of Roses. Latin is taught in a scattered way: the relic of a great if aristocratic past when the Sierra Leone missions ran small select academies to train bright creole boys for the ministry and grounded them thoroughly in Latin and Greek preparatory to going on to Fourah Bay. Such was the C. M. S. Grammar School, where in 1859 there were 'three classes in Latin reading Henry's Second Book, Young's New Latin Delectus and the London Grammar respectively; two classes in Greek, reading Greek Testament and Valpy's Delectus and Grammar respectively'. Greek has now disappeared from the C.M.S. Grammar School, and fewer Africans than ever study Latin—but few, also, study even French. There are no epidiascopes, no film shows, no domestic science, almost no art, no civics; only a little sewing for girls and a little carpentering for boys. Mr. Nichols found many teachers untrained to teach even the minimum of subjects attempted for the examinations; and when no teacher could be found the subject was simply omitted for the time being.

This is still, substantially, the condition of secondary education, though money has now been found for a few modern teachers from England with breezy modern ideas on civics and world history. Unfortunately the war over grammar and modern schools, which is raging in England, has broken out in Sierra Leone, too. The modern school, to the mind of the African 'old boy', carries the suggestion of training young Africans to be hewers of wood and drawers of water. He will have none of it. Yet there is a great demand for technical education, and for the fitting of school teaching to African requirements. Bo School was originally planned as the antithesis of the bookish missionary pseudo-grammar school. The *Royal Gazette* of September 29, 1905, proclaimed its foundation with the explanation: 'Under existing conditions, pupils educated in Freetown almost invariably return home with a feeling of contempt for the native towns and even for their nearest relatives. To prevent this both the native teachers and the pupils will be expected to wear country cloth and their lives outside school hours will be spent in a small town, the government of which will be on ordinary native lines'. The boys, indeed, lived up to the prospectus, for the punishment book records that on April 23 information was lodged against the boy Sahr by a man named Bochari of Bo that the boy had been the 'friend' of his wife for the past four months and, when she was sent away, pursued her on the train. Perhaps to improve the moral tone, a series of lantern lectures was given afterwards on 'Great Women', No. 1 being Florence Nightingale. Bo has, however, developed on public school lines; the 'towns' of mud huts with their plots of gardens (it is a grave offence not to do your gardening) have turned into 'houses', and tribal brawls into inter-house soccer.

Measured in terms of examination results the secondary schools, with 3,300 pupils on their rolls, produced in 1950 224 children as candidates for the Junior Cambridge: 52 boys and 32 girls passed. Very broadly, the university authorities find that an African boy or girl who has worked continuously is, at any stage in his scholastic career, three years behind the average English child of the same length of schooling. As against this, some Sierra Leone children stay at school longer and hammer their heads against the iron doors of the Cambridge examinations with desperate and pathetic fury. It is not uncommon to find children in their teens solemnly singing with the infants:

Row, row, row your boat
  Gently down the stream,
Merrily, merrily, merrily, merrily,
  Life is but a dream . . .

But it is an upstream pull for some, that dream of certificated education, which finds boys of 25 sitting the Cambridge for the fifth time. Until reforming zeal got to work, the Sixth at the C.M.S. grammar school used to be called 'the greybeards'.

From the secondary school, a proportion of the teachers-to-be go to Fourah Bay or St. Joseph's for teacher training, and those from primary schools go to Bunumbu, Magburaka or the Catholic college; but the output of fully trained teachers is only reaching 85 a year. What secondary education is, the teachers are; what the teachers are, determines what primary education is. For my part I found the younger teachers of Sierra Leone, both in the Colony and in the Protectorate, among the most interesting of what I may perhaps call the African professional classes. Despite the limitations of their training, the best among them evinced remarkable lightness of spirit, eagerness to serve, width of interest and general intelligence; they had a sense of vocation and of the dignity of their calling. Secondary school boys and girls gave to the question 'What do you want to do?' the answer: 'I want to raise my country; I shall teach'. (Some, it is true, confessed that they taught because there were no other openings, or because other professions required training which they could not afford.) They were proud of their schools and their children; eager to demonstrate every detail of the famous syllabus and the fidelity with which the timetable covered it; often lamenting shortcomings of equipment ('Will you send me some old magazines from England, sir?') but always insisting that the children were good and keen to learn—that the best way to punish them was to give them a half-holiday. One Sunday I beheld the specially-favoured staying in to learn a speech from *Julius Caesar*.

Teachers' lives are not easy. Though their pay has been put up, it is not easy to make ends meet when any man with a salary is a milch cow for his relatives. Relatives know exactly when the salary is paid, and arrive on that day. Some families, the moment a son or nephew attains the affluence and dignity of a teaching appointment, immediately abandon the eternal struggle with the bush and fast-growing weeds and settle upon him. In the Protectorate the teacher's relations with the chief may be delicate; he will surely have to pay for his privileged position one way or another. In Freetown there are still relatives, and high rents besides. And always there is the toil of forcing children's minds in the unfamiliar mould of a thought and a tongue the teacher himself finds hard, and can hardly ever practise with a European.

More teacher-training is the official answer; refresher courses; more European teachers; buildings and equipment—the secondary schools alone need £1½ million spent on them; adult education to stimulate parents into taking a deeper interest in schools and children; technical education to show that primary education leads to useful employment and does not merely spoil farmers or farmers' wives; more of everything. 'But', says the Deputy Director of Education (one seems always in Sierra Leone to be talking to deputies, for mysterious reasons connected with leave, promotion and Special Duty), 'but', he remarks sadly, 'we're already spending nearly 9 per cent of the ordinary expenditure and nearly a third of the development funds. The Missions aren't able to do as much as they used. The native authorities are spending a few thousands, but their budgets are pitiful. Why doesn't Freetown take a bit more responsibility—as local authorities do at home? But, anyway, what jobs would thousands of young people do when they left Central School with Standard VII? Drive tractors? Help run Pioneer Oil Mills? It's going to be quite a problem, you know. It all depends on development.'

20. MOUNT AUREOL

Senge the wise exceeded
kings in wisdom
TEMNE PROVERB[1]

WHEN Governor Fergusson, who was himself of African descent, laid the foundation-stone of Fourah Bay College in 1845, his emotions overcame him, and he burst into tears. For the site was that of an old slave factory, and the new establishment was intended to train from the new race of Liberated Africans a professional cadre of which he, as a doctor and supreme representative of Her Majesty, seemed to be the remarkable prototype. In due course there rose, in the words of the Colonial chaplain: 'The white walls of a large and noble building, rising in aristocratic loftiness, three good stories high, as if by enchantment, from the palm trees which embosom it, and displaying its parapets in the quiet moonlight, like a structure of the fancy, which Spenser's pen might not have despised'. Today, an enchanting little example of early Victorian colonial architecture, it is used by the Railway as a head office. But it should be visited and viewed with reverence; the foundation-stone tapped into place by Governor Fergusson's gavel is suitably engraved, and recalls that occasion; and the rafters are formed from the masts of slave-ships whose carcasses have rotted in the ooze of Destruction Bay this hundred years.

The high hopes with which the college was launched (its beginnings go back to 1827) were sustained almost wholly upon missionary efforts and missionary funds, as was all other education in the Colony. In 1864, the Church Missionary Society spent £4,700 on education and the Government £400—but it is only fair to say that in the early days it was not always easy to say where the C.M.S. ended and Government began. Besides, even in England the State at that period took a limited view of its responsibility for education. Fourah Bay College remained a somewhat exclusive place, accommodating rarely more than 20 pupils, the English staff continually stricken by malaria and

---

[1] Senge was king of the first world God made (see p. 127). The proverb means Thou art wiser than I; I accept thy pronouncements'.

changed by death. Yet it began the production of some notable dictionaries of West African languages, including Koelle's *Polyglotta Africana*, a comparison of over 100 languages which the philologist—'an ubiquitous little man with an ever-present notebook'—compiled in the grassy streets of Freetown.

By 1876 the curriculum covered Latin, Greek, Hebrew and Arabic, French and German, Native Languages, Political Economy, Philosophy, Logic, Mathematics, Natural Science and Music. In that year the college, whose alumni had led evangelistic expeditions in various parts of West Africa and were doing important work for the government of the settlements (Gold Coast, Gambia and Sierra Leone), was affiliated to the University of Durham, as was Codrington College, Barbados. The examination papers, in sealed packages, were sent by the last mails leaving England before candidates sat the exams in Durham. But by then Dr. Horton, a leading creole savant, was calling for a West African university, undertaking scientific research in the colonies, and training Negroes to be doctors and engineers who could take over the development of the country's resources since the English seemed incompetent to do so. Those were the years in which men were talking about a railway from Freetown to Timbuktu.

The railway came twenty years later, but got no nearer Timbuktu than Kamabai; the College remained affiliated to Durham and got no nearer the idea of a University than an increase in numbers to 40 or 50. Missionary finances began to flag, the municipality of Freetown felt no civic urge to develop its university. By 1923 the Government were spending on all education £22,447 6s. 4d., and that was 3 per cent of the total expenditure of the Colony. Students came to the stunted college from Accra and Lagos; but both the Gold Coast and Nigeria found it necessary to start their own universities. The chance of creating a great West African seat of learning in Freetown to compensate in intellectual ways for straitened material resources was lost—if it ever existed.

None the less, under its energetic new Principal, Fourah Bay College is now trying to recover some of the years which locusts and bug-bug have eaten. Under the educational reconstruction scheme set on foot at the end of the war, £350,000 were allotted from Colonial Development and Welfare funds for its development as a State-aided college, with an independent Board of Governors representing the Churches and the civic and State authorities. It forsook the cramped old building and moved up to Mount Aureol where, clustered round a fragment of a wall belonging to a seventeenth-century Jesuit mission, stood the temporary buildings of a wartime hospital. These have been adapted to house the College: wards have become classrooms and hostels, the operating theatre has become physics and chemistry laboratories, the hospital concert-hall has become the university theatre. It is scrappy and untidy, and the staff looks forward to building an impressive campus at an early date—but it is alive, it is growing, and tin roofs do not prevent high thinking, even in West African rains. In fact, some people in the Colony think that it is growing too fast and eating up money which should go towards improving primary and secondary education. It may certainly be asked whether Fourah Bay should not be content with patching temporary buildings for the next twenty years or so. 'Twenty year is no forever' is a creole proverb. But it is difficult not to sympathize with the Fourah Bay view that the enlarged college is doing an indispensable job for which money must be found somehow.

To some critics of things African and creole it is ludicrous for a country which with difficulty produces a hundred rather poor school certificates a year to have a college at all. It has to provide two years of pre-university courses to raise pupils to higher school certificate standard. But it also trains teachers, and it cannot train a better generation of teachers until it can give the sixth form teaching which the secondary schools cannot give, and probably should not try to give, in the present lamentable state of their staff and resources. The training of teachers is Fourah Bay's most important task; it is the 'University Department'—the heir to the earlier hopes of the missionary founders of the College—which excites doubt. But most of those taking the four-year university course are either going into teaching also, or into Government positions—senior positions for which the policy of Africanization requires that suitable occupants should be found. The department is a sketchy affair, no doubt. Only in the last year or two has science teaching begun to be worthy of the name. Moreover much of the money spent on the University Department goes on teaching Nigerian and Gold

Coast students, because the number of Sierra Leonians who can benefit from it are small, though increasing (in 1950 only three entered the University Department; in 1952, 22 did so). But it will improve and in time teach enough Sierra Leonians; above all, its presence and influence gives Sierra Leone an academic body—I might almost say academic lobby—which it needs.

The official mind needs to be balanced by the academic mind; the facts on the files need to be interpreted in the context of a wider outlook. For fifty years the officials have been looking down on Freetown and planning its future good from the quiet of Hill Station. It will do no harm, and probably much good, for trained minds of another kind to look down from Mount Aureol, which in the early rains is electric with lightning. It is true that the officials on Hill Station can hardly be expected to regard the fibreboard refectory on Mount Aureol with the same veneration as they would All Souls'; but then why should the staff think of the Secretariat with quite the same trepidation as they would the Treasury or the Cabinet Offices? Mount Aureol, while understanding the reasons for the tightness of the purse-strings, is entitled to argue that education in the past has not been good enough and needs some original re-thinking; the Secretariat is perhaps entitled to retort that Mount Aureol has a good deal to learn about the ease with which African interest in a new project evaporates and turns to lethargy.

The fact remains that African opinion is solidly behind Fourah Bay now. Africans, creoles and tribesfolk, want the college; and in time they may accept the necessity for paying the rates and taxes to defray its rising cost. At present they warm to its benefits. An extra-mural department, at which a man or woman can study law or prepare for matriculation, is very different from the slow process of waiting for sea mails carrying the correspondence course tutor's comments on one's exercises. I have heard an African say: 'It has meant new hope in my life. Perhaps I can get out of my rut in Government service. I'd lay down my life for the extra-mural department!' There may be nothing very brilliant about pass degrees of Durham University. But they are a beginning. And there is much to be said for a centre of enthusiasm: an institution for which people are prepared to fight and sacrifice, even if it *is* a bit beyond their means.

Fourah Bay is interpreting its title as a 'College of Arts,

Science and Technology' as including a brief to organize part-time classes in technical and commercial know-how. Hitherto Sierra Leonians had to train as accountants or electricians through correspondence colleges. Ultimately Freetown will have its technical institute—its own 'Poly'; meanwhile, there are Fourah Bay classes. Feelings sometimes run high on technical aaining. Africans feel there should be more of it at every level, nd point to the success of the modest first generation of African A.M.I.C.E.s, water engineers and so on. While granting the success of a handful of exceptionally able men, European employers declare that there is little material on which to build a tradition of skilled workmanship. The country is always short of skilled men, and the efforts of the Government Training Centre, where some 90 trainees are taught to be better carpenters, masons, motor mechanics, painters and decorators, has not as yet made much difference—the course is short, and any man with a bag of tools and a Trade Certificate gives himself out as a tradesman requiring tradesman's wages, only to prove amazingly incompetent. Many possessors of the 'Red' certificate cannot, in fact, read or write as the test prescribes, and it is rare, for example, to find electricians or toolmakers who can read drawings with any ease.

It is excruciating to observe a carpenter with a saw in Sierra Leone. He pushes it slowly into the wood away from himself, attempting to get the bite with the *upstroke*. Usually the teeth are so ineffectually set that the wood pinches the blade abominably—and the saw is then liberally greased with palm oil from a bottle which forms part of a carpenter's kit. Yet Africans keep the most decrepit vehicles on the roads, and thus provide themselves with endless opportunities for learning about motor engines. Stories of African ingenuity with machinery are endless. One hears of the trimmed branch of a tree doing duty as a temporary connecting-rod for an injured locomotive, and of a driver who kept his engine running at one time during the war when lubricating oil ran short by means of banana skins in the cylinders.

But between these heroic measures and maintaining machines in a state of high efficiency, between repeating a pattern and working out a new design, there seems to be a gap. Routine can be taught by rigorous apprenticeships, such as are insisted upon at the railway workshops, at the Marampa mines, or at the

Government sawmills and furniture factory at Kenema. Under close supervision illiterate tribal carpenters, after a five-year training, can work to a very fine finish, and may be seen at Kenema producing in fine woods beautiful jobs of cabinet-making, if in a somewhat standardized, Edgware Road style. The railway is building narrow-gauge train-sets at half the price, and with considerably better finish, than those supplied from Britain in 1945 (not a vintage year for British engineering).

At best, it is difficult to explain the theory of machines in Mende, in Krio, even in the range of English commanded by Africans who, having reached Standard III or IV, earnestly claim: 'I am *educated* man, sir'. I have been told how an aspiring mechanic, with more English than this, was carefully coached for weeks with the aid of a good textbook to understand the mechanism of the four-cycle internal combustion engine, only to produce, when requested to write out in his own words what he had learned, the impressive definition: 'The four-cycle engine is a Prince of Power and a Maid of All Work'. Instruction must be imaginative and never let go of the trainee's mind for a second, skilfully preventing parrot-learning, skilfully forcing it to grasp principles. This is an exhausting and necessarily expensive process. The African, in truth, needs more individual tutoring than the English student, not less.

A fear lurks in the African heart that, while the European may for his own purposes tell the black man some of the secrets of science and machinery, he will always hold some of them back. He will not yield 'the heart of the medicine', any more than the African would do if the positions were reversed. (Many African technical processes, the use of the Gara dye, for instance, are kept secret; secrets, like patents, are sold on licence—on condition they are kept from unauthorized persons.) And there *is* one final secret which the European can never impart—experience. The African takes his examination and possesses his diploma; yet, somehow, his book learning does not give him the grasp of the matter which he expected. Something has eluded him. He may pretend he has it. But he will feel baffled and resentful.

It is for Fourah Bay to probe these difficulties of African mentality: business men will not, and officials, with the best intentions, cannot. The African background, the traditional forms of African thought, together with poor schooling, make the grasp of western analytical and abstract thought very difficult. I was told at Fourah Bay that such tests as had been made with Sleight Non-verbal Intelligence Tests, Alexander's Passalong ('well saturated with G') and many others indicated that Sierra Leonian and Nigerian students compared favourably with the average of English students in their basic intellectual endowment. But 'intelligence' so defined is one thing; the use of it another. Consider the background of Borboh and Mariama in relation to modern techniques. 'My nurses', said a doctor ruefully, 'seem to have absolutely no idea of physical properties of things, no manual dexterity'.

How should it be otherwise, save for creoles from the richer families? 'The creole boy—what I may call the creole middle-class boy', a headmaster told me, 'has lots in him—once he has got over the idea that he knows everything already; that's just a crust over an inferiority complex anyhow.' But the headmaster, like the doctor, found that the absence of order and method at home, the lack of discipline and character-formation, were duly reflected in difficulties of tuition in school.

For the majority of children in Sierra Leone, home life anything but fits them to grapple with the discipline of western thought. How few of them have what modern psychologists call 'play material'—interlocking objects which teach 'the physical properties of things'. The Meccano set is almost unknown even to the creole boy; lack of acquaintance with mechanical objects, lack of self-expression in arts and handicrafts, like lack of understanding of natural processes, predispose the mind to accept the world incuriously. Mechanical things are just 'white man's magic'; nature as revealed by science has no real relevance to social or personal experience.

It is hardly enough to try to improve Sierra Leone education by building a few fine schools, by getting teachers through school certificate, higher certificate and college, and by paying them more. A new approach to African education based on a radical understanding of the difficulties is needed—and it can only grow from the devoted work of a university centre, staffed with men and women skilled in observation and social analysis.

But a technical tradition cannot grow where there are no object-lessons in technology, and no technological careers to prepare for. Students at Fourah Bay, like some students at

British 'Red Brick' universities, used to go into teaching or law because these were the only professions open to them. If, in the past, science and technology had been taught, those who learnt them would still have had to teach for a livelihood. Africans are now getting a few jobs as inspectors of works. Government and the Firms want trained accountants. But the tradition persists that between the professional engineer with an English degree and the semi-trained motor mechanic taking a wrench to an innocent tractor, a vast gulf of dignity is fixed. 'Please send me some money for overalls', an outraged African trainee wrote from England. 'I am expected to do dirty work *here*.'

These attitudes, these incapacities, will be overcome as the output of technically trained men and women increases, but output must be matched by the growth of a market, if more education is not to produce still more discontented clerks. More education requires a better upbringing of the young in terms of diet, regimen, play, training, conduct, ideals. This in turn can only come about by the founding of better homes, by social welfare, by adult education; all of them developments in which a college of 'Arts, Science and Technology' must be active; a centre of research and propaganda. When Fourah Bay was founded, it was sufficient to fit creoles to preach the Gospel. Today the ministry itself requires a shrewder understanding of African needs. These needs can only be met by a university in the full medieval sense of that term.

But the creation of a university, and of opportunities for creative lives for its graduates, requires more money—and more economic development. Fourah Bay College no longer depends, or could dream of depending, on missionary offerings. Its Government grant is £80,000 a year. To fulfil its mission it says it needs £115,000, even £125,000. But to take so much out of the educational budget is to cut away the supports on which it stands: the improvement of primary and secondary schools, teachers, children. A poor country either educates the few well, whereupon these lose touch with the majority, or it educates the many ill, which is wasteful of both economic and intellectual resources. Sierra Leone has actually had both these experiences, yet the budget provides more money for education than ever before. Where is the wealth to support this level of expenditure, and to double, to treble it, in the years ahead?

21. THE MINES

Iron cuts iron
MENDE PROVERB

FROM the earliest days it was hoped that the Colony would be enriched by discoveries of valuable minerals. Gold in alluvial form, as well as ivory and slaves, had come down from the interior, and from the days of the Royal Africa Company it was known that the Africans could smelt their own iron. During the nineteenth century several requests for mineral surveys were put forward; but the Colony seemed unendowed and the non-entanglement policy prevented the hinterland being explored; Gladstonian Governments were sufficiently unhappy about the political complications of mineral discoveries in South Africa. Sierra Leone had to develop on the proceeds of country produce, missionary contributions, and the upkeep of the naval coaling station.

The first geological survey, made by Frank Dixey in 1919–22, failed to reveal any minerals in paying quantities, and the Government refused to spend more. But Sir Arthur Kitson, Director of the Geological Survey of the Gold Coast, re-examined Dixey's work and persuaded the Sierra Leone Government to send out Dr. Junner in 1926 to make a new survey. Junner almost immediately recognized as practically solid hematite iron ore two large hills rising hundreds of feet out of the bush-clad plain at Marampa, and soon after uncovered the promise of alluvial gold and platinum at Tonkolili; in 1930 the first diamond was discovered in Kono country, a land poor, remote, and stricken with sleeping-sickness. Chrome ore was found in 1937, most strategically located near the railway at Hangha, thus providing the line with through hauls, though it is of such low grade that the railway has to carry it at a loss to enable it to be marketed competitively. None the less production is being steadily increased.

A Geological Department was formed, but without trimmings. The iron was inaccessible, 50 miles from the sea, near the little town of Lunsar, 55 houses, population 400. From 1926 onwards, however, a series of gold prospectors arrived, took up concessions, and began to pan for gold; along the river Makong and around Mabonto the 'Gold Missis', Katharine Fowler-Lunn, an American geologist, found them at work, some with inadequate equipment, 'but like all inveterate gold seekers, he knew everything was going to be fine. He had gold; he showed it to me, his tired, fever-ridden eyes gleaming with joy . . . he would get enough to go home to England, and live in comfort for the rest of his days'. This man in fact went home penniless —a Distressed British Subject.

The Gold Missis herself prospected for the Maroc Company, which panned the rivers and in 1932–3, on an authorized capital of £50,000, paid dividends of £42,000 after the Government had collected its royalty. In 15 years it made over £200,000. The payable gold was by 1941 worked out; but gold is now being dredged in Sierra Leone on a small scale by the Pampona Mining Company, though much gold still panned by African prospectors is smuggled out of the country.

But its royalties from the gold prospectors did not prevent the Government, during the depression, from economizing at the expense of the Geological Department (which, even so, discovered more gold, iron, diamonds and chrome). When sterling parted company with the gold standard, Maroc's profits leapt up. But it was another mining company which gave Sierra Leone its first real 'gold mine' by developing the iron ore at a time when a few pence a ton made all the difference between profit and loss, and Marampa's ore would be 2,000 miles further from a market than anyone else's. The African and Eastern Corporation explored Marampa and obtained a lease from the Lunsar tribal authority, but the commercial possibilities were not appreciated until James Campbell, an overseas mining expert, made another survey and found the finance, jointly with the corporation, to start operations. In 1930 the Sierra Leone Development Company was formed, with James Campbell as its first chairman. It received mining rights from the Government under the Concessions Ordinance; in 1932 a Minerals Ordinance was introduced after the Government had decided that wealth under the soil must be exploited for the good of the whole country, not just the locality in which it happened to occur.

The Development Company got to work. Its main task was to create an ore port, and a new railway from the port to Marampa. The loading installation was located at Pepel on the Rokel River, which involved charting the river and showing (perhaps for the first time) that ships of 10,000 tons burthen could negotiate the channel far inland. The 3ft. 6in. gauge railway was driven 52 miles through the bush. The African navvies were unused to the work and the engineering difficulties were not small. The first funds amounted to £1,000,000, of which half was found by private investment and half was loaned by the Colonial Development Fund, which has since had its money back. This compares with the £200,000 spent by the Sierra Leone Company in starting the Colony. The first shipment of ore left Pepel on 7th September, 1933. By the time Hitler straddled Europe from Norway to Morocco, Marampa was able to supply Britain with 40 per cent of her intake of iron ore. But in 1931 and 1932 the whole scheme was a colossal gamble as prices fell from month to month, steelworks closed, dole queues lengthened, governments tumbled and no man knew what lay ahead.

Today Marampa is one of the most up-to-date ore-getting and ore-transporting concerns in the world. It is run by 60 Europeans and 3,000 Africans. One of the hills of hematite has been lowered by 80 feet in 20 years' working, and most of the red hematite has been removed; a modern washery deals with the grey powder ore (soft schistose powder ore) which contains about 45 per cent iron. The washery, fitted with spiral concentration plants, concentrates this powder—which is merely scraped from the hill by bulldozers—to over 60 per cent for shipment. Over a million and a quarter tons of ore is produced every year, and is loaded into ships by a modern conveyor-loader at Pepel at the rate of 2,000 tons an hour. Ships turn round in 23 hours (which is no doubt very boring for the crew). Ore trains, carrying 1,000 tons a load, roar down the railway at speeds which considerably exceed those achieved on the Government line.

In 1923, the revenue of Sierra Leone was £845,319, of which £440,000, or over 50 per cent, came from import duties. There was no company or income tax. In 1952, the companies' tax was estimated to produce £1,313,000 out of a total revenue of just over £6 million—20 per cent—while estimates of import duties were about £1,800,000. Mineral wealth, in short, is now producing a fifth of Sierra Leone's state income (and the total cost of the Geological Survey from 1926 to 1946 was £74,000). The total value of minerals produced in 1952 was £3,750,000.

Of this amount, however, the greater part was contributed by diamonds, not iron ore. Two years after the occurrence of diamonds had been established by the Geological Department, the Consolidated African Selection Trust obtained prospecting rights and was able to show that the gems occurred in economic quantities. But the contrast between the problem of getting the diamonds and getting the iron could not have been more complete. The iron is in a lump, easy to deal with, heavy to transport. The diamonds, though presenting no transport problem once won, are scattered over some 480 square miles in the drainage system of the Sewa River. Large tracts are diamondiferous, but the treatment of the gravel is expensive. It is thought that somewhere there is a pipe of diamond, where this form of carbon was produced under geological pressures when the present rock formations were laid down; but it has not been found, and the diamonds now being won are those that have been washed out by the river system over millions of years and left lying in the beds of streams.

The concession accordingly covers a huge area of bush. It is surveyed by experts and sampled to prove its economic potentiality. In areas where the diamonds are payable the overburden and top-soil is turned up by mechanical shovels, and the gravel—the bed of former streams—is loaded into trucks, carried to washers, and concentrated by gravity methods. The concentrates go into sealed cans and are taken to the sorting house, a building into which workers can only go after changing their clothes and from which they can only emerge after stripping and search. The visitor, from a barred vantage point, can however observe the concentrate going over the sorters, whose platforms are coated with a wax to which the diamonds, being heavy, adhere. Sometimes these tables, after the passage of the concentrate, gleam with an almost phosphorescent sheen of diamond; more often two or three stones are picked off and placed in receptacles under keen supervision. Though well paid by most standards, the workers are inevitably in the position of poor men seeing fortunes in the most portable form on earth appearing regularly under their eyes.

Diamond prices are high, and demand is ahead of supply; the demand is rather for industry—especially for the armaments industry—though the bigger Sierra Leone diamonds go into jewelry. The diamond trade enjoys that least elastic of all demands—the newly engaged woman's demand for a diamond engagement ring. The workings at the Woyie River produced in January 1945 the third or fourth largest diamond in the world —770 carats. Diamonds have been found of 200 to 500 carats, but the average is 2 to 3 carats. Sierra Leone does well out of her diamonds; the company, though it keeps its accounts private, has a Government Director on the Board and pays out 45 per cent of its profit to the Government in taxes, as well as an annual contribution to the Protectorate Mining Benefits Fund. Its diamonds, in sealed containers, are flown to Britain and the prices they fetch pay for a good deal of the country's education and social services. Between 1948 and 1952 it paid over £3 million in taxes.

But anyone who knows how can search gravel for alluvial diamonds, and inevitably the Selection Trust has taught innumerable workers from Kono country and elsewhere how to treat gravel. They do so privily; and a large part of Sierra Leone's diamond output pays no royalties to the revenue at all—it makes rich men of the Illicit Diamond Buyers. The illicit diamond traffic harms the country's interests, for the illegal diamond washers pick the eyes out of the seams—the minority of biggish diamonds which their primitive methods can detect—and leave the remainder of the cut uneconomic to work by refined but expensive methods. Considerable wealth is therefore permanently lost to the Sierra Leone people as a whole by their operations.

Yengema, the headquarters of the Diamond Workings, is a pleasant place. A country of undulating hills, just on the borders of forest and orchard bush areas, it is green and varied, and bonanza for the naturalist and bird-watcher. The Diamond people have charming bungalows. The offices are laid out in streets lined with scarlet flamboyants. The workers are very well paid since the last strike—far too well paid in the view of a temperance-minded management, which points austerely to the heavy increase in the consumption of stout. But until recently there was no motorable road in the nearby African town, and (apart from the mines hospital) the nearest hospital is at Kailahun, 50 miles to the south. Kono country is backward, lacking schools and roads. The idea that its diamonds should be extracted for the good of all Sierra Leone—to build fine schools at Magburaka and Bo for instance—does not appeal much to Konos. There is no special Kono interest in helping suppress illegal diamond snatching.

In fact, men from other tribes come up to Kono country to work at night and in secret to pothole the workings and get the diamonds before the white men get them. They do not make much out of the work—about £1 per carat—but it is more interesting work than brushing the hills and trying to extract rice from the worn-out soil of the Panguma Valley. The penalties, if one is caught, are relatively mild; and in recent years police supervision has weakened and the risks have decreased. An efficient organization exists to transmit smuggled diamonds to Freetown. They change hands several times, always at a nice but reasonable profit to the middleman. Indeed diamonds are sometimes offered openly for sale on the railway. Ultimately the diamonds reach a syndicate of I.D.B. merchants in Freetown. These could not expect to make much out of the diamonds by selling on the world market at controlled prices. But they pay the suppliers well above that rate, and still make incomes estimated at £20,000 a year—and somehow manage to avoid paying the income tax that the companies pay. They probably fly most of the diamonds to Syria, whence they cross into Israel and are cut by skilled cutters trained in Holland before the war. Most of the industrial diamonds find their way to Russia. Before the war they went to Germany. They are worth paying fancy prices for (probably three times the controlled price); it is estimated that the polish given to moving parts on the Spitfire by diamond grinders increased its speed by 15 m.p.h.

Four hundred and eighty diamondiferous square miles is a lot to police, with policemen who are paid less than a carat's price a week. Meanwhile, young men with the desire to get rich quick penetrate into the area—which is, theoretically, sealed off. They are quarrelsome and give the chiefs trouble—

199

but then they can be profitably fined for woman damage and sold palm wine at exorbitant prices. Through the feuds and grievances which follow the police get information leading to arrests; even so, diamonds have been mined practically under the company's front door. It is obviously necessary to break up the organization; if it were not temptingly profitable to dig for diamonds, losses could be controlled. But British justice rules in Freetown, and millionaires must have their crimes proved against them in Court. They have a lot of money to spend. They spend lavishly—and it is not easy to bring them to book. Their one fear—those that do not possess British passports —is deportation.

The mines—diamond, chrome, iron and gold—have created a new class, in the last twenty years: the beginnings of an industrial proletariat. It is by many restless young men considered a more desirable status than that of the farmer. At Lunsar a thousand or more hangers-on wait hopefully for jobs in the ore workings, or, if discharged for any reason, hang on because they dislike the alternative. At Lunsar, and to some extent at Yengema, the 'detribalized' native has made his appearance, but not as a creole, with his eyes set on an education leading to a white-collar job. He is a workman owing no allegiances, ambitious only for his pay and what it will bring.

This is the price paid for winning the country's wealth. To the European mine manager—himself often of working-class origin—it seems no special problem. As he sees matters, if the country is to get on, if things are to be made 'efficient', then the tribal system, with its traditional outlook on land and obligation to the community, must go. In its place, individual ambition must supply the incentive which makes the good workman, punctual, responsible, apprenticed and skilled in some trade. Wages are good; indeed the companies think them inflationary; amenities and welfare are designed to set a standard of living for emulation in other occupations. The Development Company is spending over £50,000 on a magnificent hospital. Its labour lines consist of good, well-built identical cottages with tin or asbestos roofs—some are even laid out imaginatively as villages rather than as *lines*. An apprenticeship scheme has been started which is a valuable addition to the country's technical education; a British trade union official is in charge. The

200

apprentices are literate (to Standard IV), they are tested scientifically for mechanical aptitude, shown instructional films and film strips, taught maths and mechanics, given practical training in the shops by European fitters, turners, moulders and mechanics. In their sixth year they become journeymen with an appropriate wage differential (5s. 8d. a day, as compared with 3s. 2d. for a labourer). Free issues of rice are designed to overcome any tendencies to malnutrition. To the business man these things are self-evidently good—their own justification.

The official, the missionary, and particularly the anthropologist are more hesitant. Mines and development there must be, but they are concerned that the transition from tribal communism to wage-earning individualism shall not be too sudden. It amuses them to see the shock which the growth of trade unionism gives the companies. The business men are all for development and progress—but curiously enough they are less keen on the growth of the trade unionism which has accompanied industrial development in Europe. They tend to the view that while a backward country like Sierra Leone is ripe for development by sound business enterprise, it is not ripe for trade unionism. The companies do not say these things in public, but in private business men speak with some vehemence about the 'deliberate encouragement' of unionism which appears to them to have been a part of colonial policy in the immediate post-war years.

As a fact, the interest of Transport House in Sierra Leone unions has been somewhat lukewarm, and a good deal less than Mr. Siaka Stevens, who was General Secretary of the movement until he became Minister of Labour, would have liked in the interest of responsible union behaviour. Help is now being given; but unionism has been a spontaneous development and, for the organizers, a poorly paid and often thankless task. To form a union means a considerable outlay and organizing effort without pay until subscriptions come in and a fund accumulates. The employees of the mining companies are now organized in a union with a membership of 6,000, and so are those in the railways and on the waterfront. The Artisans' and Allied Workers' Union includes about 2,000 builders and masons. There are only 500 in the Transport and General Workers' Union, and the Clerks' Union is weaker still.

None the less some valuable lessons in self-help and organization related to African needs are being learned in these unions; but how far the African instinct to form into 'secret' societies for intrigue and profit will affect them has yet to be seen. Secret societies, oaths and rituals are, it may be remembered, embedded in the hallowed and historic past of British Unions. Perhaps one safeguard against retrogressive steps is the strong hold of creole officials on the present organizations.

Strikes have taken place both at Marampa and Yengema; both companies have had to swallow large wage increases, and one of them had to swallow a scathing report by a commission of inquiry into their part in the dispute. There has been violence, mostly fomented by unemployed hangers-on. But if a European manager has been stoned, at least the strikes have not been without incidents which reveal underlying good humour. In Marampa a crowd of shouting strikers dispersed abashed when an African nanny emerged furiously from her European employer's house to deliver a piece of her mind on the anti-social folly of exciting the English pickins just as she was getting them to bed; in Yengema a discredited union official was observed to run for his life into the maternity ward of the hospital, sanctuary which was respected.

Mines organizations are changing African life; the discipline of regular shifts is as foreign to the man from the bush farm as it was to the English factory worker in the 1820's. It will have its effect on mental attitudes and aptitudes. Living by cash is new. Union comradeship is new. Moreover, it will extend. The Development Corporation is considering the development of new hematite deposits in Tonkolili and an extension of the railway to them. The British iron and steel industry is in urgent need of more iron ore, and it seems regrettable that British capital should pour into the development of iron ore deposits in Conakry, in French Guinea, to the disadvantage of Sierra Leone. The geological survey has mapped the presence of many new minerals, some of which may prove economic, such as the known deposits of bauxite, manganese and lignite; the latter, if recoverable (it has an overburden of 30 feet), would give the railway cheaper fuel and lose the National Coal Board another thankful customer. Smaller deposits of many other valuable minerals may some day prove valuable.

The mines bring in the revenue; they also make a different man of Ansumana. He is under no chief's authority; after working his stint he is a free man with money in his pocket. He may send some of it back to his family farm—or he may discard all the old obligations. His wits are sharpened by working with hundreds or thousands of others in the service of the machines. He may bring up his family in a new way. They may have no farm to work on; so, unless they go to school, how is their childhood to be spent? And what are his sons to do, except follow him, and perhaps get a better job, in the mines? He listens to what is afoot in the world. He may possibly read a newspaper, or hear one being read. He goes to union meetings; he may even think about politics. He is a new and incalculable factor in the changing social scene.

'Bundu' mask worn by 'Bundu Devils' of the women's secret society. These are in fact old women who take charge of the Bundu novices. This mask is a fairly modern one and shows Ashanti influence.

22. THE CHILDS PLAN

*Da tik we man klem go op na im e go
klem kam dong*
If you climb up a tree, you must
climb down by that same tree
CREOLE PROVERB

FURTHER mineral expansion is, according to Mr. Childs' *Plan of Economic Development for Sierra Leone*, 'in the long run possibly the best hope for the territory's economic future'. But though the mines provide a fifth of revenue, they employ barely 7,000 people. Nearly 90 per cent of the people live by the land. However valuable the mines become, and whatever manufacturing industries the mines bring into being, the basic problem is the health and productivity of the soil. The land must produce more; to produce more it must be rightly used. Its use must be properly adjusted to the changes which British rule has made in tribal life.

In 1949, the Sierra Leone Government seconded Mr. H. Childs, the Chief Commissioner, to go round the Protectorate, and, with the Agricultural Department's recommendations for land use in mind, to work out just how far and how fast agricultural production and exports could be raised. A 10-year plan had already received the assent of the Legislative Council in 1946; what was wanted was something workmanlike and practical, with 5-year targets to work towards, targets expressed in round figures and accompanied by clear guidance on how they were to be hit. Mr. Childs gathered up all the loose ends of experiment and effort, all the available knowledge on crops, soils and micro-climates, and produced the Plan which now lies upon the desk of every departmental head in Freetown and of every District Commissioner up-country—the Plan which is to solve once for all the frustrations of the last thirty years. For three years Government, chiefs, tribal authorities and district councils have been working on it. The tractors lurching from landing-craft in the Scarcies and Waanje swamps; the herds of Government cattle in Musaia ('those dam' pretty, dam' expensive cows', as Someone High Up described them to me); the Produce Marketing Boards in Freetown; the Development Plans which load every D.C.'s loaded desk and loaded day; the palaver in barris up and down the land; the new, often amateur, roads that probe the bush for isolated towns and farms; the Pioneer Mills whose whirr obtrudes a new sound into the orchestra of the bush—all of them are part of the Plan.

The plan, whose workings the visitor observes everywhere, can be summed up in two columns of figures: crop production for 1948, from which Mr. Childs worked, and the targets for 1954. We are all used to White Papers and targets by now— or we are ashamed to confess otherwise—so it is proper to set out this crucial formula for salvation. To give some idea of the anticipated benefit to Sierra Leone, I have added (what Mr. Childs wisely leaves out, but which the rash unofficial may as well fill in) the approximate values of the increased production at 1948 (pre-Korean war) prices.

	Actual tonnages	1948 Actual F.O.B. value £	Target tonnages	1954 Approx. values at 1948 prices £
Palm kernels .	66,431	1,744,591	100,000	3,120,000
Palm oil . .	2,208	115,958	10,000	
Kola nuts .	1,841	166,633	2,000	180,000
Cocoa . .	1,379	102,941	3,000	220,000
Piassava . .	2,160	88,345	4,000	177,000
Coffee . .	347	73,682	700	147,000
Ginger . .	1,319	26,558	2,000	40,000
Benniseed .	349	1,497	500	2,000
Groundnuts .	890	19,148	5,000	100,000
Peppers . .	16	11,538	20	13,000
	76,940	£2,350,891	127,220	£3,999,000

A very neat and workmanlike plan, down to the four extra tons of peppers, which might by some statistical expert be translated into an astronomical number of additional curries served in London hotels. These figures show that while Sierra Leone has an interesting variety of exports, everything really depends on how far the plan achieves its objects in increasing palm products. In 1952 the export duty on palm kernels was tripled, and produced for the exchequer £1,040,000, or nearly two-thirds as much as the companies' tax; if the plan succeeds, probably another £500,000 a year will come in.

The foundation of the plan is a rapid increase in the mileage of roads. The roads are to bring out the agricultural crops, and to stimulate new plantings; if it be said that the builders of the railway had the same hopes, the answer is made that the railway and rivers provide the country with arteries, and the roads will provide the veins—one system completes the other. In 1948 Sierra Leone had but 1,325 miles of motorable roads; by 1954 there will be nearly 3,000.

The marketing of palm oil and palm kernels has also been limited to such deliveries as could be made in the number of man-and-woman-hours available for collection, preparation and porterage, *after* the ordinary work on the rice farms had been done. Motorable roads would save much of the labour of headloading kernels to the nearest collection point. But there remains the labour—'bother', the plan calls it—of boiling and expressing the pericarp oil and in cracking the nuts for the kernels. In fact, even when relegated to women and children, the hard work involved greatly restricts possible output. The plan proposed to mechanize it in centrally situated Pioneer oil mills, as is done in other palm-oil countries such as Nigeria and the Congo. Each mill is expected to serve an area of 10 square miles of good palm country, breaking even on cost of operation when it produces 180 tons of oil and 180 tons of kernels a year. Roads and paths must be built to drain the area's palm fruit to the mill—probably costing £2,000 apart from upkeep.

Roads and mills together are expected in five years to add a third to a crop which is less cultivated than collected haphazardly from a plant that grows wild. But simultaneously cultivators are expected to plant new palms round mills and along roads to facilitate collection. Such new plantings are of varieties of the oil palm which give a higher yield. Sierra Leone's precious capital stock of oil palms may well be decreasing—burnt to death in bush burnings, bled to death by unskilled tapping for palm wine. But millions more palms could be grown—provided native cultivators give up rice production on hillsides and slopes, plant these with palms (along with other tree crops), and confine rice-growing to swamps or estuaries. Thus the area of bush-burning and shifting cultivation is to be cut down, and, at least in the south, to be replaced by cash crops of palm produce, cocoa, coffee, kola, and even timber.

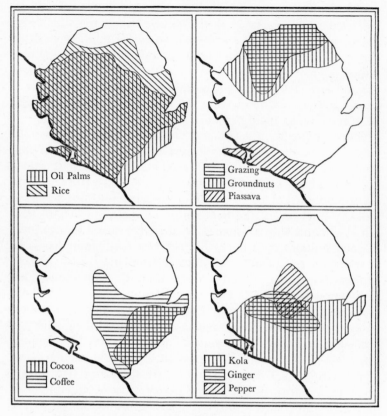

Oil Palms
Rice

Grazing
Groundnuts
Piassava

Cocoa
Coffee

Kola
Ginger
Pepper

Map to show areas suitable for growth of main agricultural crops. It does not follow that the whole area is so
used, and the reference to rice should be read in conjunction
with remarks on soil erosion in Chapters 8 and 22.

These tree crops would conserve the fertility of the soil, and
restore, though on a productive cropping basis, the balance of
nature destroyed when the great forests were murdered and the
period of bush fallow fell below seven years.

Sierra Leone could grow 10,000 tons of cocoa annually—
high-grade cocoa which commands high prices in view of an
expanding world demand for chocolate. The prosperity of the
Ashanti cocoa farmer, now threatened by the swollen shoot
disease, could be reproduced in Mendeland. Coffee, too, could
be grown in much larger quantities—as was shown by the

rapid planting of trees in response, not only to the Ministry of Food contract (as stated in the plan), but to the still higher prices given at Koindu and elsewhere by French traders. Kola output is hampered by the Gambian import duty, but the plan called for more kola. It called for more ginger, benniseed and groundnuts. To get more piassava it proposes the cutting of new waterways in the swamps to tap raffia palms now difficult of access to men equipped only with cutlasses.

There is, further, the prospect of exports of citrus, pineapples and bananas. Profitable export of pineapples depends on canning, and the Department of Trade and Industries has much to learn on this subject from Hawaii and South Africa. Citrus has been talked of for years without much result. But along the railway line and in the Scarcies occur many pockets of light silt clay loams with a water table of 12 feet or less that promise a good banana crop once the secret of cultivation has been learned. Sierra Leone is no further from the British banana market than Jamaica, and is nearer than the Cameroons. That bananas will grow and can be successfully shipped has been demonstrated by a Syrian enthusiast, M. Courban, whose pioneer plantations near Songo are now—after a long period of difficulty and loss due to bad advice and scant Government backing—doing well. It is not possible to grow the standardized, hardy Grosmichel variety in West Africa, because it is susceptible to Panama disease; the Canary variety, though more palatable, must have protective packing and be moved by rail and sea upon a strict time-schedule to permit ripening. Mr. Godbeer of the Commerce and Industries Department has invented a simple, satisfactory and inexpensive method of packing which uses local materials, rice straw and country-made netting. But shipping space is short and timing is difficult. Yet the potentiality of the market is immense. Britain alone could take another 8 million stems or 130,000 tons; against this Sierra Leone supplied 350 tons in 1952.

The plan does not set up any targets for animal products. The improvement of livestock and the introduction of mixed farming, dairying and meat production are expected to remain in the experimental stage for more than five years. The only immediate practical step is to persuade cultivators to control erosion and degradation by early burning of pastures and to discourage the merciless killing of such trees as survive the burning (it is a heart-rending sight in the north to see fires being kindled with malice aforethought in holes cut into the vitals of solitary trees. What is it in Islam that creates such intense hatred of trees?). It will take Africans years to see the logic of the argument that pigs must be fed as well as Africans, and housed even better, if they are to hoist their owners' food and housing above the superior pig standard. Knowledge of cattle is confined to the Fulas. To teach Mendes to understand animal husbandry may be an even bigger job than to get them to abandon upland in favour of swamp rice. It will require agricultural education and still more agricultural education.

Nor does the plan include any targets for the fisheries. But fish is a bigger source of protein in Sierra Leone than meat or game. Before the war, Scandinavian stockfish was sold up-country for 2½d. per lb., but the rise in Laplanders' wages has made the trade unprofitable, and now, without imports to compete, a quarter of a pound of Bonga costs a shilling. The fishermen's wants are simple and it is said that they are content to take higher prices and do less fishing. In fact, the middlemen and 'fish mammies' get most of the profit, but even if it were so, no one who has seen how the fishermen venture upon treacherous waters in their frail canoes would blame them. The fisheries along the coast will only yield their full harvest to bigger, powered boats; to trawls; to scientific understanding of the migration of surface and deep-sea fish. Soon after the war ended the Government replaced the ancient trawler which supplemented Freetown's fish supply with a modern high-speed diesel trawler of far greater capacity. But this bid to open up the fisheries came to nothing. The trawler was perpetually in dock and is now for sale. Dark stories circulated about the fishermen's medicine upon the perfidious bark that was to do them out of their profits and fatally offend the fish; one prominent politician boasted that the trawler would be made to fail. But over a glass or two on the verandah of the City Hotel I was given the candid opinion of a passing Norwegian trawler-owner on the wisdom and consequences of (a) employing that type of trawler in the tropics, and (b) entrusting its ridiculously delicate engines to African engineers. He had an infectious laugh that blew away superstition.

Today a better scheme is in operation. At Kissy in the old Admiralty Nissen huts has been located the headquarters of the West African Fisheries Research Institute, one of the series of Institutes, organized by a central body, which supplies all British West African colonies with common research services for their main crops—rice, fish, cocoa, oil-palm and so forth. Its task is two-fold: to learn the full extent of the offshore and deep-water fisheries, and to teach African fishermen to use floating-trawl powered boats co-operatively owned by fishing villages, or financed by 'fish mammies' of substance. The Director told me that the Institute would be sadly disappointed if, in five or six years, it did not establish the presence of enough fish and develop the means of harvesting them ultimately to multiply the Sierra Leone catch a thousand times. But it will take time. Just as tropical soil is harder to cultivate than soil in temperate climates, so are tropical waters less fertile in fish. In temperate climes warm layers of water are continuously rising to the surface, and cold layers are sinking, an interaction which encourages the growth of plankton, the vegetable food of the smallest fishes and the basis of fish populations. But in the tropics the hot impact of the sun reverses this alternation and no vegetable food for fish grows over large areas. Thus the lower layers are relatively poor in fish. Some intuitive knowledge of the dangers of over-fishing the impoverished tropical shallows may have informed the Tuntu Society's inhibitions: the Sherbros or Bulloms have fished these waters for thousands of years.

A big scientific fishery would produce large amounts of cheap protein for the upland farmer, many suitable species of fish for a local canning industry—an additional export—and large amounts of fish manure, rich in the phosphate which laterite soils lack. It would thus notably forward the purely agricultural objectives of the plan. But the basis of the plan lies in the big switch from upland rice to swamp and estuary rice, from a mainly subsistence to a mainly cash-crop agriculture. Can this be done? It is an extremely attractive rearrangement of Sierra Leone agriculture, one which solves all problems—on coloured maps. It would halt the loss of fertility. The habit of buying rice would increase the incentive of oil-palm and cocoa growers. The swamps would yield well, and could be properly rotated and dressed with fertilizer, which a cash-crop farmer would think worth buying. The rice farmer in the estuaries would become mechanized; he would develop into a new and efficient type of cultivator, producing a maximum crop to provide the cash to buy or hire his machines and other needs.

Finally, if all the inland swamps now unused and the full extent of riverain and mangrove swamps were put under rice, the total rice production would allow a perhaps handsome margin for export, at least until Sierra Leone's population grew to absorb it. In 1948 the West African Rice Mission visited Sierra Leone and made proposals designed to produce 50,000 tons of rice for export. The Childs Plan doubts if the way is even now clear for this fulfilment of Winston Churchill's anticipations of the 'twenties; but the results of mechanized cultivation in 1950–52 suggest that it *could* be done. If so it would fill a strategic need of the western world; and at the present (1952) unofficial price of £75 per ton, it would nearly double the export value of agricultural products as projected by the Childs Plan. To that £4,000,000 it would add another £3,750,000.

Sierra Leone, exporting twice its present output of palm kernels, cocoa, coffee and other crops, *and* exporting such a basic foodstuff as rice, *and* with a large and growing income from minerals, would be a very different economic proposition from the Sierra Leone of today. It would perhaps be the demi-paradise that settlers, creole leaders and enthusiasts from Britain once dreamed the Colony would become, had it but hinterland, railways, trade, and modern plantations. The Childs Plan is the kernel of that wider, but still practicable, possibility. Can it be made a reality? Or must it fade like so many other grandiose hopes that the rain has washed into the drains of Freetown?

It well may, unless Sierra Leonians as a whole can be inspired to play their part; unless the Ansumanas and Mariamas of the villages as well as the young men and women pursuing the higher certificate at Fourah Bay, or learning about pigs, humus and NPK at Njala, can be inspired to bring it about. Early in his report, Mr. Childs wrote:

'The foundations of economic development must be laid right down on the ground, in the villages and among the people. . . . A criticism of which a good deal has been heard in the past is that such plans have been apt to lack efficacy through being imposed, cut and dried, from the top. . . . The people must actively co-operate in the work of development if results are to be commensurate with the cost or the need. . . . This means that economic development should be conceived, and treated, as an act of partnership between Government and people and that where necessary to make partnership a reality constructive changes must be made in the system of administration. . . . Similarly it may be of even greater importance that the people of the country should themselves show capacity and readiness to adapt their local institutions and ways of life so as to increase their effectiveness. . . .'

Though it might not be easy to translate this exhortation into Mende, in fact the responsibility for the plan is being laid as far as possible on African shoulders. For every district, section plans have been drawn up which it is the job of the district councils sitting under the presidency of the D.C. to carry through. The councils discuss and work out the details of local development plans, especially for roads, the formation of co-operatives, swamp rice-growing, relations with Produce Marketing Boards, and the details of every aspect of the Childs master plan.

A Five-Year District Plan, duly cyclostyled and circulated to all chiefs and officials, is an impressive document. It begins with a condensed Domesday inventory of the district's resources, followed by the aims and targets of the plan in general terms (e.g. total mileage of additional roads to be built) and then in detail (e.g. road surveys from point to point). In the south, the plans give prominence to such projects as the creation of nurseries for seedling oil palms of improved varieties as a major objective—no polite visitor to any Mende chiefdom can escape a ceremonial inspection of the new nursery. In the north, the plans place emphasis on swamp rice with security of tenure for swamp farmers, and such subjects as the need for veterinary services. Coastal districts, in addition, plan for improved fisheries. Agricultural, Forestry and Co-operation officers have helped to shape these plans, after being cross-questioned about their recommendations, as council minutes (now also cyclostyled and duly circulated) reveal.

The councils' plans are carried out, of course, in the main by the chiefs working through their time-honoured system of allocating work and duties. But other agencies exist to push forward the plan. The need to encourage Co-operation in Sierra Leone was finally realized by the authorities in 1939; until then, neither the state of education nor the demand for crops, other than palm kernels and piassava, seemed to make Co-operation practicable. An Ordinance was enacted, and in 1949 a Registrar of Co-operative Societies, Mr. Hill, was appointed. Mr. Hill surveyed the possibilities crop by crop (including fish and pig-keeping) and also the prospects for Co-operative Wholesale—or consumers—Societies. He concluded that: 'There is now a magnificent opportunity for co-operative enterprise. . . . It has the prospect of covering . . . all the main aspects of agricultural and social life; and appears to be one of the best means of securing a substantial and increasing rise in the standard of living of the common man, and of giving a moral training of high value'. By 1950 some 43 societies were in operation, of which 27 were marketing societies and one a producers' society. Co-operatives are now organizing the marketing of bananas, cocoa and fish. A particularly encouraging sign has been the formation of a society to develop mixed farming with oxen-ploughing and crop rotations—in the heart of the Mende country where knowledge of cattle has hitherto been wanting.

To develop cash crops over a long period not only co-operation in production and marketing but stabilization of prices is necessary. Native crops are remarkably sensitive to sudden price changes. Sudden price-falls rouse ever-latent suspicions of the white man's hidden piratical tendencies. They may destroy in a season the work of years of exhortation by weary Agricultural Officers. To achieve stable prices by centralized marketing (mainly by means of contracts with the U.K. Ministry of Food) and the accumulation of revolving funds, the Produce Marketing Board was set up. It has in a few years accumulated a £5 million fund out of which it makes advances to producers for such purposes as purchase of seedling Angola oil palms, nurseries, roads to drain produce to Pioneer mills, better bagging methods for cocoa, organization of agricultural shows, and reckons that it is supplying better-graded cocoa than the Gold Coast.

At all levels these organizations call for leaders and administrative staff. 'The field staffs, particularly of the Agricultural Department and Co-operative Department, need to be strengthened. ... Whether one is thinking in terms of the much-needed Geological Survey, or of agricultural extension work . . . or of the introduction of mechanical methods . . . or of rural water supplies . . . it is not lack of funds but lack of men which impedes progress . . . everything possible must be done to speed up the training of Africans . . . everything possible must be done to assist recruitment from overseas. . . . ' So runs the refrain of the Childs Plan. The scarcity of experts with persuasive tongues (able to put their stuff over in Mende, Temne, Kono, etc.) is matched by the scarcity of local organizers in chiefdoms and district councils. In the last resort the plan has got to be explained to every Ansumana and his wives—to every Mawe. It is often easier to explain why things go wrong than how to make them go right, as this poignant extract from the Proceedings of the Tenth Meeting of the Bombali District Council held in Makeni in March 1952 suggests:

> *Mr. H. A. Bangura:* It is understood that the Native Administration Farm at Kamakwie has been closed down. Will the Agricultural Officer please state if this is (a) on account of the soil? (b) due to the fault of the Demonstrator? (c) due to the situation of the farm? Is it to be opened again? If not, why not?

> *Agricultural Officer (Makeni):* I understand that it was due to the disappearance of a large quantity of seed rice from the farm and that several of the town's big men were involved. I therefore regret that it is not possible to reopen the farm. . . .

The plan is a new attempt to assert human control over the natural and social processes which have changed the face of Sierra Leone since British rule upset the balance of tribal life. It is an attempt—whether or not those who called for it or contributed to it realized the fact—to create a new balance at a new level: a balance in which agriculture shall by its very productiveness maintain and indeed build up the land's fertility, while the wealth that agriculture and mining puts into the hands of farmers and workers and the State shall create, through education, personal incentives and higher living standards, a level of skill and understanding among Africans adequate to maintain this new, but more complex and exacting, relationship between the people of Sierra Leone and their country. This can only be done if the people produce their own leadership *at every level*, a leadership based on understanding of the tasks to be surmounted, instead of on authority sustained by tradition.

These, alas, are but windy generalizations in the modern manner. But it is difficult to spare the reader them. All I can do to make them concrete is to offer an impressionistic sketch of a transformed—indeed apotheosized—Ansumana running a cocoa or oil-palm plantation for cash profits; keeping his accounts; reading pamphlets from Njala on improved methods; attending meetings of his local marketing and credit co-operatives with weighty advice for the shaping of their policy; standing for election for the district council, or at least voting only after a careful scrutiny of the candidates' promises to build roads or schools; taking in a newspaper; appearing at agricultural shows and buying stock and implements there; purchasing his family requirements out of income—rice, building materials, furniture, education for his children—after reinvesting in his plantation's upkeep.

This is an Ansumana who keeps a weather eye on the politicians in Freetown and makes them fear his cool appraisal of their words; an Ansumana who expects steady progress in the country's development, knows how to assess it, and how to bring pressure to ensure it; an Ansumana who may offer rice to the ancestors, but will offer manure to his swamp rice holding; an Ansumana who may dance at the ceremonies of Poro, Sande, Wunde, Njaya and other societies—but who, when he feels ill or sees that his children are ill, will get on to a lorry or bicycle along the hard PWD road to the nearby hospital; an energetic, bustling Ansumana who will be proud to have one son training to be an engineer—but will be content with another son who, though gaining high praise for his work in biology for the Cambridge, yet finds plenty to interest him on his father's well-run farm, and will cherish the land after Ansumana has crossed the river and can, as an ancestor, give but shadowy advice on how to put in seedlings or distinguish between capital and income in one's trading accounts.

It may be some time before the present generation of cultivators gives place to men like these; meanwhile Africans are to be brought in at every other level to run the plan—and to run Sierra Leone. Schools may be inadequate, Fourah Bay little more than a blueprint. It may be nearly as hard to get an African who can tune an engine as it is to get an African who can run a research farm, a co-operative or a Government department. But a new teacher, an extra-mural teacher, has been installed in Sierra Leone to see what he can make of the present generation of educated Africans. His name is Responsibility. For the services are to be progressively Africanized. Indeed, the shaping of policy, the carrying out of the plan itself, is to be Africanized. Before the apotheosized Ansumana appears in any number in Mendeland or elsewhere, African ministers will be in charge of the clusters of rooms where the fans flutter papers in in-trays and out-trays—the Secretariat departments.

The ancient crafts live on precariously. Though the loom is simple, design is vigorous, and superb cloth is produced by sewing the strips together. 'Country cloth' is indispensable for ritual observances

'I know the answer . . .' First task of the Sierra Leonian child is to grasp the strange thought-forms of English, the key to western technology

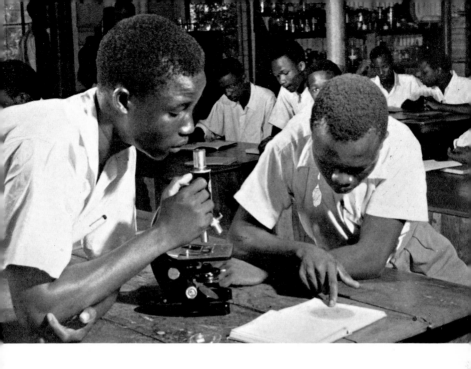

'I know the answer . . .' Science opens a new world to the African sixth form boy—but laboratories and fine schools are still few

The luckiest go on to Fourah Bay college, which has been moved to Mount Aureol from the Victorian building in which candidates for the African ministry used to learn Greek, Latin, Hebrew, and even Arabic

The chieftaincy is still coveted, and rivals from the ruling houses must state their claims before the elders when an election follows a chief's death. Secondary education is not necessarily a recommendation

One essential of the plan to arrest the loss of soil fertility is to develop tree crops, especially on sloping ground, in place of rice. Sierra Leone could grow five times the present cocoa crop, at high prices

Oil palms are, however, the most important tree crop. But larger plantations and bigger crops outstrip the capacity of the women and children to crack the nuts. This task must be centralized and mechanized in Pioneer Oil Mills

'Luk flawa, luk wata; mix!' (Here's flour and water, they must be mixed.) This creole proverb is apt to the Freetown Junior Dinner Club, where Europeans and Africans meet in friendly discussion

23. AFRICANIZATION

Don't tell the man who is carrying
you that he stinks

TEMNE PROVERB

I ONCE heard an unwary European in the last years of
the British Raj remark soothingly to Jawaharlal Nehru that,
after all, Indianization was going on rapidly. 'Indianization!'
the Nationalist leader snorted, 'what a silly word that is! Do
you think England could be Englishized?' None the less, just as
science and technology are being applied to the problems of
Sierra Leone as never before, Africanization is the order of the
day. It is not an entirely new departure; at many periods the
Colony has witnessed and critics have deplored 'laudable exertions to elevate the Negro race to that intellectual standard of
which they are pronounced capable, to the ultimate design of
superseding, at any sacrifice of English interest, in all departments, lucrative, speculative and professional, those who have
been the authors of Africa's present advancement and
prosperity'.

Africanization today takes the principal form of promoting
into the senior services of Government. Until recently there
were few such appointments, though in 1924 the Assistant
Colonial Secretary was African. In 1939, of 235 senior appointments, 26 were held by Africans, all elderly men who had
waited long for their promotion. In 1952, of 535 senior appointments (how Government grows!) 116 were held by Africans,
many of them younger men. Among them were a Puisne
Judge and the Director of Medical Services. Nearly all were
creoles. Africanization is proceeding as fast as education permits.
'It is at present only limited', an African establishment officer
said to me, 'by the ability of our schools to turn out school
certificate men.'

The process of supersession, however, has gone further than
filling one senior Secretariat post in four with Africans. The
change in the system of local government in the Protectorate
(as well as in the Colony rural areas) is intended to take initia-
tive from the District Commissioner and place it in the hands

of elected African officials. In fifty years of administrative change, the D.C. has become a different man. He is still the principal tax assessor and collector, magistrate and chief executive in his district; but he is more and more tied to his desk by the development plans, estimates, sets of statistics, paper-work, and above all by the need, as president of the district council, to teach the job of administration, of committee-rule, to the council. It is still his job to tour his district, to know the people, as well as collect tax, but though he often manages to be on trek three months in the year, he knows that according to the older theory of government he is no longer doing the real job.

The District Commissioner in the inter-war years lived a more leisurely but also more mobile life. He had but one set of estimates to prepare; he took a casual if professional view of his papers; he took a mild interest in development—it had to be mild because any actual request which he made to spend money was rejected curtly. He took, however, a great interest in his chiefs and his people. He pursued justice with a single-minded determination that awed while it amused his subjects, and today his name is often remembered where the present incumbent's is unknown. The 'thirties saw the beginnings of change. District councils had been started on an advisory basis. Some D.C.s whizzed through the district in cars.

The older generation, a few of whom had seen the Protectorate started, lived an entirely different life. They had no Provincial Commissioners to inspect them. They were directly responsible to Freetown, which had absolutely no wish to intervene in their affairs. Freetown was totally happy if they kept quiet and wrote infrequently. They in turn felt their job was done if the law was respected and the taxes collected. They reckoned that it took three months' trekking to collect tax in solid silver. But they trekked another five months, making eight months in twelve during which they could not answer letters. They expected to make comfortably on their hammock allowance. There were no roads; they went everywhere, stopped everywhere, interfered with everybody's palavers and humbugs and enjoyed the shooting. They had their own methods; they often married, by proper payment of bridewealth, into local families, and obtained a good deal of 'pillow information'. They came of a generation not afraid to express itself in eccentricity; no finer sight could be seen than a certain D.C. Kabala moving with a majestic train from the railhead at Kamabai, his hundreds of porters loaded with every delicacy that Fortnum and Mason (and those were great days for Fortnum and Mason) could supply. Upon him descended within the next six months anyone who had, or anticipated having, any business with him; for it was known that after six months of feasting he ran out of stock and calmly reverted for the next year or so to a completely native diet—rice, foo-foo, and palaver sauce on Sundays.

Roads and development bring government closer to the people. But it is not a Pa D.C. Government. It is paper government, and Africans increasingly push the paper. The present generation of D.C.s must resign themselves to standing back further and further from the administration, surrendering judicial and tax-collecting powers, surrendering contacts, becoming teachers and councillors, ultimately becoming constitutional figureheads, 'Government Agents' in the Gold Coast phrase, until their offices, too, are Africanized or abolished. At present they toil at a rate and in a way that would have appalled the first generation of D.C.s who were the younger sons of squires and took on the job because it was, if in exile, at least imperial and fit for a gentleman.

Thus emerges the African local government officer. He is, as yet, only a sketch of what he is intended to become. Will he be a success? I do not know; nobody knows. He will have the advantages, as well as the disadvantages, of being an African. He should know the mind of the people. Motor roads as well as collection of UNESCO statistics put a growing barrier between white ruler and African folk. 'Roads are no good for Fathers,' a missionary said to me; 'it's a good thing *we* can't afford cars.' The African administrator, whatever his office, will be able to get at the facts more easily—if he chooses. What sort of man he will be will depend on his education; and he must get his education from his tribal or creole family life, from the schools available, and from Fourah Bay. Senior men can be given an additional varnish at an English university, no doubt. It is conceivable that some African officials will have a good deal more education than some British rulers have had; and to the African mind that will be decisive. Character? Well—what is character? Are we claiming that character is a unique product of English professional-class origins and upbringing, of class-rooms and lecture rooms and common rooms situated in England? And if not, why then should it not be provided as a specialist course in a College of Arts, Science and Technology?

But it is not so much character that is lacking as a solid African middle-class; not just a cadre of literate clerks, but a professional and commercial bourgeoisie, with money behind them. 'Well, whose fault is that?' the European is tempted to retort. 'They let the Syrian beat them to it. Character again!' But why did the Syrians beat them to it? Commissioner Alldridge warned the creoles in 1910: 'The Syrian trader has annexed the West Coast; he has come and come to stay. . . . He is more than a clever man of business; his tact is wonderful, amounting to genius. He lays himself out to study the country people, and he succeeds wherever he goes. . . . Content with the "nimble ninepence" . . . the Syrian saves where the Sierra Leonian squanders; he makes no show; he attends strictly to business. . . . But do we find that the Sierra Leonians are taking this lesson to heart? Are they trying to carry on their businesses on similar lines? Are they as thrifty in their domestic and daily lives as the Syrians? . . . How, under the present circumstances, with the importing retailing houses on the one hand and the Syrian gleaners on the other, they are to exist, is with them one of the most serious problems of the day. . . .'

The Syrians and the 'Importing retailing houses' won, in alliance with each other. 'The Firms' found the Syrian easier to deal with; he got the produce and brought it down to Free-town, his prices were lower, his deliveries prompter—and they extended credit to him, and gradually withdrew it from the African. Alldridge thought the ruin of the creole trader was love of display and fecklessness. It often was; but one of his greatest handicaps was, and remains, the weight of the social services, which he alone carried and still carries on his shoulders. For the rule is: a man must support his relatives if he can, and even his friends if he can. The rules of African hospitality are Open House while a crust remains on the shelf. The African trader, like the African doctor, lawyer, teacher, Government clerk, is leeched by his relatives. They are poor; at any time some among them are sick or unfortunate; if he has resources it is his duty to share. This prevents him from accumulating capital. When he does accumulate it, uncertainty often causes him to consume it hastily before someone else lays claim to it. A trader gave me a case: last year a Kono who was panning gold found a nugget worth £80; his relatives descended upon him like locusts until he was cleaned out. The trader asked him if he would now start panning again. He replied: 'Not yet. For at least a year I shall go and live on *them*'. A missionary told me that his ministers were reduced to beggary by the ceaseless calls upon them, and raising their stipends hardly benefited them at all; he spoke of the immense relief expressed by one pastor when advised he could with propriety refuse to lend anyone his bicycle on the grounds that it was Church property. The African is a good trader within the limits imposed by this parasitism. A trade union leader told me that Communism was impossible in Sierra Leone 'because everyone is a small capitalist of some kind'.[1]

The Syrian won hands down because he could live as simply as the African (the Lebanese come to West Africa from one of the most poverty-stricken parts of their country; many were literally driven out by hunger); because he was given credit by his compatriots, not parasitized by them; because he could take longer views; and because he soon had the Firms behind him. That is the truth of the matter. Now after fifty years of hard work and money-making the Syrian business community is in an almost impregnable position—though their cadets still go out and trade in the villages as their first coral-selling grandfathers did. 'Business makes you old pappa', a young Syrian, atypically hungering to join the British Army, said to me. 'You shop all day for twelve hours. You fish for every customer, play him with the line like *this*—' he mimed the action of reeling in a fish. And it is true. A Syrian will let you turn his shop upside down. An African simply says: 'What do you want?' and then names his price.[2]

It would be wrong to cast the Syrian trader as villain of the Sierra Leone tragi-comedy, as many Africans and some Europeans do. It was necessary to make the railway pay, to bring

[1] Not, of course, a very convincing argument in view of events in China.

[2] You will get 300 per cent better service from an African shopkeeper or salesgirl if your first words are 'Good morning'.

in the revenue, to find the money to run the country, to finance even the meagre Government provision for education that was made in the years when missionary funds and fervour began to decline. Only the single-hearted pursuit of profits which distinguishes the Syrian could have produced that trade. The produce had to be gleaned from self-sufficient native communities in a roadless land. From the first the administration set its face firmly against alienating lands for European-run plantations, and left it to the native cultivator to produce the trade. The big firms went elsewhere—to the East; in Sierra Leone their prices were low, their interest, rebuffed, rather scanty. It was necessary for someone to take Japanese tinware and textiles up-country to create the wants which would induce the rice-farmer to collect and sell palm produce. To speed the process, the Syrian wove a web of debt; that is, no other institutions being available, he provided agricultural credit. The Firms were not capable of such work. To live native up-country and make the nimble ninepence was beneath the dignity of their counter-jumpers. They wanted to buy in bulk and make profits in bulk. They still do.

Sierra Leone owes much of its development to the Syrians, even if the consequences have been tragic for the creoles. Still, the Syrians have done well out of African and Briton alike, and there seems no good reason why some of them should be allowed to defraud the country of income tax and diamond royalties. However, the Africanization of trade is taking place in other ways. In the Protectorate, the tribal African is taking to trade upon the profits of high prices for cash crops. Perhaps more significantly, both the Syrians and the Firms are having their claws trimmed by the setting up of co-operatives and by the fixing of buying prices by the marketing boards. These bodies will ultimately be wholly run by Africans. A complete network of producers', consumers', marketing and credit co-operatives would diminish the trade of Syrians and big business alike. At this interesting moment, the United Africa Company has come out strongly for Africanization, and has introduced a scheme to train its own district and departmental managers. Some up-country branches are now run by Africans. It is a sign of grace; I hope that in view of U.A.C.'s importance in the everyday life of West Africans, in the fullness of time representatives of this new African managerial profession will find their way on to the U.A.C. Board.

Opportunities have suddenly widened to Africans not only in administration and commerce, but in the professions. Teachers for the new schools; doctors, nurses and dispensers for the new hospitals; engineers to inspect the new works, bridges, roads, mills, dams; all are wanted and at good salaries. Lawyers are less in demand, since the D.C., the paramount chiefs and the native courts are still solidly against importing British legal forms into Protectorate courts. British officials—and not only in Sierra Leone—have little time for the native lawyer. But who brought the law from England and set up the profession as almost the *only* profession at which an African might make money? It is, as a profession, still overcrowded. But development at least creates commercial litigation and conveyancing. And, for the matter of that, lawyers can run co-operatives.

The irony is that, just as the opportunity widens, the creoles and the educated tribal Africans are unready to take advantage of it. The reserves are not there; a professional middle-class cannot be created in depth by a ten-year plan. It takes generations to grow, and the opportunities available to Africans in administration, commerce and the professions have been too small to provide anything but a nucleus. Schools can be set up far more quickly than good, disciplined homes can be made. It is far easier to get a child taught English or arithmetic than to get it trained in orderliness and concentration and endowed with a sense of security, family honour and responsibility. The one is a matter of Government funds. The other is a matter of a culture growing on a reasonable standard of living for a considerable time. 'Jantri no kam bai takiti' runs the creole proverb. Gentry are not made by over-worry and fuss.

I asked a doctor in Freetown what she thought was the greatest need. Her reply was, 'Infant and nursery schools'. As I had just been given to understand by an educationist that the first need was for science labs. in secondary schools, I asked her to justify her priority. She remarked that they were needed to do what the African and even the creole home did not do: to lay in early life the foundations of character.[1] She meant more

---

[1] It is interesting that Dr. Margai's election manifesto included a demand for experimental nursery schools—'to produce good citizens'.

particularly the character needed to sustain modern organization—such as hospitals. Many doctors spoke to me of their disappointment in African nurses, male and female. It was next to impossible to inculcate method into them; they were unreliable, dishonest and disobedient, and their attitude to patients—to suffering—was unspeakable. They were often charming and amiable; but the disciplined altruism of nursing was beyond them. Yet white doctors spoke warmly of the skill and devotion of their African medical colleagues. It may be no coincidence that African doctors go through the hard training of British medical schools. It is noticeable how doctoring runs in old-fashioned creole professional families of standing and substance.

This creole professional élite is small for reasons—perhaps—that are nobody's fault. Its smallness is none the less tragic. And it may be no accident that outstanding creole men and women often die at a tragically early age. There is too much for them to do; hardly anyone to rely on; hardly anyone to whom trust can be delegated safely. Mrs. Benka-Coker, the pioneer of girls' secondary education and the organizer of the movement for raising the status of women, died recently at 49; I witnessed an impressive mourning by a community that could ill afford to lose her dynamism.

The truth is that 'Africanization' means slightly different things to Europeans and Africans. To Africans, it means unconditional superseding of Europeans by Africans. Africans are to do the job, partly in a European way, partly in an African way. To Europeans it essentially means finally Europeanizing Africans so that they can have the *same* attitudes to their jobs, responsibilities, power and temptations, as the trained European. And indeed the task of running a Sierra Leone reorganized along the lines of the Childs Plan, conforming to the recommendations of the Agricultural Department, developing mining and manufacturing, *is* one for modern western administrators.

But it is also a task which Africans must do; and if they fail, well, then, it cannot be done. Only Africans can, as the Childs Report recognizes, persuade Africans so drastically to change their ways in such a short time. At Pujehun ('the town of hot peppers', or quarrelsome town) two experiments are proceeding, though they are probably not thought of as experiments.

The assistant D.C., Mr. A. K. Hyde, D.F.C., is a creole: will the people of Pujehun District recognize in him the essential African leadership needed in the new tasks of administration? He is a remarkable man, cool and objective in his appraisal of the problem, at once a personal and a public problem of the greatest moment to himself and his people. Not far from the Government offices is the community development scheme run by a Mende, Mr. Frank Anthony, a burly man of infectious enthusiasm and high faith. Anthony organizes community development committees in the chiefdoms of the district on a self-help principle; this self-help amounts to adult education in all farming, health and welfare matters. It is simple and practical. It brings, for example, those who have successfully organized a cooperative into touch with those who would like to form one; it sets up committees for the digging of wells and latrines and the construction, by communal labour, of better houses. It seeks to drain off the discontent of the young by making life constructive.

At Pujehun Frank Anthony took me round the small demonstration farm which shows simply and unelaborately how rice is grown in a swamp and how cash crops—pineapples, bananas, palm oil, coffee, cocoa and citrus—are grown on the hillsides in contour strips. He is the centre of a mass literacy campaign, which begins with the practical job of keeping minutes of meeting, accounts in standard form, the making of social surveys, complete with cyclostyled questionnaires and statistical analysis, and the public reading of the many pamphlets on agricultural improvement published by the Agricultural Department. The Pujehun centre also trains other community development officers. 'Community development' is a horrid phrase; but it is a real and vivid thing: the basic work of teaching Ansumana and Mariama how to live better, how to get better crops while keeping their land in good heart, how to live more healthfully and care better for their children.

The progress of such experiments will reveal more of the implications of 'Africanization' than we now know.

R

24. SELF GOVERNMENT

Promis na det
A promise is a debt to be redeemed
CREOLE PROVERB

THE logic of Africanization proceeds to the day when an African Prime Minister of Sierra Leone takes his seat for the first time at one of the Commonwealth Premiers' Conferences—that grand 'hanging heads' by the tribal authorities which a multi-racial Commonwealth has evolved for the discussion of policy. The justice of history would indeed require that the first African Premier to attend should be a Sierra Leonian. For Sierra Leone spans the strange life of the British Empire. Among the first settlers were men who put their trust in the Crown and fought for George III against George Washington to avert the great schism in the English-speaking world. The first self-governing democracy established in Africa was set up in Sierra Leone in 1787; the settlers were to elect their governor and magistrate. In the ensuing anarchy King Tom showed that tribal organization was stronger than an ill-found democratic city-state; his war-boys scattered the settlers.

The Government of the Colony has reflected every stage of Commonwealth development. The failure of the free city-state was followed by company rule, a miniature reproduction of arrangements in India, except that the company was non-profit-making, and failed financially. In 1808, Sierra Leone became a Crown Colony, under the rule of Governor-in-council. When, as occasionally happened, all members of council were laid low by putrid miasmata, the Governor ruled alone, and sometimes despotically. But as the Colony grew in numbers and education, British ideals of popular representation reasserted themselves. 'All the affairs of the Colony are transacted by a Council consisting of Seven', protested Poole, the visiting colonial chaplain, in 1850. 'And its public business is carried on by this body of officials, without any reference to public opinion. . . . Houses of Assembly, acting in concert with Legislative Councils, are the best correctives for political maladministration; and the habits of business, intelligence and common good sense of the superior portion of the native population could without difficulty furnish an efficient legislature.'

The authorities had no faith in Houses of Assembly, but some years later reconstituted the Legislative Council to make it slightly more sensitive to the public opinion of the Colony, if any. The new 'Leg. Co.' consisted mainly of officials, and an Executive Council, or 'Ex. Co.', was formed, entirely of officials. But Africans were nominated to sit on the Legislative Council, whose debates were held in public and, towards the end of the century, printed in the press: and the Secretary of State warned the Governor that in nominating Africans to serve he 'should choose not those who are most likely to support Government but those who will be taken to represent and will readily inform you of the wishes of the intelligent portion of the community'.

The next significant step was the appointment of the provincial commissioners of the Protectorate to sit in Leg. Co. *ex officio* and represent the interests of the hinterland. Then, five years after the First World War had made the world safe for democracy, Leg. Co. was again reconstituted. The number of unofficial members was raised to seven, three of whom were elected by literate voters in the Colony. Three paramount chiefs were brought in to represent the Protectorate. Officialdom could always outvote the rest by a majority of one, but it was understood that in such an event the Government would submit the measure to the Colonial Office before passing it into law.

The British Commonwealth was undergoing its transmogrification into a Commonwealth in which republics and kingdoms were associated under the symbol of the Crown, when Sierra Leone, like other colonies, began to discuss the next step—a constitution which would give the majority vote to unofficial representatives of the peoples in the territory, and so pave the way to responsible cabinet government. Soon after the war, the Governor, Sir Hubert Stevenson, began to sound opinion on a constitution which would make self-government an achievable goal within the period taken by a ten-year plan so to improve education that Africans would be forthcoming in numbers for posts of responsibility. Whereupon all the old frustration and antagonisms of the past reappeared. Sierra Leone, though in the creole phrase the 'Mother Colony' of British West Africa, is once again following where in years gone by she took the lead. The first African to bear the title Prime Minister is Kwame Nkrumah of the Gold Coast.

Sir George Beresford-Stooke inaugurated, after considerable delay, a modified Stevenson constitution in 1951. It has worked smoothly—but to the accompaniment of much bitterness and recrimination from creole political leaders. It gives a majority in the new Leg. Co. to unofficial African members, of whom there are 21 as opposed to 7 officials (some of whom, however, such as the Director of Medical Services, are African), and two nominated members, one African, representing commerce. There is an Executive Council of four official members and six members appointed from the unofficial bloc in Leg. Co. Thus Ex. Co. is an embryonic cabinet. Trouble, however, arose over the allocation of unofficial seats to Leg. Co. Seven are for members elected by the Colony, fourteen for members elected by district councils and the Protectorate Assembly. In other words, the Colony, the stronghold of the creole community, though greatly over-represented in terms of simple numbers, is permanently outvoted by the Protectorate unless nearly all the officials and nominated members take the creole side in a clash of interests.

After 170 years of struggle and aspiration, the creoles ('the superior portion of the native population') found themselves inheriting no promised land, but put into the power of the unregenerate tribesmen. Not, however, directly. For while a 50 per cent literacy rate was held to justify poll by ballot in the Colony, which also had the experience of voting for the municipal council and the old Leg. Co., a five per cent literacy rate in the tribal area was held to require indirect representation of the people. Thus the 14 members elected (by secret ballot) by the district councils and Protectorate Assembly are, in considerable degree, the nominees of tribal authorities and chiefs. Some 6,000 voters elected the 7 Colony members; 500 voters put the 14 Protectorate members in.[1]

It is thus far from being a democratic assembly, though it is held that it is more truly representative of the people of Sierra

[1] But see p. 230. This is how the creole spokesmen sometimes express it. These 500 voters, of course, are themselves representatives of their people on the district council or vote as members of the Protectorate Assembly.

Leone than any democratically elected body could be at the present stage of education and what is called, in the modern cant, 'social emergence'. It has also, of course, limited powers; the Governor retains a veto on legislation, and has reserve powers connected with public order, relations with the Commonwealth and public appointments.

In the first discussions on a new constitution, the Colony leaders seemed resigned to a balance in the new chamber which would permanently outvote the creole community. But before long, under the leadership of the redoubtable Wallace Johnson and Dr. Bankole Bright, the National Council, the creole party, began to fight the proposals. They argued that, in fact, the voting arrangements did not put power in the hands of the Protectorate, which they declared they did not fear, but in the hands of a coterie of reactionary paramount chiefs and tribal authorities who were mere tools in the hands of District Commissioners and British officials generally; that, in fact, it was a means of extending, not reducing, official rule. It disenfranchised some 2,000 literate Colony-born citizens residing in the hinterland. It divided rather than united the country. Perhaps only for tactical reasons, the National Council petitioned that it was illegal to constitute an assembly in which British (Colony) representatives appeared with foreigners (tribal people). The British Protected persons of the Colony, they argued, were foreigners in the meaning of the law. This produced no very favourable reaction among the chiefs. The creoles called for a reconsideration of the constitution by a committee, and the fact that no committee has ever been appointed, other than the select committee which modified Governor Stevenson's original sketch of a constitution, is branded by them as an act of betrayal.

At the elections which followed the National Council was opposed in the Colony by the Sierra Leone People's Party, which appealed to the Colony electorate on a programme of making the constitution work until something better could be worked out. In the Colony, the National Council won four of the seven seats, the S.L.P.P. getting only two—one of which, Freetown East, elected Mr. Sanusi Mustapha on a Muslim ticket. The seventh seat went to an independent. On this basis Johnson and Bright, pledged to fight against the constitution by every means, expected to get seats in Ex. Co., as the Governor had expressed doubt whether party government has sufficiently crystallized to enable him to work even partly on party lines in allotting the unofficial Ex. Co. seats. But during the inauguration of the Council, and almost overnight, the eight paramount chiefs elected to the Council, and other Protectorate members, joined the small S.L.P.P. group, swelling it from four or five Colony and Protectorate members to fifteen. This effectively faced the Governor with a majority party. The division was deepened by a remark of Dr. Bright's, who was understood to say that, on the constitutional issue, the National Council and S.L.P.P. were as apart as two hills. The Governor therefore gave all the unofficial Ex. Co. seats to S.L.P.P. men, including one paramount chief, Bai Farima Tass II. Bright and Johnson thus found themselves excluded from the 'training class for cabinet ministers'. They chose to regard this as the result of the Governor's malevolence, though they might just as well have apportioned some blame to the chiefs and Protectorate members who evidently saw a neat way of excluding the enemies of indirect election from high office.

Indeed, the National Council to some extent created the majority party by the violence of their opposition to a constitution which gave, at long last, due representation to the tribes. The S.L.P.P. has now solidified—at least for the time being—as a party with definite views. They propose that direct election by ballot should be introduced into the tribal areas as soon as may be, but bitterly deny that the present membership is 'self-appointed'. They argue that all tribal authorities, from village headmen upwards, are fully representative of their people, and receive their appointment only after extensive negotiation and 'hanging heads', which excludes unacceptable men. The councils themselves are the result of a pyramid of choices of this kind, and include the pick of the intelligentsia of the Protectorate, including, in some districts, creoles. The councils, as electoral colleges, elect their representatives to Leg. Co. by secret ballot and deny that they are influenced by the D.C.s. The D.C.s strongly deny it too; in fact one D.C. told me that he had been asked by his council whom the Government would like elected, and had produced temporary alarm and despondency when he replied that he neither knew nor cared and that it was time they voted according to their consciences and stopped behaving like children! A lesson in political maturity which, he said, had been well learned, as they were now opposing him in the district council itself.

The paramount chiefs distrust the National Council's plea that direct election must be introduced to make the constitution workable. They see it—perhaps wrongly—as a creole method of getting control over an excitable and politically immature people, and they point to intervention by creole 'agitators' in chiefdom affairs leading to riots by malcontents. 'We have seen what happens in Liberia', one paramount chief said to me. 'Two or three hundred creole families run the place for their own benefit. The tribes are exploited at every turn. We know. They are Mendes, too. Freetown has spent our money on itself in the past, and now we want a say in government.' Even before the constitution was brought in, Government was bowing to this opinion by building expensive and, as some people think, extravagant schools in Bo and Magburaka 'lest the Protectorate should feel they were getting nothing out of taxes'.

The National Council at one time even suggested a federal constitution, with separate assemblies for Colony and Protectorate; this again fills tribal politicians with suspicions that they are not, as they declare, really working for the country's unity—except on their own terms. Though the S.L.P.P. originated as much in the Colony as in the Protectorate, at its heart lies a resolution, shared by Muslims and pagans alike, not to let a clique of ambitious creoles run the country. Personalities no doubt play some part in its feelings—at least so far as one can judge from the salvos exchanged between the *Observer* of Bo and Mr. Wallace Johnson's spirited *African Standard*.

Yet this division is a paradox. One of the first politicians to attempt to bring politically conscious people in the Colony and the Protectorate together was Wallace Johnson. His Youth League achieved considerable success, on the basis of a common front against the British—and some of his activities led Mr. Johnson into internment during the war as prejudicial to the safety of the country. Like many political prisoners before him, he solaced himself in the writing of verse. Both he and the leaders of the S.L.P.P. protest that their aim today is to unite not split the territory. Indeed, compact communities no longer exist. Today the creoles are outnumbered in the Colony by tribal, or perhaps one should say de-tribalized, natives. On the other hand, the greater part of the professional and administrative posts in the Protectorate are held by creoles. Creole and tribal attitudes often clash, but it is creole assumption of superior airs and privileges that angers the 'big men' in a chiefdom rather than Christianity, lounge suits and the possession of the junior or senior Cambridge. Moreover, at the very moment when creole culture can no longer expect to be accorded admiration because it is an African adaptation of European culture, in fact the attitudes, ambitions and motives of educated tribal Africans and educated creoles are becoming almost indistinguishable. The educated, literate African, whatever his origins, takes on something of the creole likeness. He is de-tribalized and westernized, if not Christianized. On the other hand the creole is forsaking some of his distinguishing characteristics— his Christian observance, for example, and his former pride in being the white man's client. He even makes a conscious effort to think of himself as African rather than creole. I once asked a senior creole official whether he felt creole, or Sierra Leonian, or just African? 'I feel West African,' he replied; 'I look forward to the United States of West Africa.'

This may mean that, to the tribal African, the creole still lacks the *taste* of belonging to a disciplined community; still lacks certain ideas of loyalty and fellowship which membership of the Poro imparts. But both politically and socially, the educated creole, Temne, Mende or Fula increasingly feels a sense of community—perhaps of class solidarity. No doubt this is untrue of the older generation, but as school exerts its pressure this sense of nationality should grow. Women in the tribes, moreover, however different they may feel from creole women, tend to emulate their ways. They cling to Sande, no doubt; but they desire independence and respect, and often wrest it from tribal society. It is not always a desire for monogamy. 'I don't mind being married to a man with several wives', a young lady said to me in the Harford Secondary School for Girls. 'But of course I must be a *head* wife.' In fact, the tendency is towards monogamy and a high status for women. It is perhaps in the soul of the African woman that Christianity and Islam will fight their decisive battle.

232

It may therefore be doubtful how long the Colony electorate
will put up with a creole party with such a negative attitude as
that of the National Council, and permanently excluded from
the sweets of office. Already the facts of power are modifying
parties and politicians. The S.L.P.P., monopolizing the unofficial portfolios in Ex. Co., seems in no hurry to implement
its election pledge to draft democratic reforms for conservatism
which keeps them in power. Can it be, too, that the intense
bitterness expressed by Mr. Johnson is less a matter of the constitution than of the political chances which lost him a seat in
Ex. Co.? I trembled as he banged the table, shook pamphlets
under my nose, gave me a preview of a philippic in preparation
entitled *Exit Beresford-Stooke*, and sternly warned me to get my
facts right—but I could not help noticing the stress he laid upon
his own part (which has been considerable) in the political
education of West Africa in general and Kwame Nkrumah in
particular. Wallace Johnson undoubtedly has a following in
the Protectorate as in the Colony, and did much to stir the
country into demanding a new constitution, but it cannot be
anything but irksome to see Dr. Margai inherit all this hard
work on the day that the S.L.P.P. became the majority party.
He was a member of the mission which protested in London
against the constitution—but he has since resigned from the
National Council and the 'Creole Party' is breaking up.

If Wallace Johnson had emerged as the Kwame Nkrumah of
Sierra Leone, perhaps the pressure for transfer of power would
be greater than it is. And changes in African politics blow up
with the rapidity of tornadoes in the Colony hills. But so far
the S.L.P.P. has set a course of moderate nationalism, Dr.
Margai, Albert Margai, and other members of Ex. Co. such as
Sanussi Mustapha and Siaka Stevens are perfectly frank in
their belief that they have everything to learn in the running
of Government departments even with a British head. Several
told me that they thought it would be two years before they
could shoulder ministerial responsibility, an attitude which
has brought down the ridicule of the *African Standard* on the
'Ministerial Training Class' of 'unseasoned politicians and . . .
men who have not the remotest idea how the Central Government is administered'. None the less, the goal of this modest
self-preparation is power. 'The question is not whether the

Colonial peoples will get power but when they will get it,'
observed Mr. Laminah Sankoh in the *African Vanguard*. Indeed,
though Responsibility may—as no doubt the Governor intended that it should—educate Dr. Margai and his colleagues in
the realities of running a country, suspicions sometimes animate
the African mind that the white man, by making it all look so
complicated, is seeking to extend his power by indirect means.
He may seek to perpetuate his rule, warns Mr. Laminah
Sankoh, 'not by downright suppression, but by fussiness—
development plans, educational programmes, co-operative
enterprises, etc.—all of which serve as dress-windows and entail
the employment of a host of expatriates'.

'Africanization of the civil service', declared the S.L.P.P.
manifesto, 'is the main plank in our programme.' It also
pledged itself to strip District Commissioners of 'excessive
powers' and to extend an independent judiciary to the Protectorate, which no doubt cheered the lawyers. To provide the
Africans to replace the British officials it promised to give the
country more education: 'Our aim is universal free compul-
sory education', and meanwhile primary and secondary schools
were to be built and staffed at speed; while Fourah Bay College
ambitions are backed to the hilt by members of Ex. Co. The
manifesto called, expatriates or no expatriates, for an even more
ambitious development scheme than the Childs Plan—a bigger
railway system, hydro-electric schemes, tarmac roads, better
telephones, better rediffusion, more hospitals, municipal
housing, co-operatives and 'fussiness' on a really grand scale
—even a more vigorous exploitation of the country's mineral
wealth: 'We shall need for a considerable time . . . capital and
technical skills from abroad to develop our mineral resources
. . . on a mutually acceptable partnership. . . . The country
should receive a far higher share of the revenue derived from
the mines. . . .' The S.L.P.P. manifesto had little to learn from
British political party promises.

Dr. Margai, I think, means business. He told me that he had,
as party leader, taken the portfolio of health and natural
resources, because the work of these departments went to the
heart of the matter in Sierra Leone, were the hardest and most
daunting. A Mende proverb runs: 'The man's mind is the man'.
Dr. Margai is a Mende who trained in England. In the course

of his medical career he set his medical mind to the practical task of teaching hygiene to the Bundu officials who perform 'the singular freemasonic rites of the women', as Rankin delicately described them in the 1830's. He did much to introduce into the women's societies sensible instruction in sex knowledge and post- and ante-natal care. As Minister-for-Agriculture-in-training he visits the ploughing and swamp rice schemes and insists that parties of chiefs and tribal authorities shall accompany him and learn the whole technique. 'We must grow more,' he said to me, 'export more, and find the health and energy for the effort.' A quiet, gentle-looking man, he has still about him that curious medical air of listening simultaneously to the patient and the patient's symptoms, leaving the impression of a courteous, probing, unfoolable sympathy. I do not know whether, as a politician, he can survive. But I am sure his approach is exactly the right one for Sierra Leone's leader. For from its political leaders the country needs the family doctoring that only Africans can give, combined with powers of objective diagnosis of its ills which only a scientific training can impart. A doctor can be expected to see the interrelationship of food production, land use, soil conservation, and the mental and physical well-being of a people as an organic whole, not merely as a succession of issues to be judged by their usefulness in the struggle to win power.

Postscript: *Ministers-in-training, as it happens, have not completed a two-year probationary course. As I passed the proofs of this book it was announced that the five African members of Executive Council were taking over full responsibility for their departments. This of course does not yet mean the institution of Cabinet responsibility to the degree reached in the Gold Coast—or even Nigeria under the 1951 constitution. But it is a step on the way. Change in Africa is speeding up.*

25. THE WHEREWITHAL

An empty sack will not
stand upright
MENDE PROVERB

MANY things can happen as African ministers assume
responsibility, and as the African majority in the Legislative
Council learns to deploy its strength. But whatever happens,
the cautious pace of economic or financial policy of pre-war
years is unlikely to be resumed. The S.L.P.P. manifesto is but
one indication that African politicians think in terms of expansion. Ministers-in-training find their departments engaged on
schemes of development, but their inclination is to spend still
more, to speed time-tables up, to show the public results. They
are as sensitive as British ministers to the prospect of questions
in the House. They are prone to suspect that explanations are
excuses for doing too little. They are inclined to think that
development plans—such as the Ten-Year Plan or the Childs
Plan—are the minimum which a frightened but grudging
Government will concede, not the maximum that the country's
resources will run to. 'It is true', said one to me, 'that we now
have double-decker buses in Freetown. But do you realize that
*there isn't a single coin-in-the-slot postage-stamp machine in the length
and breadth of the country*?'

The Treasury is not one of the departments for which a portfolio has been given to an African minister-in-training. The
Financial Secretary is a senior British colonial servant. His
room is high up in the four-storey Secretariat building, and looks
down, as all Treasurers' rooms should, upon the scenes of the
puppet-play which all Treasurers seek to influence for good by
laying hands on as many of the tangled strings as possible.
Mighty are Treasurers, Financial Secretaries and Chancellors
of the Exchequer. But even their power is limited. I found that
inevitably the present Financial Secretary had a good deal of
sympathy for his predecessors. Within the terms of the economic and social equation, they had found what money they
could for the development of Sierra Leone. It was little enough.
But the country's entire revenue in the 'twenties was only about a

third more than it expected to receive in 1952 as a free gift from Britain in the form of Colonial Development and Welfare funds. Inevitably, there was little money for education, so mission schools and Fourah Bay had to struggle along as best they could. Ineluctably, there was little money for roads, so trade came in slowly. Sierra Leone was a one-crop country living on a crop that was unscientifically cultivated and enjoying no monopoly —indeed, competing not very successfully with the plantations of Nigeria, the Congo and the East Indies. The Treasurer, like the treasurers of most colonies, could, in the last analysis, only get money from the export crop. Export duties are paid from the proceeds of the crop, railway receipts come from the crop, even hut tax is ultimately paid from cash crops. Import duties, on the other hand, are limited by the total imports which the country can afford—and the imports of an 'under-developed country' cannot exceed the value of exports. Thus exports are the key to development. Palm kernel exports increased from 21,000 tons in 1901 to 84,000 tons in 1936, when the mines had begun to yield a useful extra revenue; and that increase pretty well set the limits for successive Financial Secretaries, except in so far as the Home Government was prepared to find money. And Sierra Leone was not a high priority with the Home Government in those years.

And therefore the reply of successive Financial Secretaries to well-meant proposals was usually 'No'. No, no, no—until D.C.s and Provincial Commissioners learned to be content with small improvements here and there, to labour as patiently as missionaries with the knowledge that they would sow without seeing the harvest ripen. Of course, 'No' was said too often, became too much of a habit—when the question of the geological survey came up, for example. But it wasn't easy to find money in those years.

Today, the Financial Secretary's problem is still to find the money to finance the development. His resources are doubtless greater—but everybody's ideas on what can and must be done are greater still. His position is as uncomfortable and unpopular as his predecessors'. He is now getting over a million from the mines. He is getting hundreds of thousands from coffee, cocoa, piassava and so forth. But the oil-palm is still the main source of his, as of the community's income. As the S.L.P.P. manifesto remarks, 'The development of the country will increase the general revenue of the country, raise living standards, and increase the taxable capacity of the inhabitants'. Very true. But in fact it is just in the development of the major crop that the Childs Plan lags. By 1952, instead of 30 Pioneer mills being in operation, only six were working, and against a target of 82,000 tons of kernels, in the same year only 76,376 were exported. Against a target of 10,000 tons of palm oil, exports were only 833 tons—a heavy drop on 1951. A few other crops did well, but the kernel of the Plan is oil-palm development.

True, prices soared soon after the Childs Plan was issued and put all the values up. But inflation raised import prices just as much as export prices, while rearmament delayed deliveries of engineering supplies. Though produce prices went up, the cost of improving the railway to carry the additional produce expected to come from the Pioneer mills increased comparably. Budgeted to cost $£1\frac{1}{4}$ million, by 1952 the cost was probably up to £3 million. No doubt prices are easier now; but export prices are down, too. Sierra Leone cannot rely on windfall profits or world shortages to keep her going. She must have a larger and more diverse production.

Large bills are coming due for payment. The Ten-Year Plan, approved by the unreformed Leg. Co. in 1946, proposed to spend £5,256,575. This included the cost of the deep-water quay and better electricity and water supplies, but only a small part of the educational blue-print. The rise in prices since 1946 will have much increased the size of this bill. The Childs Plan added to this total another £2,924,000, made up of $£1\frac{1}{4}$ million for the railway, £820,000 for roads, bridges and waterways, £529,000 for Pioneer mills and oil-palm plantations, and £325,000 to improve other crops. On paper, the Colony should have spent £8,000,000 in building up its production potential by 1956. And perhaps if every project is completed as blueprinted, this will be nearer £10,000,000.

Ten million pounds is not a large sum in British eyes—a third of the cost of the Groundnut Scheme, to use the standard yardstick of the embittered economist. But it is a good deal of money for Ansumana and Mariama and people like them to subscribe—or to pay back, once borrowed. The Treasury got £2 million of it from the London Market at $3\frac{1}{2}$ per cent, but the balance will cost more. Some capital projects are being financed out of revenue. Indeed such works are costing about £750,000 a year. But the cost of running the country and its services on the more ambitious scale required under the plans is also rising, and rising fast.

The annual bill for education, which in 1941 was actually smaller than the vote for running the Customs Department, has now reached 12 per cent of the total expenditure of the Colony: that is £334,620, plus another £252,000 being spent as capital cost of new schools. It has nearly doubled in the last two years. Much of the increase is the result of putting up the teachers' salaries. But high as it is it does not take into account some considerable sums still spent by missions, by private bodies and native administrations outside the budget. The capital cost of the education plan was put at £2 million in 1948—but is now far higher as costs and salaries have gone up. Yet Africans feel that *far* more should be spent. So does academic opinion on Mount Aureol.

Many other departments are related to education—public relations, broadcasting, social welfare and so forth. Africans want more of these services. Mass literacy, for example, would be speeded up by broadcasting educational programmes, while the decline of morals in Freetown requires the case-worker's attention. Increased human energy, no less than increased training of hand and brain, must also be paid for—health expenditure has doubled in the last five years. When the Protectorate has all the hospitals and doctors it needs the annual cost will be many times more than the present £310,000. To those engaged in production, however, their work seems most important of all—since only if it succeeds can the rest be paid for. Expenditure on agriculture, forestry, industry and commerce, on co-operatives and research, has leapt up as the Childs Plan has got into its stride.

The cost of personnel is also rising. Not only do the development plans require besides trained Africans many more 'expensive expatriates', but the expatriates themselves expect to be paid enough to make ends meet. Almost every research and agricultural station is short of staff. When I called at Rokupr Rice Station, whose work is of crucial importance not only to Sierra Leone but also to Nigeria, it had two agricultural officers to keep it going against its scheduled complement of seven scientists. In July 1949, according to Mr. Childs, senior service departments had 100 unfilled vacancies. Though some of these gaps have been plugged, many remain—and the need for first-class men is as acute as ever. Nobody costs as little as a first-class scientist or technologist, no matter what you pay him. But the salaries offered by the Colonial Service are hardly such as to attract the first-class mind, unless he most fortunately also is animated by a burning urge to serve in Sierra Leone. Salaries must go up simply to attract the competent.

The day-to-day cost of administration is rising for the same reason.

D.C.s struggle along with worn-out cars and live, in some cases, as nearly as possible on country chop. There is a painful contrast between what a young man earns for organizing the movement of earth shifters in the Yengema mines and what is earned by the man who lives and works beneath the flag at the D.C.s office, maintaining law and order, upholding justice, and teaching the district council clean and efficient administration. Africans, like Indians, may sometimes be tempted to think that a cheaper, if somewhat corrupt, administration would do. They concede that the technicians understand geology or machinery and nobody else does; but not that highly paid administrators are essential. They find it hard to realize that the technician cannot work at all unless his way is made smooth by an efficient administration. 'Now look here', said a Memsahib to me on the second or third evening I spent in Freetown. 'You want the truth about this place—I'll tell it to you. Nobody else will *dare*.' I inclined an eager ear. The deadly truth was—that British officials are monstrously under-paid and that honest, hardworking African servants are impossible to get. But there is certainly something in the first contention, even if it cannot be held to constitute the whole truth about Sierra Leone.

In 1952, expenditure was estimated at £5,486,828. Not perhaps a very large sum—but the largest in Sierra Leone's history and likely to go on rising. Revenue was expected to realize £6,085,068 of which the British taxpayer was to find nearly £566,000 in Colonial Development and Welfare, mostly for health and education. Revenue in 1946 was £2,195,474; in 1938 it was £1,000,000. In 1923 it was £845,000. To put these figures in perspective, in 1897, the year after the Protectorate was proclaimed—and when the attempts to extract hut tax was causing the Poro leaf to be secretly passed from hand to hand—revenue was £100,000. A sixty-fold increase in revenue in half a century is a considerable achievement for a small country in which the basic agricultural technique has, in all that period, hardly changed at all and yields can have increased but fractionally, while hardly a factory has been set up, and mining is barely fifteen years old. It has been done by peace, by the doubling of the population, by working the land ruthlessly hard.

To meet demands for accelerated development the finance department must raise still more revenue. But it is not easy either to impose or to raise taxes in Sierra Leone. Income tax falls on the mining firms and salaried people—hardly at all on the traders. The men and organization to put on the tourniquet of income tax properly do not exist. The plain fact is that three-quarters of the revenue comes from the income tax paid by half a dozen companies, and from the customs duties. Thus to increase the revenue depends absolutely on mining more iron and diamonds, and exporting more palm kernels and other produce. The value of outgoing trade fixes the value of incoming trade—trade is taxed both coming and going. There are limits. To tax heavily the imports of a country that buys from abroad all its manufactured goods, from rails to motor spare parts, is simply to increase the cost of living, put up wage demands and stimulate inflation. While prices are high and world demand is keen, export duties can be slapped on exported produce—duties on kernels brought the revenue £178,000 in 1950, but in 1952 were expected to produce a million. Very nice: but when prices fall the money will not be so easy to get.

Everything, therefore, turns upon the further expansion of trade, upon carrying through the Plans, hitting the Targets, etc., and converting Sierra Leone into a country which not only produces a wide variety of crops but exports them in large quantities. In the last resort, only Ansumana and Mariama and people like them can do this—though the geologists can make a big contribution. 'What you need here', I said brashly, some days after my arrival, 'is a big find of uranium.' 'We've looked', came the reply, 'and there doesn't seem to be any—

thank God! Just imagine this lovely country stiff with security, spies and strategic complications! Diamonds are quite enough to be going on with!' But in terms of sober practicalities Sierra Leone has only to achieve a sizeable rice surplus for export to put a solid prop under her economy. Rice would pay for a good deal of education, social welfare, plant and machinery. The market for iron and diamonds may be firm, but in a world whose population is increasing at the rate of twenty million mouths a year, the market for staple foodstuffs is still firmer. A country with cereals and fats—rice and palm-oil—to sell will be in a strong bargaining position for as far ahead as man can foresee.

Meanwhile the Financial Secretary must find the money for the work that has been started, and do what he can to ensure that it is productively spent. For him, as for every other department, the gentle, genial, immemorial pace of life and events in this green land is deceptive; they are all engaged in a race against time.

Typical scarf dance used on all festive occasions.

26. STIRRUP CUP

An go, an kam
A hand stretched out
will be clasped by another
CREOLE PROVERB

'WELL, there it is,' said the Financial Secretary, 'add it up for yourself. I think you'll find we've stretched our resources as tight as a drum. We're really going as fast as we can. . . .'

The Red Queen might have known how to get the last word, but I could only tuck the weighty volume entitled *Estimates of Revenue and Expenditure for the Year 1952* under my arm and bow myself out. I went down the Secretariat lift for the last time, out into the eternal calidarium of saturated and sun-warmed tropic air, down Oxford Street to the West African Airways Office. I passed over the counter a ticket, worn and grubby with handling, a passport chopped with the smudgy official cognizances of nearly a dozen African territories—for mine had been a round trip. *Citizen of the United Kingdom and Colonies:* yes, I felt I really was as officially described. I felt that I had now some infinitesimal civic significance and part in this country that had been little more than a name to me a few months previously. I felt I wore a garment of kinship fabricated, however tenuously, of experiences shared, of problems and controversies made intimately mine, intimate with true parochial passion by virtue of hard argument in bars, in boats, in trains, in thatched round houses and wooden gauzed-in bungalows; mine by virtue of an authentic sense of indigestion caused more by the conscientious consumption of Sierra Leone Government reports than of groundnut stew.

As my last days ran inexorably out, I found myself sometimes inattentive during periods of instruction on geology or administrative method. I was preoccupied with a private plan for developing a tourist industry in Sierra Leone. I saw it all. What could any book do to bring to the British-domiciled citizen of U.K. and colonies the beauty and strangeness, the colour and sensuous embrace of this corner of his inheritance? Little indeed; and what was wanted, I felt, was something to bring the holiday-makers here. I saw the vivid travel posters in Cook's windows—

and they could not exaggerate the contrast of sea and sky and the gleaming sand of the Colony beaches. They could not promise more ease, more genuine hallmarked Blue Lagoon escapism than the palm colonnades of the Colony beaches could provide. I planned the visits to the historic monuments of Freetown—King's Yard, Wilberforce Hall, Portuguese Lighthouse, Fourah Bay College—in coaches under the aegis of guides primed by Mr. Utting's school history; I planned launch trips to Bance Island; I planned expeditions to the Colony villages. I saw, I confess, a somewhat synthetic production of curios for the trade. But I also saw the flow of pounds and dollars into the territory's coffers, and thus made visible what the Financial Secretary would call invisible income. I even bid for the tourist from America, chartering launches to put to the proof my contention that the barracuda fishing off Shenge and Sherbro offers better sport than that off the Florida coast.

I saw travellers driving into the Protectorate along the new PWD roads with hired equipment, camp beds, chop-boxes and the like, ready to enjoy the simple hospitality of the chiefdom resthouse, in the spirit in which they would go to a Youth Hostel in Britain. I saw this sort of thing organized; not too expensive, of course, but very profitably for the chiefdoms. There would be the minority of tourists who would go into the Protectorate much as they would go into the Pyrenees; for the majority, I saw Mr. Butlin, the Workers' Travel Association, or somebody, providing in the Colony accommodation rather less—Graham Greene-ish, shall I say?—than that available at the City Hotel. (None the less, the City Hotel takes a treasured place in my memories along with the Zanzibar Hotel, Zanzibar, and the Highlands Hotel, Kenya. I like atmosphere: I like it strong.)

Why not? Sierra Leone is only a ten-days' cruise, and the development of the banana industry might give it a service of fast banana-passenger liners. It is 24 hours by air (tourist fares could be introduced) from Thos. Cook in Berkeley Street. It is the nearest British African colony, if we except the Gambia. It has a good climate, just before the rains or in the months succeeding them, when the harvest is being brought in and the drums throb through the night. A yellow fever and T.A.B. inoculation need upset nobody, and paludrine is on every table, next the salt-cellar and the H.P. sauce. Sierra Leone is healthy. And it offers a more complete change of scene, a greater adventure, than any Continental resort. Besides, it is on Sterling, and you can spend as much as you like. I kept these ideas to myself, for the people who love Sierra Leone are no keener to have it 'spoilt' by incursions of tourists in incongruous and undignified attire than by the consequences of the discovery of uranium. But some cruise ships used to put into Freetown before World War II. Even now, students and young people might think of Sierra Leone as a place for an educational holiday. If we, in Britain, are to understand our problem and our responsibility in Africa, there must be more eye-witnesses of that problem at the plain citizen's level. Sierra Leone is the ideal territory to provide such contacts and first-hand experiences—accessible, understandable, and reasonably representative of a British colony in transition.

Personal contacts are of infinite importance; the history of the British Commonwealth is proof of that, if of nothing else. As I left the West Africa Airways offices, my departure fixed, my heart heavy, I noticed a name-plate on the stairs leading to the offices above. I was up them in a flash, and sent in my name. A few moments later I was in the presence of a Pickwickian and puzzled but polite legal gentleman. 'And how are you?' I asked cheerfully. 'Really, my dear sir, I'm afraid I don't quite—I mean, do we know each other?' murmured Lawyer Dobbs. 'We used to, very well, a quarter of a century ago', I said. 'Good heavens!' he exclaimed with a burst of laughter. '*It's Lewis of the Remove*. How you've changed!'

So it was with Lawyer Dobbs (formerly of the Remove) and his elegant and amusing creole wife that I went to the Freetown Junior Dinner Club on the last evening of my tour. There is also a Senior Dinner Club, where speeches are made and distinguished persons foregather. The Junior Dinner Club conducts its proceedings with considerable informality. It brings together men and women of good will of all races and occupations. Its convivialities, its use of lighthearted sociability as a medium for more serious social purpose, brings the younger European professional people, colonial officials and executives of the Firms into contact with their opposite numbers in the creole community and with the educated élite from the Protectorate. At least one Syrian is a member, and there should be more.

'Everybody, everybody, everybody likes Saturday night', sing the Junior Diners as they join hands and circle slowly round each member imprisoned in turn in the ring, where he is expected to do an individual dance. Hill Station dances; Mount Aureol dances; Government jigs; commerce capers. The Public Relations Officer, the British Council representative, the headmaster, the District Commissioner visiting Freetown, the Army officer—everybody likes Saturday night. I liked it very much myself, danced long, left last (so far as I recall), and wrote my name, address and telephone number in a variety of diaries, on the backs of envelopes, on snapshots, on matchboxes, and, I rather fancy, on the label of a bottle of Vimto. Or it may not have been Vimto. I hope they'll remember, those Freetownese. *Fodom fo me, ah fodom fo yu.*

A few hours later the country was spread below me, a mottled map, sliding westwards. Bad weather lay ahead, and every now and then we smashed through rainstorms. The plane grew dark and the land was veiled in vapour. But hidden or green and glittering, in the pockets of sunlight, it was no longer just a stretch of Africa. It was a scene, the detail filled in, a perspective provided by its history: the scene of a great, and as yet undecided, struggle to create a new and stable environment in which African capabilities should emerge, develop and finally make a new (and much needed) contribution to the wider problems of all mankind.

That struggle began when the Colony was first founded, and if it has been waged at times half-heartedly—if momentarily the earlier vision has been lost—at least it must be recalled how little knowledge of what was involved there was when men like Clarkson and Wilberforce planned it by candlelight. We know better now. But equally our greater scientific knowledge has shown us how much needs to be done, how much capital invested in works and brains, in education, understanding and good will, if we are to gain control over the natural forces which the first immigrant tribes into the virgin forest disturbed with such well-founded trepidation, with supplications and sacrifices to avert the wrath that their presumption might entail.

I saw the land in the mind's eye, at once as a map and as I had travelled through it: the women in the bush weeding and ever weeding as the rain brought up the fast-germinating seed,

246

their backs bent, their eyes turned down to the earth, the weight of their babies pressing them down; the men repairing and ever repairing their frail defences against wind and rain and sun. I saw the sick who had not gone to the fields that day; I visualized the almost unbreakable chain of disease, inertia, failure, ignorance, malnutrition, disease. I heard the endless inconclusive discussions in the barris; I knew the pressure on poor men to put personal gain—some little easing of the burdens on their backs—before a putative, theoretical communal good. I saw the little gangs at the slowly advancing roadheads; the officials struggling with the weight of paper; the Syrians playing their customers like fishermen; the diamonds slipping from hand to hand; the Financial Secretary turning from tax to loan, and from loan back to tax. I imagined the triumphant tractor scoring its furrows into the astonished tilth, and the tractor silent for weeks for want of a fan-belt. I conjured up, far below me, the heat, and the heartbreak, and the hopelessness of it all; and the extraordinary energies of men that kept the work going, and welled up endlessly into hope and laughter, dancing, love and song.

I saw through the triumphal arches of two great rainbows the land which nourished men and animals and plants together —high bush, low bush, bare rock; savannah, marsh and forest. I refocused it in my mind's eye, a living organism, a universe; a thing that lived, brought forth men and cities, died. And from three thousand feet it rolled on endlessly in its patterns of lush or faded greenery, intersected every so often by brown and turbid rivers, which flowed by the million tons of water between high banks still lined with forest trees, flowed on ceaselessly and silently save for an occasional low sob—or chuckle—as they carried the good earth down to the mangroves and the rice fields and out to sea.

BOOKS CONSULTED

For an authoritative history of Sierra Leone in the light of modern research we await the appearance of the work now under preparation by the Government archivist, Mr. C. H. Fyfe, some of whose broadcasts on Freetown radio have been of great use to me. The standard history is J. J. Crook's *History of Sierra Leone*, an official and somewhat pedestrian chronicle which carries the story little beyond the proclamation of the Protectorate in 1896. Utting's school history, *The Story of Sierra Leone*, published by Longmans, gives as much of the tale as most general readers require. The early history of West Africa is given, if through rose-tinted spectacles, by Raymond Michelet in *African Empires and Civilisation*, 1945.

Many aspects of this fascinating country's early history have been the subject of researches published in *Sierra Leone Studies*, an invaluable source of information in 18 volumes appearing between 1915 and 1939 at irregular intervals. The most vivid descriptions of the country at various periods in its history are given by travellers, among which I have made use, in this book, of the following: *Narrative of Two Voyages to the River Sierra Leone* by A. M. Fauconbridge (wife of the Company's agent), published in 1793; *An Account of the Native Africans in the Neighbourhood of Sierra Leone* by T. Winterbottom, M.D., 1803; *The White Man's Grave* by F. Harrison Rankin, 1834; *A Residence in Sierra Leone* by A Lady, 1849; *Life, Scenery and Customs in Sierra Leone and the Gambia* by T. Eyre Poole, D.D., 1850; *Sierra Leone, or, The White Man's Grave* by G. A. Lethbridge Banbury, 1889; *Sierra Leone After a Hundred Years* by Bishop E. G. Ingham, D.D., 1894. These books—and there are several others—most forcibly portray the social development of the country and the Liberated Africans. Luke's Bibliography of Sierra Leone provides many other references.

The state of the Protectorate, when it was first taken over, and ten years or so later, is fully described by Commissioner T. C. Alldridge, in *The Sherbro and its Hinterland*, Macmillan, 1901, and *A Transformed Colony: Sierra Leone as it was and is, its progress, peoples, native customs and undeveloped wealth*, Seeley & Co., 1910. The Temne country was described more fully under the title *Sierra Leone* in 1915 by Newland, with a particular view to developing plantation agriculture. In 1926 appeared F. W. H. Migeod's *A View of Sierra Leone*, the first careful and scholarly first-hand account of the whole territory and tribal society, before the abolition of slavery (Kegan Paul, 1926). In the mid-thirties, Katharine Fowler-Lunn published her experiences as a prospector for gold soon after the first mineral deposits had been verified by the Geological Department (*The Gold Missis*, Unwin, 1936).

Recent judgements on Sierra Leone have perhaps been influenced by Graham Greene's novel, *The Heart of the Matter*, and earlier travelogue, *Journey Without Maps*. Greene portrays a decayed and stagnant colony; but Sierra Leone was of interest to him, one feels, rather as a ready-made *décor* for his particular genre of theological melodrama (which I admire, though few Europeans in the country do) rather than as a serious attempt to get to the heart of the matter so far as a complex African society is concerned. A charming modern pen-picture of the Colony is contained in Linyard's *Morning on Mount Aureol*.

The most authoritative account of native life and the secret societies is Dr. Kenneth Little's *The Mende of Sierra Leone*, to which my debt will be obvious; also his invaluable study *The Mende Rice Farm and Its Cost*, published by Editions Universitaires, Brussels. I have also referred to the Rev. Max Gorvie's pamphlets, *Our People in the Sierra Leone Protectorate* and *Old and New in Sierra Leone*, in Africa's Own Library series, published by the United Society for Christian Literature in 1944. For the customs of tribes other than the Mendes, one has to rely upon Sierra Leone Studies, especially the many contributions by E. F. Sayers on the Temnes, Korankos, Susus and Mandingos; much of the information available is summarized in M. McCulloch's volume on *The Peoples of the Sierra Leone Protectorate* in the ethnographic survey of Africa ed. Daryll Forde for the International African Institute. Group-Capt. L. W. C. Pearce-Gervis, in his *Sierra Leone Story*, provides a vivid account of the rites of some of the secret societies. The legal aspect is summarized in J. S. Fenton's *Outline of Native Law in Sierra Leone* (1932). No study of the Protectorate is complete without at least a brief glance at F. W. H. Migeod's fascinating study in philosophical philology, *The Languages of West Africa* (Kegan Paul, 1913), and Schlenker's *Temne Grammar and Fables*, published in 1864. Fourah Bay College is now beginning to make its own researches, of which I have read *An Adventure in Community Study* by Students reading for the diploma in education, 1951–2.

For an understanding of the economic, ecological and agricultural situation in Sierra Leone, one is dependent—apart from discussion on the spot—upon a series of recent Government reports, of which the most important are *Soil Conservation and Land Use* (Sessional Paper No. 1 of 1951) and *A Plan of Economic Development in Sierra Leone* (the Childs Plan), published in 1950 by the Government printer. The really earnest student will, of course, supplement his readings in the Childs Plan with frequent reference to the 12 District Plans, which burst my portmanteau on two occasions at least.

I have, however, had occasion to refer for confirmation to many departmental reports, a brief list of which follows: Sierra Leone Protectorate Handbook, 1951; Report on the Sierra Leone Protectorate for the Years 1949 and 1950; Annual Report on the Sierra Police Force, 1950; Report on the Development of Education in Sierra Leone, 1948; Survey of the Secondary Schools of Sierra Leone (Nichols Report), 1950; Draft Syllabus of Instruction for Use in Central Schools in Sierra Leone, 1950; Education Department Annual Report, 1950; Report on Co-operation in Sierra Leone,

1949; Annual Report of the Labour Department, 1950; Annual Reports of the Social Welfare Department, 1950 and 1951; Estimates of Revenue and Expenditure for the Year 1952; Annual Report of the Registrar of Co-operative societies, 1948-9 and 1949-50; Annual Report of the Railway Department, 1950; Something About the Sierra Leone Railway, 1950; A History of the Sierra Leone Railway by J. Ralph Best, 1951; Annual Report of the Mines Department, 1950.

The Agricultural Department, besides its succinct annual report, publishes—or used to publish—many useful pamphlets on individual Sierra Leone crops, of which I possessed myself of many. For the natural history of this beautiful country the reader will naturally turn to Bannerman's monumental *Birds of West Africa* in 7 volumes, George Cansdale's handier *Animals of West Africa* and the detailed botanical studies, *Useful Plants of West Africa*, published by the Crown Agents for the Colonies. It would seem that most plants are useful. Many individual studies in Sierra Leonian natural history appear in the periodical *Nigerian Field*.

One of the most illuminating sources of information about any country is its newspaper and periodical press. I have spent many hours fascinated by the leaders, features, letters to the editor—and the advertisements—of such publications as the Bo *Observer*, the *African Vanguard*, the *Daily Guardian*, *The African Standard* and the *Sierra Leone Daily Mail*. Now that this latter journal has been taken over by the British *Daily Mirror*, it may be feared—if I may use the expression—that a big change will come over the nineteenth- and even eighteenth-century appearance of Sierra Leone journals and journalism. There are those, of course, who will welcome the change.

INDEX

Accra, 8, 17
Administration (see also British rule, Local Government, etc.), 60, 62, 65, 67, 69, 72, 212, 214, 219, 240
Administration, African, tribal, 63, 67, 69, 71, 110
Advertising, 6, 101
African Institution, the, 33
Africanization, 3, 11, 12, 36, 212, 216, 217pp., 226, 228, 234, 246
After-life, 141
Agricultural Dept., 73, 74pp., 95, 158, 174, 204, 209, 212, 213, 214, 224, 225, 235, 239, 241, 246
Agriculture (see Crops, Farming, etc.), 33, 37, 66, 74pp., 122, 142, 208pp., 214, 239. And Art, 163
Alldridge, 64, 105, 220
America, 3, 31, 41, 244
American influence, 49, 59, 102, 157
American War of Independence, 31, 41, 226
Ancestors, rites for, 86, 92, 140, 141, 215
Anglicanism, 12, 24, 157
Animals, wild, 106, 115
Anthony, Mr. F., 225
Ants, 102
Architecture, 4, 5, 11, 25, 58, 124
Army, 7, 31, 66, 110, 151, 152
Art, 10, 132, 134, 154, 160pp., 192
Artisans and Allied Workers Union, 201
Aureol, Mount, 7, 188
Australia, 4, 17, 35
Avocado, 48
Axes, 82

Bai Bureh, 65
Bai Farima, 116
Bai Farima Tass II, Hon. P. C., 230
Balangi, 18, 163
Ballot, the, 70, 230. See Elections
Banana Islands, 24
Bananas, 49, 96, 208, 225

Banbury, Lethebridge, 165
Bance Island (Bunce I.), 16, 244
Bandajuma, 69
Barbot, 16
Barri, the, 23, 70, 205
Basket-making, see Crafts
Bathurst Street, 17
Bathurst Village, 24
Bats, 37, 107
Bauxite, 202
Benguema, 27
Benka-Coker, Mrs., 176, 224
Benniseed, 208
Beresford-Stooke, Sir George, 233
Betrothal, 38, 145, 146. See Marriage
Bilharzia, 171
Birds, 95, 107, 115
Blyden, Dr. E., 59
Bo, 53, 60, 62, 63, 66, 69, 72, 73 74, 176
Bo School, 62, 69, 183, 231
Bombali, 214
Bonthe, 34, 99, 100, 101, 102
Borfima medicine, the, 112
Breadfruit, 20, 102
Bridewealth, 146, 153. See Wives, Women, Marriage, etc.
Bridges, 238
Bright, Dr. Bankole, 229, 230
Bright, John, 64
British, the, 19, 64, 218, 227
British rule, 19, 53, 60, 62pp., 100, 105, 117, 204, 214, 218, 226, 227
Brushing farms, 85, 108
Buedu, 69
Bulloms, the, 12, 14, 15, 108, 116, 117
Bullom boats, 14
Bullom shore, 2
Bundu devil, 145, 146
Bundu rites, material, bush, 8, 9, 109, 145, 162, 235. See Sande
Bunumbu College, 184
Bunumbu Press, 62
Burial rites, creole, 39

253

Burning farms, 85, 108 (see Fire), 206
Buses, 5, 236
Bush, secondary, see Vegetation, Agriculture, etc.
Business men, British, see Traders, European
Butterflies, 21

Cabinet government, 228pp. See Executive Council
Calypso, the, 44, 50, 51
Campbell, James, 195
Camwood, 15
Cannibalism, 110
Canoes, dugouts, 29, 81, 98, 99, 209
Carving, 161
Casely-Hayford, Gladys, 46
Cassava (Cassada), 15, 25, 29, 56, 85, 87, 88, 111, 120
Catholic Mission, the, 53, 154, 157, 166, 219
Cattle, 26, 57, 87, 114, 119, 120, 122, 208, 213
Caulker, Chief, 81, 103
Character, African and British, 219, 223. See Mentality
Charlotte Village, 24
Charms, see Fetish
Chief Commissioner, 63
Chiefdoms, 67, 212, 215
Chiefs, Chieftaincy, 63, 65, 67, 68, 70, 71, 72, 108, 134, 136, 151, 180, 204, 223, 227, 229, 231
Child, Mr. W., 211, 240. See Childs Plan
Child-bearing, 147, 168, 174
Children, 27, 31, 35, 39, 57, 91, 123pp., 139, 143pp., 176pp., 206, 225
Childs Plan, the, 113, 204pp., 214, 224, 234, 236, 238
Chimpanzees, 107
Christianity, 28, 32, 36, 40, 116, 152pp., 231, 232
    African attitude to, 152pp., 232
    British attitude to, 40, 155, 158

Cholera, 166
Chrome, 194
Churches, Freetown, 12
    Parish, 23, 25
    Bonthe, 100
Church Missionary Society (CMS), 33, 117, 156, 166, 186
Church Missionary Society Grammar School, 182, 184
Churchill, Rt. Hon. Sir Winston, 84, 211
Cinema, 13
Cinnamon, 26
Cintra, Pedro de, 75
Circumcision, female, 145, 235
    male, 129
Citrus, 208, 225
City of London interests, 67. See Firms, Minerals, etc.
Civil Service, see Colonial Service
Clarkson, Thomas, 246. See Slave trade
Clerks' jobs, 33, 70, 158, 193, 200, 220
Cline Town, 13, 53
Clitoris, excision of, 145, 235
Cloth, see Weaving
Clothes, see Dress
Clubs, 13, 14
Coast, the (West African), 3, 8, 9, 32
Cocoa, 26, 96, 112, 113, 206, 207, 213, 225, 237
Codrington College, 187
Coffee, 26, 56, 66, 96, 111, 112, 113, 206, 207, 225, 237
Colonial Development and Welfare funds, 172, 176, 188, 236, 240
Colonial Office, 30, 59, 67, 166, 227
Colonial Service, 7, 13, 166, 247, 234, 236, 239, 240 (see Commissioners)
Colony, the, 19pp., 32, 53, 55, 60, 63, 81, 89, 100, 178, 211, 217, 226
Commerce and Industries Department, 111, 208
Commercial men, see Traders, European
Commonwealth, British, 227, 244

Commissioners, see under District, Provincial, Chief, Alldridge
Community Development Schemes, 225. See Welfare, Social organization, etc.
Compagnie Française de l'Afrique Orientale (CFAO), 14, 101
Conakry, 60, 203
Constitution, Stevenson, 229pp.
Cook, Thos., & Co., 243, 244
Cooking, 47pp., 143
Co-operative Societies, 98, 153, 212, 213, 214, 216, 222, 234, 239
Cormorants, 95
Corn, cereals, see Maize, Rice, Millet, etc.
Corrugated iron, see Roofs
Costume, see Dress
Cotton, 26, 87, 113
Cotton tree, the, 11, 20, 85
Courban, Mr., 208
Court Messengers, 66, 99, 151, 169
Courts, 68, 70, 218 (see Justice)
Courtship, see Betrothal, Love
Crafts, African, 16, 25, 130, 139, 145, 160pp., 191, 192, 244
Credit, 37, 89, 93, 95
Creepers, 79
Creoles, the, 5, 13, 28, 30, 31pp., 41, 43, 46, 53, 57, 60, 153, 202, 211, 219, 222, 224, 228, 231, 232, 245
Creolization, 33, 158, 232
Crocodiles, 115
Crops (see under Rice, etc.), 25, 29, 86pp., 95, 204pp., 225, 241
Cultivation, 26, 55, 57, 72, 80, 82, 85pp., 90, 95, 96, 110, 120, 121, 206, 222, 235, 246
Culture, African, 37, 46, 49, 67, 128pp. See Creoles, Social organization, etc.
Customs Department, 239

Dakar, 60
Dancing, 113, 128, 139, 141, 142, 145, 163, 164, 245
Daru, 81, 152

Dawes, Governor, 11
Death, rites, 38, 141, 166
Debt, 85, 140, 222. See Credit
Decker, Mr. T., 43
Deepwater Quay, 8, 18, 54
Degradation, see Erosion, Soil, etc.
Democracy, 28, 70, 113, 212, 215, 226pp.
Demongo, 76
Detribalization, 200
'Development', 70, 71, 175, 200, 218, 222, 234, 236pp.
Development Company (Delco), the Sierra Leone, 195, 200, 202
Devils, see Spirits, Religion, etc.
Diamonds, 67, 111, 197, 198, 199, 241
Diet, 13, 27, 47, 111, 113, 124, 219, 240, 243, 244
Dinner Clubs, 245
Disease, 91, 125, 128, 150, 166pp., 181, 226, 227, 235, 244, 246
Disraeli, 20
Distribution, see Shops, Traders, etc.
District Commissioners (D.C.s), 28, 29, 65, 66, 67, 68, 70, 72, 73, 74, 83, 93, 156, 159, 169, 204, 205, 212, 217pp., 229, 234, 237, 240. See Local Government
District Councils, 70, 71, 212, 214, 218, 230pp.
District plans, 212pp.
Divorce, tribal, 139
Dixey, Frank, 194
Dobbs, Mr. A. E., 245
Doctors, see Medical Profession
Domestic science, domesticity, see Home life
Drainage, see Rainfall, Water, etc.
Dreams, 124, 150
Dress, African, male, 5, 6, 31, 54, 158
female, 6, 31, 57, 146
children's, 125, 129
Drums, drumming, 9, 128, 141, 244
Durham University, 187
Dysentery, 166

Easmon, Dr. M. F. C., 46

Education (creole), 23, 28, 29, 31, 33, 35, 39, 44, 71, 102, 173, 174, 176pp., 190, 222, 227, 246
  (primary), 102, 148, 180, 216, 223
  (secondary), 62, 69, 155, 183, 184, 189, 214, 216, 217, 219, 224, 227, 234
  (of tribal Africans), 155, 157, 159, 212, 214, 227, 232
  (traditional tribal), 124pp., 129, 145, 146
  (chiefs), 69, 104
  (technical), 97, 152, 154, 174, 187, 190, 191, 193, 200, 209, 214, 216
  (agricultural), see Agricultural Dept.
  (cost of), 193, 239

Elections, 228pp.

Elephantiasis, 171

Elephants, 122

Employment, 27, 29, 33, 39, 60, 151, 158

Endemic Disease Control Unit, 172, 174

English, teaching of, 178, 179, 180

Equality (of races), 32, 33

Erosion problem, the, 76, 78, 81, 88, 93, 113, 115, 119, 122, 206, 208. See Soil, Vegetation, etc.

Executive Council, 11, 33, 227pp.

Expatriates, see Colonial Service, British, etc.

Exports, 26, 204, 205, 211, 241, 242

Extra-mural teaching, see Fourah Bay College

Falaba, 117

Family organization, 39, 125pp., 133, 135, 139, 220. See Home life, etc.

Farming, farms, farmers, 26, 56, 72, 76, 82, 85pp., 110, 113, 119, 120, 133, 140, 206, 208, 214, 215, 225. See also Crops, Agriculture, Laziness, etc.

Farming and missions, 155, 225

Fauconbridge, Mrs. A. M., 32, 165

Feed for cattle, see Pasture

Fergusson, Governor, 35, 167, 186

Ferries, 105, 123

Fertility, human, 36, 137, 173. See Mortality, infant
  soil, 25, 76, 80, 82, 83, 112, 137, 210, 225, 241

Fertilizers, 27, 82, 86, 210, 211

Fetish, 15, 27, 37, 38, 125

Finance (railway), 60, 221, 237
  (Government), 185, 186, 193, 196, 204, 236pp.
  (Chiefdoms), 69

Financial Secretary, 236, 237, 243, 247

Fire, use in cultivation, 55, 79, 82, 86, 108, 114, 120, 122, 208

Firms, trading, 14, 66, 159, 193, 211, 220, 222, 245. See United Africa Co., etc.

Fish, 95, 107, 209

Fisheries and fishermen, 8, 12, 25, 26, 29, 98, 99, 104, 209, 213

Fisheries Research Institute, West African, 210

Flowers, 8, 20, 23, 79, 88, 114

Food supplies, 74, 89, 95. See Diet

Foo-Foo, 15, 29, 48, 101, 219

Forests, 78-9, 80, 105, 106, 112, 113, 122, 246. See Trees
  ecology of, 3, 20

Forestry Department, 55, 105, 106, 112, 122, 212, 239

Fort Thornton, 11

Fourah Bay, 6, 7, 54
  College, 7, 33, 104, 156, 158, 176, 183, 186pp., 211, 216, 219, 234, 236, 239, 244

Fowler-Lunn, Mrs. Katherine, 195

Freedom, 33, 113

Freetown, 2, 4-5, 8, 11pp., 23, 27, 30, 31, 32, 52, 53, 60, 61, 65, 71, 74, 100, 115, 146, 166, 185, 218, 244

French, the, 16, 64, 111, 117, 118, 208

French Guinea, 1, 69, 74, 89, 108, 110, 113, 115

French influence, 49, 58
French West Africa, 16, 60, 64, 74
Frontier Police, 64, 65
Fruit, 48, 101
Frustration, 18, 40, 77, 158, 173, 204, 227
Fulas, 14, 15, 117, 118, 122, 209, 232
Futa Jallon, 115, 117

Gambia, the, 64, 187, 208, 244
Games, 61, 125
Gbangbar River, 95
Geological Department, 76, 194, 195, 202, 214, 237
Geology, geologists, 76
George III, 16, 226
George Street, 16
Ginger, 26, 101, 208
Gladstone, Rt. Hon. W. E., 64
Gloucester Village, 25
God, the African concept of, 127, 141, 157, 160
Godbeer, Mr., 208
Gola Forest, 80
Gold, 194, 195
Gold Coast, 1, 7, 12, 17, 32, 64, 76, 112, 187, 194, 213, 227
Gorvie, Rev. Max, 109
Government House, 11, 13
Governor (of Sierra Leone), 9, 11, 63, 64, 67, 226, 227, 229
Grass, 26, 79, 81, 82, 95pp., 114, 120
Grazing, see Pasture, Cattle, etc.
Greene, Graham, 13, 244, 249
Groundnuts, 88, 91, 207, 208
Groundnuts stew, 48, 120

Hamilton Report, 60
Hanno of Carthage, 2, 75
Harbour, Freetown's, 3, 8, 15
Harmattan, the, 75, 79, 115
Harris, Rev. T., 81, 124, 158
Hastings Village, 25, 26
Hawkins, John, 116
Head loading, see Porterage
Headman, the, 71
Health, 36, 165pp.

Health Department, 134, 175, 234, 235, 239, 244. See Disease, etc.
Heat, see Temperature
Hill, Mr., 213
Hill station, 7, 9, 11, 13, 36, 166, 167, 189
Hippopotamus, 106, 115
Hoe, the, 83, 87
Holy Cross, Fathers of the, see Catholic Mission
Home life, creole, 40, 46, 47, 49, 192, 219, 223
tribal African, 123pp., 140pp., 155, 219
Hornbills, 107
Horton, Dr., 187
Hospitals, 170pp., 200, 215, 239
Hotels, 8, 209, 244
Houses, housing (see Architecture), 40, 58, 81, 85, 96, 123, 134, 154, 209, 234
Humidity, 85
Humoi Society, 135, 140, 147, 150, 153, 174
Humus, see Soil, etc.
Hunger, hungry months, 17, 89, 96
Hut tax war, 60, 65, 81, 104, 241
Hyde, Mr. A. K., 224

Illicit diamond buying, 199
Imperialism, bouts of, 36, 64, 117, 118, 219
Imports, 237pp. See Traders
Income, National, 17, 211pp., 236pp.
India, 4, 226, 240
Ingram, Bishop, 165
Insects, 115, 135
Intelligence, African, 192
Iron, 67, 194pp., 241
Ironwood trees, 20
Islam, see Mohammedanism

Jackson, Father Joseph, 54
Jamaica, 17, 208. See West Indies
Jobs, job-hunting (see Employment), 26, 33, 39, 60, 151

T

INDEX

Johnson, Bishop, 27
Johnson, Mr. Wallace, 229, 230, 231, 233
Joloffs, 16
Jones, Mr. M., 23, 28
Jong River, 95
Judges, 13, 218
Junner, Dr., 194
Justice, 218

Kabala, 57, 60, 79, 114, 118, 167, 219
Kai Kai, Hon. P. C. Jaia, 97
Kai Lundo, Chief, 110, 119
Kai Samba, Hon. P. C., 68
Kailahun, 112
Kakoia Hill, 118
Kamabai, 60, 118, 187, 218
Kenema, 111, 191
Kent Village, 24, 25
King-Harmon, Sir Charles, 167
King's Yard, 244
Kissi pennies, 111
Kissis, the, 24, 111, 116, 172
Kissy, 6, 7, 12, 14, 24, 33, 54, 210
Kitson, Sir Arthur, 194
Koelle, 187
Koindu, 111, 208
Kola nuts, 15, 20, 89, 111, 130, 133, 206, 208
Kono Country, 70, 71, 118, 194
Konos, the, 70, 114, 116, 118, 122, 131, 172, 178
Kontogi medicine, 99
Korankos, the, 12, 116, 118, 122, 163, 178
Krakas, the, 104
Krio language, 15, 41pp., 49, 178, 191
Krootown, 7

Labour problems, 200–202
Lakka Village, 90
Land, rights and customs, 66, 212, 222. See Soil, etc.
Language, 41pp., 85pp., 111, 128, 148, 161, 177, 178, 179, 180, 214

Laterite, 27, 75pp.
Law, African, 65, 66, 70, 139
Law, British, 24, 54, 65, 68, 218, 229
Law Courts, 8, 11
Lawyers, 7, 220, 223
Laziness, 26, 33, 175. See Mentality, Health, Medicine, Worms, etc.
Legislative Council ('Leg. Co.'), 8, 9, 11, 34, 70, 71, 204, 226, 227, 228
Leicester Village, 24
Lemburg, Philip, 59
Leopards, 106
Leopold Village, 25
Lewis, Sir Samuel, 5
Liberated Africans, 3, 12, 23–26, 32, 34, 40, 57
Liberia, 1, 3, 64, 74, 80, 81, 106, 110, 111, 231
Lignite, 202
Limbas, the, 12, 89, 116, 118, 122
Literacy, 33, 151, 181, 225, 228, 239. See Education
Little, Dr. K., 17, 250
Livestock, see Cattle, Pigs
Loans, Government, 238. See Credit
Local Government, 28, 29, 68, 70, 212, 214, 215, 217, 219. See Self-government
Lokos (Bulloms), 15, 116
Looms, see Weaving
Lophira, 79, 114
Love, parental, 37, 125
  sexual, 46, 135, 136, 137, 145, 147, 153, 158
Luawa, 110
Lumley Beach, 9
Lumley Village, 24
Lunsar, 195, 200
Lyttelton, Rt. Hon. Oliver, 44

Mabonto, 195
MacCarthy, Sir Charles, Governor, 12
MacFoy, 33, 34
Magbureka, 176, 231
Magic, see Witchcraft

Mahogany, 20, 106
Maize, 115
Makeni, 60, 114
Makong River, 194
Malaria, 138, 166, 172
Mambolo, 122
Manatee, the, 95
Mandingoes, 111, 116
Manga Sewa, 117
Manganese, 202
Mango tree, 100
Mano River, 1
Manufactures, 25, 241
Manure, 120, 215. See Fertilizers, Cattle
Marampa, 191, 194, 195, 196, 202
Margai, Dr., 62, 146, 223 Note, 233, 234
Margai, Mr. Albert, 233
Markets, 15, 101, 111. See Trade
Maroc Company, 195
Marriage, creole, 38
   tribal, 93, 133, 136, 139, 145, 147, 153, 158
Masanke, 55
Mask, the, 132, 160-1, 162, 203
Mattru, 102
Medical profession, 3, 36, 169, 174, 217, 220, 222, 224, 235, 239
Medical Service, 217, 228
Medicine (scientific), 36, 147, 157, 173pp., 244
   (African), 15, 99, 125, 138, 140, 154, 167
Medicine man, see Witch doctor
Melon, 48
Mendeland, 59, 69, 104, 207, 216
Mendes, the, 12, 17, 40, 59, 65, 69, 71, 85pp., 104, 105pp., 127, 130, 131, 178, 209, 212, 213, 231, 232
Mentality, African, 9, 12, 17, 41, 43, 72, 77, 104, 124, 142, 147, 168, 191, 193, 203, 209, 214-15, 219pp., 232
   British, 17, 31, 36, 40, 41, 123, 200, 201, 214-15
   creole, 31pp., 220, 232
Methodism, 81, 157

Middle class, 220, 227. See Professions
Midwifery, 130
Migeod, F. W. H., 33
Millet, 91, 116
Minerals, 66, 71, 75, 77, 82, 194, 211. See Iron, Diamonds, Chrome, etc.
Minerals Ordinance, 195
Mines, 71, 118, 156, 159, 194pp., 204, 234, 237, 241, 245
Ministers (in Executive Council), 11, 17, 227pp., 233, 235 postscript, 236
Ministry of Food (U.K.), 207, 213
Missions, missionaries, 2, 3, 12, 27, 28, 32, 33, 65, 68, 69, 81, 101, 102, 116, 147, 148, 152pp., 170, 174, 177, 187, 193, 219, 221, 239
Moa River, 95, 108
Mohammedanism, 12, 37, 114, 116, 119, 125, 131, 155pp., 164, 208, 232
Money, 119, 140, 148, 151, 153, 225. See Traders, etc.
Money-lending, see Credit
Monkeys, 107
Morality, African, 12-13, 102, 137, 140, 148, 153, 156, 170, 199, 239, 240, 247
   British, 13, 33, 40, 219, 224
   creole, 26, 27, 102, 240
Mortality, infant, 125, 173
Moslems, 6, 40, 70, 141, 229, 231
Mosquitoes, 97, 172
Motor transport, 53, 60, 111, 218. See Roads
Mountains, colony, 19, 75
Moyamba, 60, 81, 104, 110
Municipal Government, 16
Musaia, 118, 204
Music, 44, 51
Mustapha, Mr. Senussi, 229, 233

Names, 29, 104, 131
National Council, 229pp., 232
Native Administrations, 69, 70, 185, 239. See Administration, Local Government

Ndama, see Cattle
Ndawa, Chief, 110
Nehru, Pandit Jawaharlal, 217
Newspapers, 46, 231
Newton, John, 103
Ngewo, 127. See God
Nichols, Mr., 180, 182
Niger, 60, 64, 113, 116
Nigeria, 65, 187, 206, 237
Nightingale, Florence, 166, 183
Njala, 73, 74, 215
Njayei Society, 140, 150
Nkrumah, Dr. Kwame, 227, 233
Nomoli, 10, 161
Numeration, 126
Nurses, 192, 222, 224

Officials, 13, 30, 33, 72, 219, 227.
    See Colonial Service, Commis-
    sioners, etc.
Oil palm, see Palm
Old age, 141, 148, 149, 153
Orugu Gorge, 19

Pademba Road, 7, 8, 11, 16
Paganism, see Religion, African
Painting, 161
Palaver Sauce, 47, 219
Palm kernels, 88, 89, 105, 113, 134,
    148, 205, 211, 238, 241
Palm oil, 15, 20, 29, 48, 55, 66, 86,
    88, 89, 96, 112, 133, 206, 207, 213,
    237
Palm wine, 55, 85, 112
Palms, coconut, 98
Pampona Mining Co., 195
Panga, 97
Panguma Valley, 82
Paramount Chiefs, see under Chiefs
Parkin, 114
Parrots, 107
Pasture, 79, 114, 115, 119, 122, 208.
    See Grass
Paterson Zochonis (P.Z.), 14, 101
Paw-paw, 48, 101
Pelicans, 95
Pendembu, 60, 81

Pepel, 195
Peppers, 15, 48, 207
Pests, control of, 91
Piassava, 35, 97, 98, 208, 237
Pigs, 157, 208, 213
Pineapples, 101, 208, 225
Pioneer Oil Mills, 115, 142, 205,
    214, 238
Pirates, 3, 102, 103
Plant life in Sierra Leone, 9, 21,
    75pp.
Plantain Islands, 103
Plantain, John, 103
Plantation companies, see Firms
Plantation crops, 95. See Crops
Ploughing, 87, 96, 120, 213. See
    Cattle, Tractors
Poetry, 44, 137, 148
Police, 11, 13, 64, 66, 69, 200. See
    Court Messengers
Political parties, 40, 229pp., 233
Politics, 34, 40, 140, 158, 203,
    229pp., 234
Polygamy, 68, 91, 125, 136, 139,
    146, 147, 152, 156, 232. See
    Wives, wifehood, Marriage
Population, 82, 83, 97, 173, 174,
    241
Poro Secret Society, 40, 65, 71, 86,
    109, 117, 129pp., 178, 180, 232
Port Loko, 116
Porterage, 53, 59, 73, 118, 134, 218
Portuguese, the, 15, 19, 116
Pottery, see Crafts
Produce Marketing Board, 89, 205,
    213
Production, see Exports, etc.
Professional cadre, professionalism,
    13, 33, 35, 72, 159, 190, 193, 211,
    214, 219, 220, 222, 239, 245
Protectorate, the, 36, 37, 40, 53, 61,
    62pp., 217, 227, 230, 231, 241
Protectorate Assembly, 63, 70, 228
Proverbs, 44, 45, 46, 128
Provincial commissioners, 63, 237
Psychology, see Mentality
Pujehun, 69, 90, 224
Punishments, 130, 136

P.W.D. (Public Works Department), 5, 7, 11, 215

Race relations, 40, 43, 44
Radio, 44
Raffia palms, 208
Railway, Sierra Leone Government, 13, 17, 19, 20, 52pp., 72, 74, 105, 112, 118, 159, 186, 194, 208, 211, 221, 234, 237; Development Company, 196
Rain, rainfall, 9, 34, 57, 74, 75, 78, 79, 91, 92, 100, 115, 246
Rankin, 165, 166, 169
Regent Village, 24
Religion, African, 86, 93, 100, 109, 118, 119, 126, 127, 128, 153, 160pp. See Missions, Christianity, Anglicanism, etc.
Reserve powers, Governor's, 229
Revolt of 1898, see Hut tax war
Rheumatism, 91
Rice, 26, 48, 56, 74, 82, 83, 84, 86pp., 96, 104, 111, 112, 113, 120, 121, 122, 209, 211pp., 235, 242
Rice mills, 122
Rice Research Station, Rokupr, 122, 239
Rivers, 19, 75, 95, 105, 114, 238, 246. See Moa, Mano, etc.
River transport, 97, 121, 238
Roads, 19, 29, 60, 70, 112, 118, 151, 205, 206, 212, 215, 218, 219, 234
Rocks, 76pp. See Geology, Minerals, etc.
Rokel River, 2, 196
Roofs, 4, 58, 135
Ross, Sir Ronald, 36, 166
Rotation of crops, 82, 96, 213. See Agriculture, Cultivation, etc.
Rotifunk, 60
Royal Houses, African, see Chiefs
Royal West Africa Co., 16, 194
Rubber, 26, 112

Sahara, the, 75, 85
St. George's Cathedral, 12, 24

St. Joseph's College, 184
Salaries, African, 39, 71, 220, 223. See Family organization
European, 240
Samodu, Alimami, 64, 117
Sande (pron. 'Sanday') secret society, 9, 71, 117, 131, 135, 136, 139, 145pp., 158, 176, 180, 215, 232
Sanitation, 125, 143, 166, 167, 172
Sankoh, Mr. Laminah, 234
Savannah, 79
Scarcies River, 96, 115, 117, 121, 205, 208
Schools, 23, 62, 154, 176, 182, 184, 192, 223, 231
Secretariat, the, 17, 189, 216, 217, 236
Section Chiefs, see Chiefs
Self-government, 12, 113, 215, 226pp., 233, 235, 244
Serabu, 113, 154, 157
Settlers, first, 32, 37, 165, 244
Sewa River, 95, 110, 197
Shenge, 81, 103, 104, 244
Sherbro Island, 95, 173, 244
Sherbros, the, 89, 108, 109, 131
Shifting cultivation, see Cultivation
Shops, shopping, 9, 101, 221
Sickness, see Disease, Health, etc.
Sierra Leone Company, 226
Sierra Leone Government Railway, see Railway
Sierra Leone People's Party (SLPP), 62, 229pp., 233, 234, 236, 237
Simon, Lady, 73
Simongama, 135
Slave trade, 37, 63, 65, 100, 103, 108, 112, 116, 117
Slaves, 3, 8, 18, 33, 37, 63, 67, 73, 108, 112
Sleeping-sickness, 172
Smeathman, Dr., 25, 60
Social barriers, 13, 36, 217, 245
elevation, 35, 36, 158, 214, 225, 229, 246
organization of tribal Africans, 67, 147, 151pp., 202, 211, 214, 219, 220, 223, 232

Social science, need for, 193
Société Commerciale de l'Ouest Afrique (SCOA), 14
Societies, African, secret, 29, 109, 117, 131, 135, 140, 145, 202, 215. See Sande, Poro, etc.
Sofas, the, 117
Soil, 25, 27, 75, 79, 93, 120, 121, 204, 235, 247
Soil Conservation Team, 82, 122
Soldiers, 32
Songo Town, 54, 208
Sorie Manga, 117
Sour-sour, 87
Sowing seed, 87
Spiders, 106
Spirit, the Great, see God
Spirits, 77, 85, 93, 118, 119, 127, 128, 138, 140, 160pp., 168. See Religion, African
Squirrels, 106
Stevens, Siaka, Mr., 201, 233
Stevenson, Sir Hubert, 227, 229
Stories, African, 44, 128, 143, 149, 150
Sugar, 26
Sulima, 98, 103
Susus, the, 12, 58, 116, 117, 122
Swamp rice, see Rice
Swamps, 75, 79, 80, 83, 95pp., 104, 112, 115, 121, 206, 209, 215, 235
Swearing, 138
Sweet potatoes, 89, 101

Taxation, 65, 70, 112, 119, 156, 196, 234, 238, 241
Teachers, 39, 178, 180, 181, 182, 183, 184, 192, 220, 222. See Professions
Technical training, 97
Technicians, African, 190
Telephones, 11
Temnes, 4, 11, 12, 19, 25, 65, 71, 85pp., 114, 116, 127, 131, 178, 232
Temperature, 85
Timber, see Wood and Trees
Timbucktoo, 59, 118
'Tin Pan', see Roofs

Tobacco, 26
Tombo, King, 4
Tonkalili, 194, 202
Tornadoes, 9
Tourism, 104, 243, 244, 245
Tower Hill, 7
Towns, see Villages
Tractor ploughing, 83, 96, 97, 104, 121, 185, 246
Trade and Industries, Department of, Sierra Leone, 208
Trade Unions, 70, 201, 202, 221
Traders, European, 14, 16, 63, 65, 66, 156, 192
    African, 8, 72, 111, 112, 115, 143, 149, 220, 221
    Syrian, 14, 25, 59, 63, 134, 220, 221, 222
    creole, 14, 16, 26, 30, 34, 54, 59, 66, 72, 101, 220
Transport, see Railway, Roads, Porterage, Motor transport, River transport
Trawlers, 8, 209. See Fisheries
Treasury, 236pp.
Treaties (with Chiefs), 63, 64, 66, 109
Trees, importance of, 20, 76, 78-9, 80, 106, 112, 115, 208
Trevelyan, Sir C., 33
Tribal custom, see Law, African
Tribal life, see Social organization, Mentality, etc.
Tribes, 6, 12, 28, 36, 40, 58, 61, 67. See under each tribe also
Tribute, 70, 108
Trypanosomiasis, 120
Tsetse fly, 172
Tuntu Society, 99
Turberville, Mr., 108
Turner's Peninsula, 63
Turtle Islands, 99

United Africa Co., 14, 55, 101, 222
University, 27 (see Fourah Bay College)
Uranium, 241
Utting, Mr., 75, 244

Vais, the, 115, 131
Vegetables, 27, 48, 87, 89
Vegetation, 9, 20-21, 24, 25, 55, 56, 59, 76pp., 112, 114, 246, 247
Venner, Mr., 52
Victorian influence, 5, 12, 17, 24, 32, 64, 100
Villages, Colony, 21, 24, 28, 32, 74
African, 1, 58, 109
Vivekananda, Swami, 131

Waaima, battle of, 118
Waanje River, 95, 100, 205
W.A.F.R.I., see Fisheries
Wages, 70, 151, 200, 201, 241
Walpole, General, 17
War, inter-tribal, 68, 108, 117, 129
Washington, George, 226
Water devils, 95
Water Street, 54
Water supplies, 8, 15, 27, 234
Waterloo Village, 24, 25, 29, 54, 56
Weaving, 139, 162
Weeds, 87, 91, 96
Welfare, 135, 193, 200
Welfare Department, 12, 13, 17, 28, 239
Wellington Village, 25
Wesleyanism, 24
West African Airways, 1, 243
West Indies, 24, 25, 31, 32, 36, 41
Western civilization, 3, 40, 154, 178. See Christianity, Missions
Widows, 139, 149
Wilberforce Hall, 16, 59, 244

Wilberforce, Samuel, 16, 246
Wilberforce Village, 20, 24
Winds, 85. See Harmattan
Winterbottom, Dr., 167
Witch doctors, 15, 37, 138, 155, 167, 168, 170
Witches, witchcraft, 11, 37, 86, 125, 138pp., 140, 147, 153, 154, 167pp., 209
Wives, price of, 119, 133, 139
Wives, wifehood, African, 68-9, 71, 91, 119, 133, 136, 139, 232. See Women
Woman damage, 138, 199
Women, creole, status of, 31, 158, 224
tribal African, status of, 145pp., 158, 232
work of, 87, 91, 113, 138, 139, 147, 148, 206, 246
attitudes of, 113, 147, 148, 153, 168, 169, 232
Wood, 25, 81, 106
Worms, parasitic, 171, 173
Wright, Mr. Ralph, 44
Wunde Society, 140, 215

Yalunka, the, 114, 117, 118
Yams, 29, 56, 88, 101
Yaws, 171
Year, the Farmer's, 85pp.
Yengama, 79, 118, 200, 202
York Village, 24, 25

Zanzibar, 20, 244